What Your Colleagues

This book goes beyond being a primer of how to implement and needed ideas of project-based learning (PBL) in any mathematics classroom. It is a book that enthusiastically embraces a wide scholarship of ideas while communicating them with a lightness and whimsy that inspires you to take the needed journey that is intimated in its title. The future of math education lies in imagining classrooms that are not only equitable in their design, but also equitable in their implementation. The best mathematical experiences lie in wait with PBL. This book must be considered the gold standard for creating those student and teacher experiences.

Sunil Singh
Author, International Speaker, and Mathematics Educator
Pickering, ON, Canada

With compelling stories and practical strategies, McHugh gives us a vision of mathematics education that empowers all learners to experience engaging, effective, and meaningful learning. In the scenarios that McHugh brings to life, students use math to tackle projects that matter to them. When guided by teachers who know how to support each learner's journey, these projects deepen students' understanding of rigorous content. More importantly, students build their confidence to use math as a tool for asking questions, seeking answers, and making contributions.

Suzie Boss
PBL Author and Advocate
Portland, OR

I have not seen and cannot imagine a more comprehensive book about project-based learning and math than this one. It feels like the time has finally come for new approaches to teaching math, and McHugh provides a detailed yet readable road map, based on her own practice and drawing from many expert sources. I love how she includes so many classroom-tested examples, stories, and practical tools. Her depth of experience and compassion for students shines through!

John Larmer
Senior PBL Advisor, Defined Learning
Mill Valley, CA

I couldn't stop smiling while reading this book. McHugh shows how students can experience math in ways that not only are memorable and relatable, but spark curiosity as well. I cannot wait to implement what I've learned from this book into my teaching practice.

Howie Hua
Mathematics Lecturer, Fresno State
Fresno, CA

From start to finish, McHugh offers a unique glimpse into mathematics classrooms in which all students see themselves as mathematicians—a place in which they experience the joy, beauty, and wonder of mathematics. Her personal stories, abundance of examples and strategies, and clear guidance provide a detailed blueprint for the reimagined teaching and learning of mathematics. This book is a must-have for those who want to finally answer the question, "Why do I have to learn this?"

Tammy Moynihan
Associate Director of Curriculum, Instruction and Assessment, Cooperative Educational
Service Agency 8 (CESA 8)
Past President, Wisconsin Mathematics Council
Falls, WI

Most of my experiences as a math educator have been with problem-based learning, not project-based learning, because getting started felt daunting. This book helped me better understand the differences and gave an actionable plan to implement meaningful project-based lessons with students. Educators say we want students to be college and career ready, yet we're using the same practices that we used decades ago. If you want your students to authentically use mathematics in their lives, this is the book for you.

Robert Kaplinsky
Author and Consultant
Long Beach, CA

Through this book, McHugh makes project-based learning come to life in the mathematics classroom. The stories shared throughout the book from both students' and teachers' perspectives help us see ourselves in this important work and show the thought process in creating PBL mathematics experiences. The examples throughout help illustrate the key components in utilizing PBL to develop student understanding of mathematics.

Kevin Dykema
President, 2022–2024, National Council of Teachers of Mathematics
Eighth-Grade Mathematics Teacher, Mattawan Middle School
Mattawan, MI

Bringing Project-Based Learning to Life in Mathematics will support mathematics teachers with creating learning environments where students see mathematics as relevant to their lives and where students have opportunities to answer questions that matter to them. McHugh's book provides practical strategies to enact this approach to mathematics teaching.

Amanda Jansen
Professor, School of Education, University of Delaware
Author of *Rough Draft Math: Revising to Learn*
Newark, DE

This book can help teachers plan and implement authentic experiences for students. With project-based learning, students are less likely to say, "When am I going to use this?," and instead receive individualized mathematics learning opportunities that are relevant and meaningful.

Christine Koerner
Executive Director of STEM Education, Oklahoma State Department of Education
Norman, OK

In *Bringing Project-Based Learning to Life in Mathematics*, McHugh articulates how project-based learning can transform the learning experience for students and the teaching experience for educators. Working with students and teachers around the world, I see how PBL can be a tool to empower students to be thinkers and problem solvers. Reading this book, a teacher learns why and how to implement PBL in their classroom.

Chadd W. McGlone
Co-Founder/Mathkind
Chapel Hill, NC

Bringing Project-Based Learning to Life in Mathematics

K–12

Bringing Project-Based Learning to Life in Mathematics

K–12

Maggie Lee McHugh

For information:

Corwin
A SAGE Company
2455 Teller Road
Thousand Oaks, California 91320
(800) 233–9936
www.corwin.com

SAGE Publications Ltd.
1 Oliver's Yard
55 City Road
London, EC1Y 1SP
United Kingdom

SAGE Publications India Pvt. Ltd.
Unit No 323-333, Third Floor,
F-Block
International Trade Tower
Nehru Place
New Delhi - 110 019
India

SAGE Publications Asia-Pacific
Pte. Ltd.
18 Cross Street #10–10/11/12
China Square Central
Singapore 048423

President: Mike Soules
Vice President and Editorial Director:
    Monica Eckman
Associate Director and Publisher,
    STEM: Erin Null
Senior Editorial Assistant:
    Nyle De Leon
Production Editor: Tori Mirsadjadi
Copy Editor: Melinda Masson
Typesetter: Integra
Proofreader: Eleni Maria Georgiou
Indexer: Integra
Cover Designer: Scott Van Atta
Marketing Manager:
    Margaret O'Connor

Library of Congress Cataloging-in-Publication Data

Names: McHugh, Maggie, author.
Title: Bringing project-based learning to life in mathematics, K-12 / Maggie McHugh.
Description: Thousand Oaks, California : Corwin, [2023] | Includes bibliographical references and index.
Identifiers: LCCN 2022059682 | ISBN 9781071880722 (paperback ; acid-free paper) | ISBN 9781071915622 (epub) | ISBN 9781071915639 (epub) | ISBN 9781071915646 (pdf)
Subjects: LCSH: Mathematics--Study and teaching. | Project method in teaching.
Classification: LCC QA11.2 .M395 2023 | DDC 510.71/2--dc23/eng20230327
LC record available at https://lccn.loc.gov/2022059682

This book is printed on acid-free paper.

23 24 25 26 27 10 9 8 7 6 5 4 3 2 1

Contents

SECTION I. THE WHY

CHAPTER 1.

CHAPTER 2.

SECTION II. THE WHAT

SECTION III. THE HOW

Visit the companion website at
https://qrs.ly/56ensfy
for downloadable resources.

Acknowledgments

This book would not have been possible without so many people cheering me on. First and foremost, thank you to the dedicated team at Corwin, most especially my editors Jessica Vidal and Erin Null. You continually provided me with insightful comments that brought me closer to my ideal as a writer.

Thank you to the educators who opened their classroom to me. I'm especially grateful to Jasmine, Allie, Stephanie, and Katy. Your willingness to allow me to learn alongside you and your students was a true gift.

So much gratitude to the mentor whose dedication to my educational career has lasted twenty years! Dr. Richardson, I remain transformed by your devotion to the education of all students. I proudly tell people I am a branch on the "Dr. Richardson" teaching tree.

I'm beyond appreciative to my friends and colleagues at PBLWorks, especially Cohort Remix. Your collective wisdom led me to "Show My Sketch" of this work.

An immense thank-you to my Polytechnic colleagues—Katy, Kelsey, Leah, Naomi, Bri, Josh, Matt, Susan, Julie, and Garrett. Your dedication to our students is second to none. You inspire me to keep innovating and meeting the needs of our students.

Lots of love and thanks to my family and friends who cheer me on through whatever crazy project I take on. A special thank-you to my mom, dad, and sisters who are proudly part of the four generations of educators in our family.

Thank you to my closest circles of friends—The Posse, Poly Peeps, and The Gurlz—whose belief in me and unwavering friendship remains a source of strength and joy.

To my bestie who makes life an adventure. Couldn't do this without you, Jenn.

Lastly, the biggest thank-you to my husband, John, whose incredible love and support fills me with the strength to continue pouring my heart and soul into my students and this field of education. You mean the world to me.

Publisher's Acknowledgments

Corwin gratefully acknowledges the contributions of the following reviewers:

Kevin Dykema
Mathematics Teacher, Mattawan Consolidated Schools
Mattawan, MI

Suzie Boss
Author and Consultant, PBLWorks National Faculty Emeritus
Portland, OR

Kelley S. Miller
Secondary Instructional Coach, Napa Valley Unified School District
Napa, CA

Richard Cox Jr.
Assistant Professor of Elementary Education, Winthrop University
Rock Hill, SC

Allyson Lam
Sixth-Grade Mathematics Teacher, San Francisco Unified School District
San Francisco, CA

Tammy Moynihan
Associate Director of Curriculum, Instruction, and Assessment, Cooperative Educational Service Agency 8 (CESA 8)
Past President, Wisconsin Mathematics Council
Oconto Falls, WI

Laurie McDonald
Mathematics Teacher, Atlantic Coast High School
Jacksonville, FL

Christine Koerner
Executive Director of STEM Education, Oklahoma State Department of Education
Norman, OK

Kaneka M. Turner
Independent K–5 Mathematics Specialist
Charlotte, NC

About the Author

Dr. Maggie Lee McHugh believes all students are creative, compassionate, intellectual learners who, when given the right educational conditions, grow to be insightful, engaged citizens in our society. For Maggie, project-based learning (PBL) lays the foundation for every learner to find success. As the Innovation Specialist at La Crosse Polytechnic, a project-based secondary school in La Crosse, Wisconsin, Maggie has the honor of exploring the world alongside her students, guiding classes such as STEM, Humanities, Makerspace, and Mathematics. Additionally, Maggie has the pleasure of serving as a national faculty member for PBLWorks, traveling the United States to work with educators on implementing PBL in their classroom and district. To uplift the mathematics community, Maggie serves as the Wisconsin Mathematics Council Annual Conference co-chair. She is also a member of the National Council of Teachers of Mathematics (NCTM) Classroom Resource Committee. Maggie is the 2021 Midwest regional winner of the National University Teacher Award and the 2019 Wisconsin Middle School Teacher of the Year. She received the state honors for the Presidential Awards for Excellence in Mathematics and Science Teaching (PAEMST). Maggie has her National Board Certification in early adolescence mathematics. Maggie's dedication to empowering all learners is fueled by her "kiddos" who daily remind her of the courage, compassion, and perseverance needed to continuously become a better "you."

This book is dedicated to all my students–past, present, and future–and the experiences we create together. Be Amazing.
Love, Dr. McHugh

Introduction

BECOMING A MATHEMATICS STUDENT

Her name was Shirley. She was my friend, and she brought mathematics to life for me. She was just what I needed when I was a seventh grader: goofy, flexible, and pink. Yup. Pink. Shirley was the name of a flamingo I created when I was 12 years old. Not just any flamingo. A working marionette flamingo. Shirley was also the name of my seventh-grade mathematics teacher, a kindhearted, gentle soul who let my creativity shine.

During a unit on creating nets, we students were tasked with folding and gluing a certain number of nets. That's it. For some reason, I got the crazy idea to put multiple nets of three-dimensional objects together to make a flamingo marionette. I meticulously colored each net in pink marker, delicately glued the flaps of the nets together, borrowed fishing line from my dad to string the nets together, and used wooden dowels to make the puppeteering control bars. Along with some hot pink feathers and googly eyes, I crafted my flamingo and named her Shirley. Pride beamed from my face as I handed in my creation.

I remember Shirley hanging up in my seventh-grade classroom almost all school year. If a feather or googly eye fell off, I would stand on a chair and meticulously glue it back on. I know my teacher took Shirley home at the end of the school year. I have no idea what happened to that puppet after that, but to this day, I still treasure the memory of Shirley, and credit her with being the first time I saw mathematics as a tool that could inspire my own creativity and innovation.

BECOMING A MATHEMATICS TEACHER

Despite my passion for creating Shirley, I did not pursue a career as a marionette puppet maker; rather, I became a mathematics teacher. Now, sixteen years into my career, I continue to evolve and grow in my practice. After teaching in traditional classrooms for six years, I was feeling stuck. I didn't feel like I was reaching students in a way that would stick with them years into the future. I wanted to create experiences that would be memorable—that would impact my students and our community. With that belief,

1

I sought a position teaching middle school in a project-based learning (PBL) environment. I had no idea what I was getting into, but I knew the setting was ripe with opportunity to explore new teaching and learning practices.

With my middle school memory of Shirley the flamingo, I presented my students the project idea of creating a creature out of nets of three-dimensional objects. For over a week, students traced and cut nets out of cardstock, carefully glued shapes together, attached googly eyes, and affixed felt, fabric, cotton balls, and feathers to make their toys. At the end of the project, I marveled at my shelf filled with so many cool-looking creatures.

As I geared up to assess and reflect with my students on the project, I expected students to have the same excitement and pride as I did when I made Shirley the flamingo. Sadly, my students were underwhelmed. Although they enjoyed the hands-on nature of the project, the students didn't really care about making a toy to sit on my bookshelf. Students reflected that they didn't grow extensively in their mathematics skills. When I looked at traditional pacing guides, I realized we could have explored and mastered the concept of nets in about two or three class periods, instead of the eight it took us to build the toys. Where did I go wrong?

BECOMING A PBL MATHEMATICS EDUCATOR

Since my first project did not go as envisioned, I spent time reading, researching, and attending professional development on PBL. I watched webinars and scoured the internet for resources on PBL. I came to realize that PBL is not about making something cute or flashy at the end of a unit of study. Rather, PBL is an educational practice where learners identify an authentic problem and work toward finding a solution, engaging in academic content and developing success skills as part of their journey. As a student-centered practice, PBL leverages student voice and choice, honoring student strengths and identities to meet their needs.

With this definition in mind, I recognized the toy creature project I implemented as a "dessert project," or a project often tacked on at the end of a unit that does not advance the learning of content and success skills (PBLWorks, 2021). What I needed to create was a "main-course project," or an experience where students learn rigorous academic content and success skills throughout the entirety of the project. In a true PBL experience, students become immersed in the process of answering a driving question by exploring solutions from a variety of standpoints (PBLWorks, 2021).

As I researched PBL specifically for mathematics ideas on design and implementation, I found a lack of materials that truly embraced PBL as a main course. Most of the books and resources I found highlighted dessert projects—tacked-on ideas with little to no authenticity.

For the past decade, I have explored how best to implement PBL into the mathematics classroom. This journey has led me to research best practices in PBL, to converse with leading PBL experts as well as leading mathematics experts, to reimagine what PBL mathematics could look like, and, most importantly, to design, implement, reflect on, and revise PBL mathematics experiences.

As I continue to engage in PBL, I feel affirmed by both tangible and intangible results, especially gratifying when equitable practices are uplifted by students and their families. Students continue to cite the relationship building and strong culture of the PBL classroom; families cite the welcoming environment and consistent, high expectations that all students can and will achieve academically. I firmly believe PBL has a place in the mathematics classroom, but it's important to share that PBL is not the only methodology I use. In any given year, I may implement a full project two to six times in my mathematics classroom, depending on the course I am teaching and the students in the class. When not fully engaged in a project, my students explore mathematical concepts through problem-solving tasks, performance tasks, and rich inquiry (see Chapter 3 for more). Yet, I can't imagine *not* engaging in PBL mathematics.

Just like perfecting any art or sport or hobby, it has taken time, mentoring, and practice to become the PBL mathematics educator I am today, one who is still learning and refining my practice. I wrote this book as a way to continue my journey, to share ideas with those interested in exploring how PBL can transform their mathematics classroom. My sincere hope is that your journey in PBL mathematics can be filled with the same excitement and rejuvenation in teaching and learning that I find when engaging my students in a PBL mathematics experience.

WHO THIS BOOK IS FOR

All educators can (and should) engage in PBL practices in their classroom. Whether you are in a school or district that practices PBL or you personally are curious about how to engage students in PBL mathematics experiences, this book has practical tips and stories to illustrate best practices in PBL mathematics. PBL is not an "all or nothing" practice. Perhaps you are looking to bring PBL to your classroom during a particularly tough stretch of the school year. Perhaps, like me, you are looking for more authentic ways to engage students or ways to bring a stronger community focus to the classroom. This book elevates practices to build the culture for PBL. To all the preservice teachers I regularly work with, this book is for you and all future educators who bring such hope and optimism to our schools.

HOW TO ENGAGE IN THIS BOOK

This book is organized into three sections. Section I highlights "The Why"—namely, why PBL mathematics is a teaching and learning practice needed to increase engagement and equity practices for our students today. Section II explores "The What," elaborating on the Six Essential Attributes of a PBL mathematics classroom. Lastly, Section III describes "The How" of designing and implementing a PBL mathematics experience. Through interactive activities, Section III invites you to design a project while reading about best practices in

PBL mathematics. Whether you read this book in one sitting or peruse the sections and chapters as needed, my hope is that this book becomes a resource to enhance your teaching and learning practices.

Throughout this book, we'll explore our **Driving Question**, "How can I bring project-based learning [PBL] to life in the mathematics classroom?" Then, within each chapter, you'll encounter the following:

- **Need to Know questions:** These questions open each chapter to facilitate your thinking and learning. Mimicking the project process, Need to Know questions are smaller, focused questions to facilitate movements toward answering the Driving Question.

- **Vignettes:** Throughout the book, you'll read vignettes of students and educators engaging in PBL mathematics. Each vignette is simply a snapshot in time of that classroom, describing projects that span multiple days and class periods, each of which encountered stumbling blocks and successes. These vignettes illustrate the moments of a project I felt best exemplified a PBL mathematics topic.

- **PBL Plus Tips:** Engaging in PBL is not an all-or-nothing experience. This book highlights the many ways you can lay the foundation to engage in PBL in your classroom. Throughout the book, you'll see a set of PBL Plus Tips or ideas to take steps toward engaging in PBL.

- **Strategies:** From ways to build a culture of PBL to formative assessment and reflection questions, this book is filled with strategies. Many of these strategies will be familiar to you. That's excellent! PBL does not ask mathematics educators to throw out all of the best practices they already use. Rather, it focuses on repackaging these strategies in a way that engages students through an authentic experience. When you encounter something familiar, my challenge to you is to consider what this looks like within the context of a project.

- **Your Turn! activities:** These activities are designed to encourage you to actively connect ideas in the chapter to your practice, prompting you to try something in your classroom. What you try might happen outside of a project. That's fantastic! When designing a PBL mathematics experience, take the high-leverage teaching practices you already engage in and repackage these practices into a sustained, authentic focus for students.

- **Additional Resources:** Some of the topics included in this book cannot be fully addressed. Check out the many resources I reference as further reading to continue growing as a mathematics educator.

- **PBL Points to Ponder:** Concluding each chapter are PBL Points to Ponder through a thinking routine, adapted from Project Zero (Harvard Graduate School of Education, 2022). As you grow in your PBL mathematics practices, your final product and culminating experience will be implementing a project in your classroom.

SOME CONCEPTS TO NOTE

Think back on your life. What vividly stands out in your memory? To me, it is the experiences I've had with family and friends. I remember family vacations, my first trip overseas with my husband, conferences attended with colleagues, parties and celebrations with friends, weddings, baptisms, birthdays. Perhaps one word to encompass all of these memories is this: *experiences*. I remember my experiences with the world and others.

This word highlights the first of two concepts I want to make particular note of in the introduction: a **PBL mathematics experience**. When engaging in PBL, practitioners might refer to conducting a PBL unit or engaging students in a project. I have chosen to call this a PBL mathematics experience. To me, PBL is more than a unit or a chapter in a textbook. Likewise, it is more than a "project," which may connote the idea of a dessert project. Naming PBL an *experience* brings to life the true nature of what students engage in when PBL is authentically implemented. If we create experiences for our students, what they learn and what they remember has the chance to become part of their forever memories and their deep learning.

The second critical concept to highlight is **equity**. Because we all experience our world from unique lenses, I want to address my ongoing work toward equitable practices. To me, equity in education means that all students—regardless of gender identity and expression, race, socioeconomic status, religion, sexual orientation, ability, language, culture, nationality, and so on—deserve access to high-quality teaching and learning practices. My belief is that educators can equitably serve students through rigorous PBL experiences, particularly in the mathematics classroom. (See more about equity in Chapter 2.)

As I continue my own journey to understand, strive for, and support equity in my classroom, I recognize that I am a white female who experienced a solidly middle-class upbringing where schooling was highly valued by my parents, both public school educators. Now, a fourth-generation teacher myself, I teach students in the same city I grew up in. Much has changed since I was in school in this same city—changes that reflect a diversifying society, changes that bring incredible assets to the community, changes that radically altered education due to the COVID-19 pandemic.

I serve a student population where just over half of the students receive free or reduced-price lunch, where the racial and linguistic diversity continues to rise, where many interests and activities compete for student attention, where gender expression is more widely accepted, where technology bridges distances yet also isolates. I teach students eager to attend postsecondary school, others ready to enter the workforce, and yet others unsure of what life after K–12 schooling may hold for them.

I imagine my personal context differs from your own in some ways. Perhaps this makes you question whether PBL can work in your context. In my work across the country, I have seen PBL experiences transform classrooms, students, and educators, bringing with it vitality and purpose. My lived experience with PBL, combined with research and the PBL stories of educators and colleagues throughout the United States, leads me to stand firm in my stance that PBL remains an equitable teaching practice for all students.

CONCLUDING THOUGHTS

I'd wager that if I talked to my fellow seventh-grade class-mates, very few (if any) would remember folding nets. So, why do I recall this mathematics lesson? Because I made it into an experience. This is my hope for all of you: to transform part of your mathematics curriculum into a PBL mathematics experience so that five, ten, twenty, or forty years from now, your students just might come back to you saying, "Remember in math class when . . . ?" What a beautiful story that would be.

The Why

Section I explores the **_why_** of project-based learning (PBL) mathematics.

Chapter 1 dives into the question, "Why does the mathematics education field need PBL?" This chapter addresses the renewed focus in mathematics education for students to embrace the role of a mathematician and experience mathematics in authentic situations. This chapter also highlights attributes of the ideal mathematics classroom and the relationship to the PBL mathematics classroom.

Chapter 2 examines the question, "Why is PBL mathematics an equitable, engaging, and effective teaching practice?" A discussion of the intersection between equity-based mathematics teaching practices and PBL equity levers is highlighted. This chapter also examines the cognitive, behavioral, and emotional dimensions of engagement found in PBL mathematics. Lastly, Chapter 2 looks at the eight effective instructional practices identified in _Principles to Actions_ (National Council of Teachers of Mathematics, 2014) and their implementation in the PBL mathematics classroom.

Finally, Chapter 3 asks the question, "Why should I engage my students in PBL?" This chapter distinguishes between the characteristics of a problem-solving task, a performance task, and a project as well as the ways these three teaching practices leverage equity-based mathematics teaching practices.

Why Now?

Need to Knows

- Why does the mathematics education field need project-based learning?
- How do current mathematics education shifts connect to project-based learning?
- How do attributes of the ideal mathematics classroom align to the project-based learning mathematics classroom?
- Why should I consider project-based learning as a teaching and learning practice?

Nina, a second-grade student whose eyes sparkle with mischief, aspires to be a skateboarding mathematician wizard when she grows up. Of course, she has "always known" that she is a wizard. There is no convincing her that wizards do not exist as she truly already is a wizard with wizarding powers and a wizarding wand. Nina doesn't like to show people her wizarding wand for fear someone will break it, so we will just have to trust her that her wand is full of wizarding powers.

I asked this young student to share more about being a skateboarding mathematician along with her obvious choice as a wizard. "I like to skateboard. I'm not very good at it, but I saw a girl win the Olympics on her skateboard, and with my wizarding powers, I bet I can be really good someday. I won't use my powers to win, but maybe just to jump really, really high." I was totally enthralled with this dream, yet I was most curious about her intended job as a mathematician.

All in one breath, Nina shared, "Well, Miss Allie said mathematicians do math, and wizards need to do math when they make potions. So I will be doing math, so I am a mathematician. And skateboards have wheels, which are round, and wheels are like circles, which is math. So I need to be a mathematician to be a skateboarder, too. So all three jobs just make sense together."

With valid arguments like that, I have no doubt this little dreamer will most certainly live up to her aspiration to be a skateboarding mathematician wizard.

A few weeks later, I was visiting with Naomi, a high school student in Algebra II. I have known Naomi since she was a sixth grader, having seen her work hard in each class, put in extra time to understand complex topics, and often work with her peers before coming to those light bulb moments. I remember her as a middle schooler, bringing me to the whiteboard to show me her work with a big smile.

Now, as a high school student whose first two years were impacted by COVID-19, Naomi is trying to navigate the waters of Algebra II. As the class moved from an exploration to independent work time, Naomi said, "I just don't see the point anymore. I'm just going through the motions these days, completing homework problems and taking quizzes. I guess, you know, I just want math to *mean something* for my life, to have a purpose, other than just doing math to do math. I want it to *mean something*, because sine and cosine mean nothing to me."

WHY THESE STORIES?

Nina and Naomi represent two different scenarios—one eagerly embracing her identity in the mathematics classroom and another struggling to find meaning and purpose. Yet, students like these can be found in our classrooms, and both represent current educational priorities in the state of mathematics education. One major emphasis in mathematics education centers on students doing mathematics in order to think, act, and reason as a mathematician. A second emphasis is the increased call for authentic connections to the mathematics classroom. Let's look deeper at each emphasis.

EMPHASIS 1: THE NEED TO EMBRACE THE ROLE OF MATHEMATICIAN

What does it mean to be a mathematician? Who is a mathematician? These questions continue to be asked, challenged, and reinvented in our mathematics community. This emphasis toward embracing the role of mathematician can be found in the position statements of mathematics education associations and in landmark publications like the Catalyzing Change series from the National Council of Teachers of Mathematics (NCTM, 2018, 2020a, 2020b), where a key recommendation is the development of positive mathematical identities. While being attentive culturally and personally to each student, educators can foster this mathematical identity by guiding students to "develop deep mathematical understanding; understand and critique the world through mathematics; and experience the wonder, joy, and beauty of mathematics" (NCTM, 2020b, p. 7).

Aguirre and colleagues (2013) contend the identity a student holds as a mathematician connects to the student's other identities, and these identities can impact one another. The identity a student holds as a mathematician is directly tied to the instructional strategies and choices we make as educators, and can be elevated through our ability to debunk the myth of "who" is a mathematician and "what" makes a good mathematician. Thus, it is imperative that we develop positive and productive mathematical skills, dispositions, and beliefs in our students.

Embracing the Identity of Mathematician Through Mathematical Habits of Mind

One of our aims as educators is to help students see themselves as mathematicians. A crosscutting way to embrace the role of a mathematician is to engage students in the Mathematical Habits of Mind. Levasseur and Cuoco (2003) define Mathematical Habits of Mind as "modes of thought . . . useful for reasoning about the world . . . and for reasoning about the mathematical content itself" (p. 27). These are the skills and dispositions students should utilize as they engage in mathematics in the classroom and the larger society.

Figure 1.1 shows a picture of the six Mathematical Habits of Mind my school shares with our sixth- to twelfth-grade students. These Mathematical Habits of Mind were developed by weaving together mathematical frameworks including the Standards for Mathematical Practice (National Governors Association Center for Best Practices & Council of Chief State School Officers, 2010), the Mathematical Habits of Mind (Levasseur & Cuoco, 2003), and the 16 Habits of Mind (Institute for Habits of Mind, 2022) to create an accessible, student-friendly list of characteristics. As my colleagues and I engage students in mathematics, we regularly discuss the Mathematical Habits of Mind and intentionally ask students to reflect on them.

Figure I-I • Mathematical Habits of Mind

Communicate Mathematically

Mathematicians . . .
- use accurate notation and representation
- share thinking using vocabulary, examples, and counter examples
- respond to others' arguments with precision and clarity

Develop Connections

Mathematicians . . .
- contextualize math concepts to authentic situations or problems
- connect algebra, numbers, geometry, statistics, and probability concepts
- find and create equivalent representations of the same concept

Question & Persist in Problem Solving

Mathematicians . . .
- persist numerically, algebraically, and geometrically in solving problems
- ask probing and extending questions
- monitor progress
- verify solution(s) using multiple strategies and approaches

Reason & Justify

Mathematicians . . .
- provide mathematical evidence for solutions or conjectures
- evaluate conjectures by generating special cases
- justify why a generalization will work all or some of the time

Search for Patterns

Mathematicians . . .
- generate multiple cases and generalize patterns
- look for short cuts based on patterns
- use prior knowledge to enhance a solution

Use Tools Strategically

Mathematicians . . .
- choose tools that help advance and verify a solution strategy
- explore new and unconventional tools
- deepen conceptual understanding through technological tools
- use tools for math modeling

Source: Courtesy of La Crosse Polytechnic School

YOUR TURN

What Mathematical Habits of Mind resonate with you? Are there any you would add or change for your classroom?

_____

_____

Activities to Promote Mathematical Habits of Mind

Purposefully teaching students about each of the Mathematical Habits of Mind leads to a stronger classroom culture centered on embracing the mindset of a mathematician. I engage students in various activities throughout the school year to establish each of these Mathematical Habits of Mind. Here are some tasks to bring the Mathematical Habits of Mind to life in your classroom.

Task 1: Patterns in Nature

Task: Patterns in Nature	Grade Level: PK–2
Task Goal: Students will be able to generate and identify simple or sequential patterns.	
Mathematical Habits of Mind:	Materials (per group):
• Search for Patterns	• Pinecones, leaves, twigs, flowers, etc.
• Communicate Mathematically	• Chalk
• Reason & Justify	• Buckets or baskets

Directions for Educators:

- Put students in partners. Give partners one bucket to collect nature items. Direct students to collect at least three different types of items (pinecones, leaves, twigs, flowers, etc.) and at least three to four examples of each type.

- Have students generate a pattern by laying out the items they have collected. For example:

    ○ pinecone, pinecone, leaf, twig, pinecone, pinecone, leaf, twig . . . (AABC, AABC)

- Ask another set of partners to label the pattern using accurate notation (i.e., AABC) with chalk.

- These partners will then explain with evidence how they labeled the pattern.

- Rotate partners as many times as you want. Challenge partners to create new patterns.

- Draw connections between the activity and the Mathematical Habits of Mind by asking reflective questions such as the following:

    ○ What patterns did you see?

    ○ Can anything be a pattern?

    ○ How can you prove something is a pattern?

Task 2: Our Classroom Measurements

Task: Our Classroom Measurements	Grade Level: 3–5
Task Goal: Find measurements of the classroom using a variety of tools, using both metric and U.S. customary units.	

Mathematical Habits of Mind:	Materials (per group):

• Use Tools Strategically
 	
• Question & Persist in Problem Solving
	• Measurement tools
	
	  ○ Rulers
	
	  ○ Yardsticks
	
	  ○ Metersticks
	
	  ○ String
	
	  ○ Protractors
	
	• Grid paper
	
	• Pencils

Directions for Educators:

- Provide a variety of measurement tools for students.

- Task students in partners with finding as many measurements of the classroom as possible. Leave the directions purposefully vague. Do not indicate a unit of measurement.

- By leaving directions vague, ask students to do a quick Think-Pair-Share to generate questions. Anticipate questions such as these:

  ○ What things can I measure in my classroom?

  ○ What are appropriate units of measurement?

  ○ How do I use this tool?

  ○ Is there a better tool?

  ○ How do I record my measurements?

- Have students record their measurements using drawings and numbers.

  ○ For example, if students measure the area of the classroom, they should create a two-dimensional, bird's-eye view diagram.

  ○ If students find the height of a desk, they should draw the desk indicating the appropriate dimensions.

  ○ If students find the angles of the doorway, they should label the angles using degrees.

- Ask partners to share all the different measurements they found—lengths, areas, angles, volumes, and so on—in a variety of units, both metric and U.S. customary.

- Draw connections between the activity and the Mathematical Habits of Mind by asking reflective questions such as the following:

  ○ What tools were most effective during this task?

  ○ What mathematics did you learn or solidify by using those tools?

  ○ How did you monitor your progress throughout this task?

  ○ What questions did you ask in order to persist in completing this task?

Task 3: Local to Global Ratios

Task: Local to Global Ratios	Grade Level: 6–8
Task Goal: Students will be able to create equivalent ratios using a variety of representations (tape diagrams, tables, double number lines, graphs, and equations).	

Mathematical Habits of Mind:	Materials (per group):

• Develop Connections
 	
• Question & Persist in Problem Solving
 	
• Communicate Mathematically
	• Slips of paper highlighting ratios in context
	  ○ Access to safe drinking water
	  ○ Literacy
	  ○ Poverty
	  ○ Access to housing
	• Information highlighting populations of the classroom, school, city/town, state, nation, and/or world
	• Poster paper
	• Markers

Directions for Educators:

- Form groups of two to three students.

- Give each group a ratio in context and the corresponding populations.

  ○ Ratios can be found on websites like Our World in Data (https://ourworldindata.org).

- Ask students to use the ratio and the population to solve problems using equivalent ratios. For example:

  ○ Globally, one out of four people do not have access to safe drinking water (Ritchie & Roser, 2021).

  ○ If there are thirty people in the classroom, how many would not have access to safe drinking water? Show using at least two representations.

- Ask students to repeat for three different populations, using different representations each time.

- Students should display their work mathematically on posters.

- Have students share their posters with the class, explaining their representations and contextualizing to the broader population.

- After all groups present, pose the question, "So what? Now what?" Engage in critical dialogue.

- Draw connections between the activity and the Mathematical Habits of Mind by asking reflective questions such as the following:

  ○ What connections did you draw between the context and the mathematics?

  ○ How did you verify your solution using multiple strategies?

  ○ How did using accurate vocabulary affect your mathematical communication?

Task 4: Construct a Square

Task: Construct a Square	Grade Level: High School
Task Goal: Create a square using limited tools and geometric properties.	
Mathematical Habits of Mind: • Question & Persist in Problem Solving • Use Tools Strategically • Communicate Mathematically	Materials (per group): *Outdoor Grass Option:* • Four nails • String *Indoor Option:* • Bulletin boards or cardboard • Four pushpins • String

Directions for Educators:

• Form groups of two to three students.

• Provide materials to each group.

• Optional: Move to appropriate outdoor location.

• Direct students to construct a square using only the materials given.

• Encourage student-generated questions such as these:

    ○ What makes a square a square?

    ○ How is a square different from a rectangle?

    ○ What are the properties of a square?

• Prompt students to share their thinking using accurate vocabulary such as *hypotenuse, Pythagorean theorem, right angle,* and so on.

• Draw connections between the activity and the Mathematical Habits of Mind by asking reflective questions such as the following:

    ○ How did you persist in solving this problem?

    ○ What did you do when faced with a challenge?

    ○ What tools could have made this task easier?

Each of these tasks could be incorporated into a project-based learning mathematics experience or serve as stand-alone tasks. As you incorporate these tasks, consider how you will purposefully connect them to the Mathematical Habits of Mind. During the task, assign students roles connected to each Mathematical Habit of Mind, such as the Communicator, Tool Manager, or Pattern Finder. After the task, ask students to reflect specifically on the Mathematical Habits of Mind used during the task. I've had students reflect on sticky notes I then post around the Mathematical Habits of Mind poster hanging in my classroom.

Activities to Get to Know Your Mathematicians

YouCubed.org (Stanford Graduate School of Education, 2019) shares a fabulous activity called "And I'm a Mathematician" where students illustrate their ties to various communities, with the intent to see that being a mathematician is an identity that can coexist with other identities, not something that is distant or irrelevant to students' lives. I have launched the school year with this activity to set the tone for my goals as a mathematics educator, helping my students embrace the role of being a mathematician.

These posters can be made by hand or digitally, or a combination of both, and be hung around the room or in a hallway. By publicly displaying these posters, students build connections to a community of learners whose lives are diverse, yet all ground themselves as being mathematicians in my classroom. I like to print all the posters and put them in a binder as part of a classroom portfolio of learning for the year. See Figure 1.2 for a student example.

Building the identity of a mathematician takes intentional time and practice, and by no means can be fully realized in a few back-to-school activities. However, these activities lay the foundation for a student-centered classroom culture. By engaging students in activities specifically tied to embracing the role of a mathematician, we as educators can help students—those like Nina who may someday become a skateboarding wizard mathematician—develop positive identities in mathematics.

Here are some other ideas that can be implemented early in the school year as you begin establishing students' mathematical identities.

- Create mathematician statements (Wedekind, 2011).
  - Create identity-building statements by asking students, "What do mathematicians do?"
  - Examples from Wedekind (2011, p. 13) include "Mathematicians are curious" and "Mathematicians ask themselves questions."
  - Ask students to reflect on how they already embody the role of a mathematician. For example, you can ask students, "How do you show curiosity?"

Figure I-2 ◆ Student Example of "And I'm a Mathematician"

Source: Images from Ewig, J. S. (3 Dec 2019). "Baby Yoda Eating Theme Park Food." Instagram; Calvert, D. (4 Dec 2019). "Pizza I love." Instagram; Oga, K. (1988). *My Neighbor Totoro*; Gore, M. (3 Feb 2022). "Perfect Buttered Noodles." delish. com; Julian Herbrig/Getty Images/EyeEm; Dawn (Feb 28 2014). "How to Draw a Peace Plant, Peace Lily." dragoart.com.

- Take pictures with an "I am a math person" frame (Hua, 2020).
  - Create a large, cutout frame with the words "I am a math person" on it.
  - Snap photos of students inside the large frame. Print and post publicly.
  - Hua (2020) suggests showing students their photograph at the end of a semester or year, asking students to reflect on how they have grown as a math person.

EMPHASIS 2: THE NEED FOR MATHEMATICS TO MEAN SOMETHING

In the opening story, Naomi voiced she wants mathematics to "mean something." Naomi's words bring to light the call for mathematics to be strongly connected to authentic, relevant learning contexts. This emphasis is highlighted in the many state standards that call for connecting mathematics to real-world situations. Implementing a rigorous curriculum, one of the key shifts in mathematics called for by the Common Core State Standards Initiative (2020), requires teachers to "pursue conceptual understanding, procedural skills and fluency, and *application* with equal intensity" (emphasis added). Whether or not you are using the Common Core State Standards, this call for application through authentic contexts is being echoed by mathematics leaders and researchers at the national, state, and local levels who desire to address the needs of our changing world while ensuring all students find relevance and meaning in the mathematics classroom.

Furthermore, creating authentic experiences in the mathematics classroom is an issue of equity (see Chapter 2). While learning mathematics in a traditional style engages some students, quite often not all students' needs are met when mathematics is presented through disconnected or contrived topics. Providing students with authentic and integrated experiences engages students who were formerly less engaged or lower performing (Lee & Galindo, 2018). As mathematics educators, when we contextualize mathematics in the lived experiences of students, including their cultural and community histories, we innately support student interest, engagement, and motivation in our classrooms (Berry et al., 2020). For mathematics to mean something, our role as educators is to bring to light the vibrant ways mathematics can be used to explore and make sense of our society.

Additional Resources

Explore more ideas to help engage your students in authentic, meaningful mathematics.

Books that support meaningful mathematics:

☐ *Dear Citizen Math: How Math Class Can Inspire a More Rational and Respectful Society* (Ani, 2021)

☐ *Engaging in Culturally Relevant Math Tasks: Fostering Hope in the Elementary Classroom* (Matthews et al., 2022a)

☐ *Engaging in Culturally Relevant Math Tasks: Fostering Hope in the Middle and High School Classroom* (Matthews et al., 2022b)

☐ *Rethinking Mathematics: Teaching Social Justice by the Numbers* (Gutstein & Peterson, 2013)

☐ Mathematics Lessons to Explore, Understand, and Respond to Social Injustice series, written for early elementary, upper elementary, middle school, and high school (Bartell et al., 2022; Berry et al., 2020; Conway et al., 2022; Koestler, 2022)

Websites with meaningful mathematics connections:

☐ Global Math Stories (Mathkind): https://mathkind.org/global-math-stories/

☐ Slow Reveal Graphs: https://slowrevealgraphs.com/

YOUR TURN

Which of your current teaching and learning practices create authentic, meaningful mathematics engagement? What would you like to try?

_____

_____

THE IDEAL MATHEMATICS CLASSROOM

The emphasis on developing students who embrace the role of a mathematician, as well as the call for authentic, meaningful mathematics, is just part of the larger reform movement in mathematics education, a movement providing the much-needed opportunity to reimagine the mathematics classroom. In a session at a virtual conference, I facilitated a conversation with over forty mathematics educators from across the United States. In this nationwide group of PK–12 teachers, we reflected on just this notion: *What does the ideal mathematics classroom look like? Sound like? Feel like?* Some of the ideas from that conversation, which I clustered around six big themes, are presented in Figure 1.3.

As this diverse group of teachers continued to highlight characteristics of their ideal mathematics classroom, I realized that what these educators described is achievable through project-based learning. These big ideas form the essential components of a project-based learning mathematics experience, which is explored more in Section II. So, with this reimagination, I propose embracing project-based learning as a transformational practice.

Figure I-3 • Description of the Ideal Mathematics Classroom

Theme	Description of the Ideal Mathematics Classroom
Rigorous Content (Chapter 4)	• Students are actively engaged in learning rich, deep mathematics the entire class period. • Students are open to learning "hard" things through perseverance. • Mathematics is scaffolded to challenge all students. • Students can navigate the mathematics needed to understand and critique our world.
Productive Inquiry (Chapter 5)	• The classroom hums with productive debate and discussion of ideas. • Students inquire about best ways to explore mathematical concepts. • Students manipulate items, ask questions of their peers, and then discuss their different strategies to solve the problems.

(Continued)

(*Continued*)

Theme	Description of the Ideal Mathematics Classroom
Identity & Agency (Chapter 6)	• Students take ownership of their learning. • All students have access to high-quality teaching and learning. • Students see themselves as capable learners and doers of mathematics. • Students use mathematics to impact society.
Authentic Connections (Chapter 7)	• Students engage in numerous focused conversations around real-life situations involving a mathematics objective. • The mathematics of the home and community is intentionally woven into the fabric of the classroom. • Students explore authentic topics and critique society using a social justice lens.
Meaningful Assessment (Chapter 8)	• Ongoing formative assessments propel learning forward. • Assessments emphasize conceptual understanding as well as procedural fluency while de-emphasizing speed. • Assessments focus on application of learning and allow students to show their learning through multiple avenues, not just tests.
Growth Through Reflection (Chapter 9)	• The classroom community values mistakes as learning opportunities. • Teachers provide timely and specific feedback beyond "right or wrong" to help students grow as mathematicians. • Students develop a growth mindset through written and verbal reflection.

WHAT EXACTLY IS PROJECT-BASED LEARNING?

Project-based learning (PBL): is a teaching and learning practice where students sustain exploration into an authentic question, challenge, or problem while engaging in academic content and developing critical success skills, such as communication, collaboration, and critical thinking.

Project-based learning (PBL) is a teaching and learning practice where students sustain exploration into an authentic question, challenge, or problem while engaging in academic content and developing critical success skills, such as communication, collaboration, and critical thinking (Boss & Larmer, 2018; PBLWorks, 2021). As they journey through the project, students demonstrate what they learn, engage in inquiry-based activities, collaborate with peers and experts, and assess themselves and one another. PBL is the culmination of rigorous learning throughout the experience, not simply a comprehensive test or product created at the end of instruction.

Much of what makes a vibrant PBL classroom is found in the great teaching and learning practices already occurring in classrooms nationwide. As strong practitioners, when you embrace PBL in the classroom, you should not abandon what you already do and start from scratch. I aim to highlight how you can build off your current high-leverage teaching practices and implement them throughout a project.

When designing and implementing a project, the goal is to repackage these high-leverage teaching and learning practices into a sustained, focused experience centered on a driving question leading to an authentic product. Because students are actively working to address a critical question or tackle a problem through mathematics, embracing the role of a mathematician becomes inherent to the PBL process. Additionally, PBL flourishes as a student-centered teaching and learning practice due to its authentic nature, the second emphasis in current mathematics education research and practice.

Furthermore, PBL fully encapsulates the characteristics of the ideal mathematics classroom described by educators across the United States, which I clustered to become the Six Essential Attributes of the PBL mathematics classroom—rigorous content, authentic connections, productive inquiry, identity and

Figure I-4 • Six Essential Attributes of the PBL Mathematics Classroom

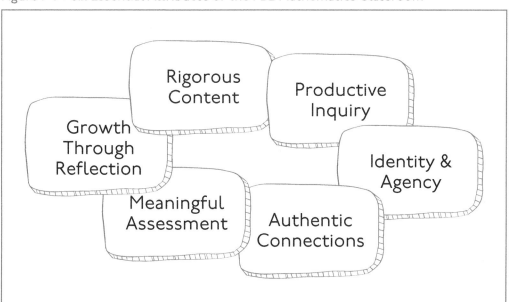

agency, meaningful assessment, and growth through reflection (see Figure 1.4). Each of these attributes most likely already comprises part of the high-quality educational experience you provide your students. In order to effectively reconceptualize and repackage these concepts into a PBL experience, we will examine the Six Essential Attributes through a PBL mathematics lens in Section II of this book.

ADDRESSING HESITANCIES ABOUT PBL MATHEMATICS

I have had the incredible pleasure to work with educators from all grades—PK–12—as well as content areas across the United States in creating a PBL classroom. I have listened to these educators and seen them in action. I believe you are one of those educators as, by reading this book, you are seeking the resources to continually engage your students and improve your practice. For that, I thank you.

Yet, even the most energetic educator may have some hesitancy about embracing PBL in the mathematics classroom. During workshops and trainings, mathematics educators often voice similar concerns:

1. PBL fits in other content areas like English, social studies, and science, but it doesn't fit in the mathematics classroom.

2. PBL works for some students, but other students just need direct instruction.

3. My mathematics curriculum is so jam-packed, I don't think I have time for PBL.

4. PBL is exciting, but because of standardized tests, I need to prepare my students by assessing them through summative tests and quizzes.

I hear and understand these hesitancies when considering implementing PBL in the classroom. My goal is to address these concerns throughout the book, but here is a quick glance at some initial responses.

Hesitancy 1: PBL doesn't fit in the mathematics classroom.

My response echoes that of Ferlazzo (2021), who asserts, "Don't make the math classroom a project-based-learning-free zone." Students deserve to experience how mathematics can be used to authentically engage with their world. At first, PBL may not seem a "fit" because not every standard lends itself to a project. That's okay. We shouldn't force standards into a project. More on this idea will be explored in Chapter 14.

To help break through any final hesitancies about mathematics and PBL, I often use the analogy of basketball (or any sport, art form, hobby, etc.). Players spend hours practicing skills like dribbling and shooting free throws outside of playing a game. However, if players never engage in a game, the hours of practice dribbling and shooting the ball quickly lose their excitement. Similarly, if our students only experience the hours of practice on mathematics skills devoid of authentic contexts, they never get the thrill of applying their skills while playing the game (PBL).

Hesitancy 2: PBL only works for some students.

When I hear this, I immediately counter this false assertion. PBL is an instructional approach that benefits all students. Lucas Education Research (2021) highlights four studies showing that rigorous PBL improved student outcomes for students from diverse racial and socioeconomic backgrounds as well as students struggling with reading and language proficiency. These research studies "dispel the misguided belief that disadvantaged students aren't ready for student-led forms of instruction like PBL and must first master basic content through more traditional methods, like direct instruction" (Lucas Education Research, 2021, p. 2). More on PBL as an equitable teaching practice is examined in Chapter 2.

Hesitancy 3: I don't have time for PBL because I have so many mathematics standards to cover.

When I hear teachers voice this hesitancy, I visualize what Singh (2018) wrote: "If math education were a pizza, it would have 5000 toppings on it. The curriculum is almost morbidly obese." Eventually, the conversation turns to the discussion of depth versus breadth. Is our goal as mathematics educators to "cover" our curriculum or to create authentic experiences for our students to embrace their identity as a mathematician?

Through a rigorous PBL experience, students can meet curriculum goals at a similar pace as in a traditional unit of instruction, yet we may need to realign our practices and reenvision how we assess students for growth and content mastery. More on meeting rigorous content goals is explored in Chapter 4.

Additionally, PBL doesn't have to be an all-or-nothing approach. The aim of this book is to help educators take small steps toward implementing PBL as one approach on their instructional menu. Chapter 3 highlights the use of problem-solving tasks and performance tasks in addition to PBL.

Hesitancy 4: I need to traditionally assess my students to prepare them for standardized testing.

Remember, PBL is just one instructional tool to use with students in your mathematics classroom. Traditional tests and quizzes can be used during units throughout the school year.

High-quality PBL mathematics experiences center on both formative and summative assessments, more of which is explored in Chapters 8 and 16. While summative assessments focus on authentic products shared during a culminating event, formative assessments in PBL can include traditional assessment practices like quizzes or tests. Research has also shown that students can perform stronger on standardized testing with PBL as the main instructional practice. Lucas Education Research (2021), for example, cites a study where high school students taking PBL-focused courses of Advanced Placement U.S. government and politics and AP environmental science outperformed students in traditional classrooms on their AP exams by 10 percentage points.

It's important to set up our students for success in standardized testing; however, I always urge educators to consider what they want students to remember about their mathematics classroom experience. Is our ultimate aim as educators to have our students perform well on a test or to have them see mathematics as a useful, essential tool used to examine problems and challenges in society?

SO WHAT? NOW WHAT?

PBL engages students by providing a real-world relevance to mathematical learning. Students work collaboratively to develop solutions to problems, thereby generating a creative and analytical mindset. This is the type of learning described by educators as ideal and needed by our students, especially now. Given the increased emphasis on student-centered mathematics and reform movements that have taken place in our mathematical community, we must respond to the urgent need to connect learning to relevant experiences—to provide a *why* for students.

With this in mind, I consider the needs of my students, of all students, of students like Nina and Naomi. Nina needs a classroom that will foster her intellectual curiosity and provide her with rich and rigorous mathematics, a classroom where her identity as a mathematician—as a learner and doer of mathematics—is celebrated and reaffirmed. Naomi needs a classroom where mathematics is purposefully connected to real-world situations, where she can question and discuss mathematical topics, and where she is able to show her learning through authentic means. Both girls would thrive by engaging in PBL mathematics. In fact, I truly believe all students, especially students furthest from opportunity, would find immense success in a PBL mathematics classroom.

CONCLUDING THOUGHTS

I'll end with a few questions for you to consider:

- Are you curious about what PBL looks like specifically in the mathematics classroom?

- Are you open to taking small, but concrete, steps toward implementing PBL?

- Do you want to explore the foundations of a robust PBL mathematics classroom?

- Are you ready to design and implement a project with your mathematics students?

If you said yes to any of these questions, then let's keep exploring the *why*, *what*, and *how* of PBL mathematics together by exploring our Driving Question, "How can I bring project-based learning [PBL] to life in the mathematics classroom?"

PBL POINTS TO PONDER: COMPASS POINTS

At the end of each chapter, I invite you to make your thinking visible by reflecting via a thinking routine (Harvard Graduate School of Education, 2022). Thinking routines are meant to be just that: routine. These can be used in your classroom with students to scaffold their thinking. Consider using this Compass Points routine at the beginning of the school year or a new unit to help students name their excitement, worries, "need to knows," and suggestions for the classroom.

As you make your thinking visible, consider writing your ideas down in a journal, conversing with a colleague, or sharing your learning with the world on social media with the hashtag #PBLmath.

- ☐ **E = Excited:** What excites you about PBL in the mathematics classroom? What's the upside?

- ☐ **W = Worrisome:** What do you find worrisome about PBL in the mathematics classroom? What's the downside?

- ☐ **N = Need to Know:** What else do you need to know or find out about PBL in the mathematics classroom? What additional information would help you to evaluate things?

- ☐ **S = Stance / Suggestion Moving Forward:** What is your current stance on PBL in the mathematics classroom? How might you move forward in your understanding of PBL in the mathematics classroom?

CHAPTER 2

PBL Mathematics as Equitable, Engaging, and Effective

"Math is math. It's not something I need. It's just another school subject." These are the words of Kala, a basketball-loving sixth grader in a small urban middle school. Although Kala scores above average in mathematics, this eleven-year-old African American female did not see the value of mathematics in her personal life. This became my goal as her teacher, to help Kala and all my students see mathematics as needed in their lives.

Need to Knows

- Why is project-based learning mathematics an equitable, engaging, and effective teaching practice?

- Why should you consider adapting your practice to include project-based learning mathematics?

I created a project for my sixth-grade students focused on the mathematics goal of connecting fractions, decimals, and percentages to social inequities in our society. Students chose topics of interest such as mental health, women's rights, or education in developing countries, then conducted research on the topic to find fractions, decimals, percentages, graphs, and charts to use as a starting point for analysis. Students communicated mathematically as they presented data, received feedback, asked critical questions of one another, and shared mathematical work.

Kala decided to focus on the issue of gangs in the United States. When asked why she was interested in this topic, she said,

> For my last project, I did smoking where I heard about DARE [Drug Abuse Resistance Education], and then I heard there was GREAT [Gang Resistance Education and Training], and so I chose that. Another reason is because I wasn't really hearing much about gangs in [our community], so I wanted to look more into that.

During her research, Kala found the percentage breakdown of gang members based on race/ethnicity as well as the approximate total number of gang members (National Gang Center, 2011; U.S. Census Bureau, 2011). As I helped Kala make sense of the data, she questioned, "Why are there so many Hispanic gang members? And Black, too?" In response I questioned Kala how the percentage breakdown for the race/ethnicity of gang members compared to the percentage breakdown of the race/ethnicity of people in the United States. This prompted Kala to continue researching and finding more data to advance her understanding of the topic mathematically.

As Kala explored the data, she learned the skill of finding the percent of a number. When she found out that the estimated number of gang members in the United States was around 1.25 million people, she used the data and the percentages to estimate approximately how many Hispanic, African American or Black, Asian, and white gang members that would be (see Figure 2.1). As Kala shared her findings with the class, one shocked peer shouted out, "There are more Hispanic gang members in the U.S. than live in this whole city . . . like lots more!"

Kala continued to engage in her research and mathematical exploration. She interviewed the school resource officer and an African American female police officer, learning about gang activity specific to our community and the efforts to promote gang resistance through the GREAT program. In her research, Kala also learned that gang activity costs the United States around $100 billion each year. As part of the mathematics project, I urged my students to imagine what could be done to solve the critical issue they explored. In working with Kala, I asked her how the $100 billion used for gang violence could be used differently. To this, Kala said, "I wouldn't be able to figure that out. One hundred billion is a lot of money, so I just don't know where to begin." I encouraged Kala to think about it for a while, perhaps seeing how her classmates were solving their critical issues.

After talking with peers, Kala decided to investigate what it would take to send gang members to college at a local four-year university. By the end of her research and mathematical problem solving, Kala realized she could send almost all, if not all, of the gang members in the United States to college for four years for the same cost of handling gang violence for one year. Kala's reflection on her realization was powerfully straightforward: "Why isn't the government just doing this, then? Putting money into education instead of fixing gang problems and putting them in jail?"

Throughout this project, Kala and her classmates engaged in rigorous mathematical learning, which they applied to a topic of their choosing. In the end, Kala and her peers made info-graphic posters highlighting the topic they explored and their mathematical critiques on society (see Figure 2.1). Kala gave copies of her infographic poster to her law enforcement experts and hung her infographic up at area Boys & Girls Clubs.

A key component of high-level mathematics projects is critical reflection by students (see Chapters 9 and 17). In this project, students reflected on their work using a thinking routine called "I used to think . . . Now I think . . . , " sharing how their thoughts have changed or grown from the beginning of the project to the end. Kala's final reflection highlighted her growth in academics as well as her mathematics identity: "I used to think math was just something to do in school and not part of my life. Now I think that math is important to help people understand our world and change things for the better."

Figure 2-1 • Kala's Infographic

 # All About Gang Violence and how to solve it

some math facts

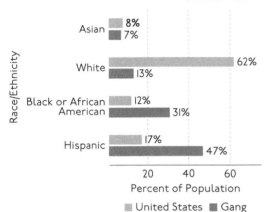

Race/Ethnicity / Percent of Population

- Asian — 8% / 7%
- White — 62% / 13%
- Black or African American — 12% / 31%
- Hispanic — 17% / 47%

■ United States ■ Gang

There are **1,150,000** gang members in the U.S.A.

That means there are **540,500** Hispanic gang members, **356,500** Black gang members, **149,500** white gang members, **80,500** Asian gang members, and **23,000** other gang members in the U.S.A.

37% of gang members are under the age of 18.

100% of cities with a population of more than 250,000 report gang activity.

 thats all of them!

$100,000,000,000

How much that U.S.A. spends on gang violence every year.

Cost of College for One Year

Tuition: $8,942

Housing: $4,000

Food: $3,000

School Needs: $2,000

Clothing/Personal Items: $1,000

Transportation/Travel: $1,000

Total: $19,942

        rounded that's $20,000

College for Gang Members

$20,000 per year for 4 years = $80,000

I divided $100,000,000,000 (100 billion) by $80,000.

I found that with 100 bilion dollars, I could send 1.25 million people to college for 4 years.

That could send almost all of the gang members to college for 4 years!

Note: This figure is a reproduction of student work; spelling errors have been left in for authenticity.

Source: Icon from iStock.com/BRO Vector

THREE REASONS FOR PBL MATHEMATICS

Kala is just one student in one classroom at one particular point in my teaching career. Yet, she inspired me to strive to bring the relevance of mathematics to all students. Kala inspired me to consider so many students in my classroom—for example:

- Students who don't see themselves as mathematicians

- Students whose previous schooling didn't make them hate math, but didn't help them see the beauty, joy, and wonder of mathematics either

- Students who have all the potential to use mathematics in their future but who could also easily dismiss mathematics as "just another school subject"

- Students whose community and cultural funds of knowledge have yet to be invited into the classroom

- Students who love mathematics and want to keep being challenged

Kala is just one student who brings equity to the forefront of my mind as I continually develop my classroom teaching and learning practices. If someone asks me why I teach, I don't say, "I teach to be equitable." I say, "I teach for my students. I teach to empower my students. I teach to help my students become change agents through mathematics. I teach for Kala." This is my *why*.

What is your *why*? Or, perhaps more importantly, who is your *why*?

YOUR TURN

Think about your lived experiences, your classroom, and your students. What is your *why*? Who is your *why*?

_____

_____

For Kala and all my students, I have chosen to center my mathematics classroom practice on project-based learning, or PBL. I find PBL mathematics to encompass what I see as the three *E*s of choosing a teaching and learning practice:

- *Equitable*
  - Is the practice equitable? Does it empower all students by building identity and agency?

- *Engaging*
  - Is the practice engaging students? Will students be engaged emotionally, behaviorally, and cognitively?

- *Effective*
  - Is the practice effective? Does it provide opportunity to explore rich content knowledge while developing the skills of a mathematician or the Mathematical Habits of Mind?

PBL mathematics connects to my personal belief of what a mathematics classroom experience should look like, sound like, and feel like. It connects to the Six Essential Attributes of the PBL mathematics classroom shared in Chapter 1. Let's explore how PBL mathematics connects to teaching and learning practices that are equitable, engaging, and effective.

PBL Mathematics as an Equitable Teaching Practice

A driving question: is the overarching question that guides student inquiry throughout the duration of a project.

PBL shifts the classroom narrative from students receiving information from the teacher to students being active players at the center of learning. This occurs from the onset of a project where teachers share a driving question and seek student "need to know" questions to continue sustaining the learning. A driving question is the overarching question that guides student inquiry throughout the duration of a project; for example, the Driving Question of this book is "How can I bring project-based learning [PBL] to life in the mathematics classroom?"

From there, each chapter highlights Need to Know questions, questions that stem from the Driving Question. Need to Know questions are the wonderings and curiosities of students that guide learning throughout the project process in order to successfully answer the Driving Question. Therefore, these student-generated Need to Know questions drive the learning in a PBL mathematics experience, positioning student curiosities at the heart of instruction (read more about this process in Chapter 13).

Need to Know questions: are the wonderings and curiosities of students that guide learning throughout the project process.

Authentic connections to students' lived experiences are critical to a successful project. Students engage deeply in learning academic content while also developing success skills like collaboration and communication. Being situated in a real-world context, students embody the role of mathematician, affirming their identity and authority in the mathematics classroom. PBL draws from student strengths, engaging with students from an asset-based lens. Kala's story represents an equity-focused mindset in the mathematics classroom and the PBL classroom.

Kala's experience, and that of her classmates, aligns with the five equity-based mathematics teaching practices called for in the book *The Impact of Identity in K–8 Mathematics Learning and Teaching* (Aguirre et al., 2013):

1. Going deep with mathematics

2. Leveraging multiple mathematical competencies

3. Affirming mathematics learners' identities

4. Challenging spaces of marginality

5. Drawing on multiple resources of knowledge

This framework can be further supported by examining the equity levers found in PBL. A leading organization for project-based learning, PBLWorks (Field, 2021), has put forward a set of equity levers in the classroom that both align with and enhance the Aguirre et al. (2013) framework:

1. Knowledge of students

2. Cognitive demand

3. Literacy

4. Shared power

Figure 2.2 highlights the intersection of the Aguirre et al. (2013) framework and the PBLWorks (Field, 2021) equity levers as they relate not only Kala's story but also general PBL mathematics connections to equity as exemplified by the Six Essential Attributes of the PBL mathematics classroom, first introduced in Chapter 1 and later explored in Section II.

Figure 2-2 • Equity Frameworks and PBL Mathematics

Aguirre et al. (2013)	PBLWorks (Field, 2021)	Kala's Story	Six Essential Attributes of PBL Mathematics
Going deep with mathematics	Cognitive demand	Kala connected the concept of percentages and percent of a number with her researched data. Kala analyzed and synthesized her information using mathematics to create new knowledge and solutions to a problem.	**Rigorous Content:** Rigor of content moves students to the highest levels of Bloom's taxonomy (Bloom et al., 1956). PBL centers on rigorous academic instruction where students move from understanding to application of a concept, requiring deep mathematical knowledge. Students synthesize and develop new knowledge through the creation of a product or sharing of their learning.
Leveraging multiple mathematical competencies	Knowledge of students and cognitive demand	Kala worked on a project in a non-tracked classroom and used visual representations in her infographic as part of her assessment, instead of a traditional skill and drill test.	**Identity & Agency:** PBL engages students through an asset-based lens. Students use their community and cultural funds of knowledge to examine an issue and create new knowledge. Students draw upon their strengths to display learning in an authentic way.
Affirming mathematics learners' identities	Knowledge of students	Kala developed the identity of a competent problem solver through multiple iterations of her work. Through individual conferences, I learned about Kala's interests and strengths.	**Authentic Connections:** Mathematics situated in the context of a project creates multiple points of entry. Mistakes are viewed as opportunities for growth. Teachers gain valuable insight into the identity and interests of their students during individual or small-group conferencing.

Aguirre et al. (2013)	PBLWorks (Field, 2021)	Kala's Story	Six Essential Attributes of PBL Mathematics
Challenging spaces of marginality	Shared power	Kala's research and expertise positioned her as having legitimate mathematical authority among her peers. Kala explored an authentic topic of her choosing. Kala exercised voice and choice in the exploration of her topic.	**Identity & Agency:** PBL increases student voice and choice, centering work on collaboration, asking students to bring their knowledge to the table for the betterment of the group or entire classroom. In a PBL mathematics experience, students collaboratively discuss critical world topics while gaining mathematical knowledge and life skills.
Drawing on multiple resources of knowledge	Literacy	Kala learned about gang activity in the community from law enforcement, asking each expert for local stories and data to enhance her mathematical understandings. Kala communicated her findings via an infographic poster, where she accurately represented her mathematics through numbers, graphs, and words.	**Productive Inquiry** and **Meaningful Assessment:** In addition to leveraging the knowledge of the teacher and other students, PBL experiences often include a component of learning from family or community experts to gain knowledge. PBL requires research outside of a textbook, highlighting resources from primary sources to newspaper articles to websites of organizations. Students increase verbal and visual communication skills by using accurate vocabulary, charts, graphs, drawings, and diagrams.

PBL Mathematics as an Engaging Teaching Practice

Have you ever sat in a workshop, training, or professional development experience without truly engaging? Perhaps you went through the motions of nodding your head in agreement, opening presenter slides on your computer to follow along, and turning to a neighbor to discuss a topic. However, at the conclusion of the experience, you walked away with little to no true engagement in the experience.

As educators, we often know what lessons or units engage students. We can describe what engagement looks like, sounds like, and feels like, but how can we distinguish true engagement by our students? Researchers have described student engagement as the intersection of three important dimensions: behavioral, emotional, and cognitive (Fredricks et al., 2004). When all three dimensions are present, learners remain fully engaged, leading to increased school success (Appleton et al., 2006). Figure 2.3 defines each of these three dimensions (Fredericks et al., 2004).

Figure 2-3 • Dimensions of Student Engagement

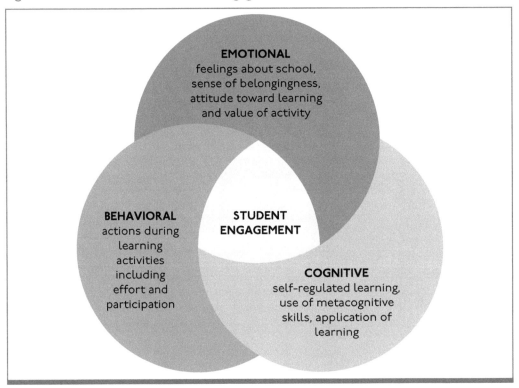

Source: Adapted from Fredricks et al. (2004).

In many mathematics classrooms, students are engaged cognitively and behaviorally. Cognitively, rich and rigorous mathematics experiences occur daily. Behaviorally, students show effort and participation in mathematics tasks. The third dimension, emotional engagement, is often the dimension that is hardest to accomplish. Creating a community of learners in the mathematics classroom certainly leads to feelings of belongingness in school; however, student perception of the value of an activity becomes increasingly difficult as mathematics moves to the abstract. Students may not see the importance of multiplying two fractions using an area model or finding the area under the curve of a sine function. Short-term emotional engagement may occur through the use of problem-solving tasks and performance tasks (see Chapter 3); however, long-term emotional engagement occurs when utilizing PBL.

Let's explore how Kala embodied all three dimensions of student engagement and how those dimensions connect to the Six Essential Attributes of the PBL mathematics classroom (see Figure 2.4).

Figure 2-4 ◆ Kala's Story Connected to Engagement Dimensions and Essential Attributes

Student Engagement Dimension (Fredricks et al., 2004)	Kala's Story	Six Essential Attributes of PBL Mathematics
Emotional	I created the opportunity for students to exercise strong voice and choice as they individually chose a critical societal topic to research. Kala chose gangs because of a connection to a prior project where she learned about the DARE program and a desire to learn more about the GREAT program. Her emotional investment was heightened when she initiated conversations with two police officers.	**Identity & Agency** and **Authentic Connections:** In the creation of a project, one of the main goals is to connect students emotionally to the topic at hand. Providing for voice and choice contributes to a student's further emotional connection to the project. A strong project centered on an authentic context meaningful to students naturally leads to stronger student emotional engagement.
Behavioral	Kala showed continued effort and participation in classroom activities. Her behavioral engagement allowed her to draw connections between the general mathematics topic of fractions, decimals, and percentages and her application of the mathematics into her chosen topic.	**Productive Inquiry:** Behavioral engagement can be observed in a project during productive inquiry, where students work to sustain their interest in a project. Students ask questions in order to engage in learning activities that further their knowledge.
Cognitive	Kala showed self-directedness and regulation in her learning as she researched data related to gang violence. Kala applied mathematical concepts and learning to her self-chosen topic. She engaged in critique and revision with her peers, reflecting upon her growth as a learner.	**Rigorous Content, Meaningful Assessment,** and **Growth Through Reflection:** Rigorous content lays the foundation for cognitive engagement, while meaningful assessment practices highlight continued cognitive engagement. Metacognitive strategies like ongoing reflection further solidify cognitive engagement.

PBL Mathematics as an Effective Teaching Practice

Teachers and researchers across the education field define *effective* differently. How exactly do we know a teaching and learning practice is effective? What characteristics and qualities should we generally look for? The National Council of Teachers of Mathematics (NCTM, 2014) explored the idea of effective mathematics teaching in its publication *Principles to Actions*, citing eight practices. Each of these practices is met in the PBL mathematics classroom, as highlighted by Kala's story as well as a general connection to the Six Essential Attributes of the PBL mathematics classroom (see Figure 2.5).

Figure 2-5 ◆ Kala's Story Connected to Effective Teaching Practices and Essential Attributes

Effective Mathematics Teaching Practice (NCTM, 2014)	Kala's Story	Six Essential Attributes of PBL Mathematics
Establish mathematics goals to focus learning.	Kala's mathematics goals centered on using fractions, decimals, and percentages from real-world sources to analyze a societal problem. Kala visually and numerically compared fractions, decimals, and percentages as well as learned how to calculate the percent of a number. Kala applied her understanding gained from mathematics workshops to her own data, showing the ability to move from surface and deep understanding to transfer levels of mathematical knowledge (Hattie et al., 2017).	**Rigorous Content:** PBL mathematics is centered on rigorous content instruction. Instruction taught at a surface to deep level lays the foundation for application of knowledge, solidifying transfer-level understanding. (See more in Chapter 4.)
Build procedural fluency from conceptual understanding.		
Implement tasks that promote reasoning and problem solving.		
Use and connect mathematical representations.		

Effective Mathematics Teaching Practice (NCTM, 2014)	Kala's Story	Six Essential Attributes of PBL Mathematics
Facilitate meaningful mathematical discourse. Pose purposeful questions.	Both Kala and I, as the teacher, posed purposeful questions about the data, specifically surrounding the race/ethnicity of gang members. These questions led to the natural discussion of percentages and how to find a percent of a number, extending Kala's mathematical content knowledge.	**Productive Inquiry:** In PBL mathematics, student questioning plays a central role in the project process. Kala's questions allowed for just-in-time learning about how to find the percent of a number. This prompted Kala to conduct more research, leading to sustained engagement in the topic and the mathematics. (See more in Chapter 5.)
Support productive struggle in learning mathematics.	Kala struggled to conceptualize how to use $100 billion to positively impact the issue of gang violence. Instead of providing her an answer, I prompted her to explore the work of her peers to generate ideas. Her growth solidified in her final reflection when Kala realized mathematics can be used "to help people understand our world and change things for the better."	**Growth Through Reflection:** Productive struggle occurs when students face problems they don't immediately know how to answer. When persevering through the struggle, students may not immediately recognize the benefit of the struggle. Through reflection, students can name the struggle and grow as a mathematician and learner. (See more in Chapter 9.)
Elicit and use evidence of student thinking.	Kala created an infographic of her mathematical research and thinking, publicly hanging it in area Boys & Girls Clubs. She visibly expressed her thinking based on research and mathematics on the poster. Drafts of her work allowed me to assess progress toward her mathematical understanding, providing just-in-time learning and instruction to support Kala. From Kala's drafts of her work, mathematical thinking was critiqued and revised by peers as well as me as her teacher.	**Meaningful Assessment:** Using evidence of student thinking as both formative and summative assessments provides both students and educators the opportunity to reflect on progress toward learning goals, thus informing teaching and learning practices. Most importantly, in PBL mathematics, students believe in the *why* behind the assessment or final product. Evidence of student learning should be highlighted in a final public product. (See more in Chapter 8.)

CONCLUDING THOUGHTS

Kala was my sixth-grade student in 2015. She has since graduated high school. Curious, I emailed her to see if she recalled this sixth-grade project. Here's her response:

> To be honest I don't remember much of the math I did in that project. I know I had to find a lot of percents. I remember my mom didn't believe me that I needed to make a phone call to a police officer at night because she [the police officer] worked third shift. I also remember being sad that there was only one Black female police officer in our area. I hope that's changed. I kinda remember making a poster because I hung it up at the Boys and Girls Club but I don't remember what I put on the poster. Sorry. I know you probably want me to remember more of the math LOL.

Thrilled to hear from her, I responded, "Actually, I don't care that you don't remember the exact math. What warms my heart is that you remember the project at all, that calling experts and seeing our community in a different light resonated with you. Whether you remember what was on your poster or not, the fact that you remember putting it up and being an active member of society is a beautiful gift."

Truly, if every student responded to me eight years after leaving my classroom with a memory of productive inquiry and engagement in school and the greater community, I'd feel incredibly blessed. In the end, mathematics is an accumulated skill, a developed understanding and mindset that happens over years of schooling.

Kala is my student. Kala is why I teach. Again, I ask, "What is your *why*? Who is your *why*?" My sincere desire is for PBL to transform your classroom, transform your students, and transform our world as you deepen your *why*.

PBL POINTS TO PONDER: THE FOUR Cs

In the four Cs routine, consider each of the questions as a starting point for discussion or reflection. This routine allows you to make connections, ask questions, identify key ideas, and consider application.

Connections: What connections can you draw between this chapter and your personal practice of engaging in equitable, engaging, and effective teaching?

Challenges: What ideas, positions, or assumptions do you want to challenge or argue with in this chapter?

Concepts: What key concepts or ideas do you think are important and worth holding on to from this chapter?

Changes: What changes in attitudes, thinking, or action are suggested by this chapter, either for you or for others?

CHAPTER 3

From Problem to Project

FROM TASK TO PROJECT

Need to Knows

- How is project-based learning different from a problem-solving task or performance task?

- Why should I choose to engage students in project-based learning in addition to problem-solving and performance tasks?

- How do I turn a textbook problem into a problem-solving task, performance task, and/ or project?

Diving into project-based learning (PBL) can seem like a gigantic jump for many mathematics educators. However, you can take smaller steps to ensure you and your students feel ready to tackle a project. One way is to begin implementing problem-solving tasks and performance tasks.

Most mathematics educators are familiar with problem-solving tasks, but let's clarify this idea. The National Council of Teachers of Mathematics (NCTM, 2010) recognizes the term *problem solving* in conjunction with tasks that "have the potential to provide intellectual challenges for enhancing students' mathematical understanding and development." These tasks help students view mathematics conceptually while furthering Mathematical Habits of Mind, especially Communicate Mathematically and Question & Persist in Problem Solving.

Problem-solving tasks have been likened to the phrase "low floor, high ceiling," meaning students can access the problem without much difficulty but room exists for exploration and growth. Problem-solving tasks ask students to determine a way to move from what is known to what is desired through multiple potential pathways that build upon prior knowledge and allow for creative risks. Liljedahl (2021) asserts that "good problem-solving tasks require students to get stuck and then to think, to experiment, to try and to fail, and to apply their knowledge in novel ways in order to get unstuck" (p. 20). I recommend further exploring the work of Liljedahl who examines what he calls "highly engaging thinking tasks" in his book *Building Thinking Classrooms in Mathematics*. Throughout the book, Liljedahl provides several examples of highly engaging problem-solving tasks for K–12 educators.

Additional Resources

Here's a list of other problem-solving tasks and mathematics educators I regularly consult:

- Open Middle Problems (Kaplinsky, 2019)

- 3-Act Math Tasks (Fletcher, n.d.; Lomax, n.d.; Meyer, n.d.; Pearce & Orr, n.d.; Wiernicki, n.d.)

- Visual Patterns (Nguyen, 2020)

- NRICH (University of Cambridge, 2022)

There is an option between a short problem-solving task and a full project, and that is what I'll call a performance task. According to Defined Learning (2015), a performance task is an open-ended application of knowledge and skills where students are asked to perform, create, or produce a tangible product to demonstrate their learning and proficiency. Performance tasks are similar to a shortened form of a project, where students grow in academic content and success skills through a transferable real-world application. Like a PBL experience, performance tasks emphasize cooperation, problem solving, and authentic, hands-on learning while de-emphasizing memorization or rote mathematics.

Figure 3.1 is a glimpse into the differences between a problem-solving task, a performance task, and a PBL experience. The similarities and differences between each level are on a continuum. The nuances between a performance task and a project are subtle, focused mainly on duration, depth of learning, and extent of resources.

Figure 3-1 • Comparison of Problem-Solving Task, Performance Task, and PBL Experience

	Problem-Solving Task	Performance Task	Project-Based Learning Experience
Time Frame	I class period or less	2–5 days	6 days +
Number of Content Standards	I content standard (one content area)	I–2 content standards (may include more than one content area)	3+ content standards (often includes multiple content areas)
Strategies and Solution	Open-ended strategies toward one or limited solutions	Open-ended strategies and multiple solutions	Open-ended strategies and multiple solutions
Real-World Context	Authentic connection possible	Authentic connection likely	Authentic connection required
Student Collaboration	Independent or collaborative	Independent or collaborative	Collaborative
Potential Role(s) Played by Student	Problem Solver, Materials Manager, Time Keeper	Researcher, Designer, Presenter	Engineer, Architect, Sports Statistician, Environmentalist, Advertising Agent, Software Designer
Outcome	Mathematical explanation	Presentation, model, prototype, diagram, sketches, public service announcement, infographic	3D-printed item, video, artwork, scaled map, fundraiser/ event, business, community presentation
Resources	Limited: Written or digital problem-solving task and solution	General: Technology for research (optional), classroom supplies	Extensive: Technology for research, experts, physical product supplies, technology for creation

WHEN PROBLEM-SOLVING TASKS AREN'T ENOUGH

Using high-quality problem-solving tasks with multiple entry points in the mathematics classroom is an effective and engaging teaching strategy. Like all quality teaching strategies, problem-solving tasks have their place in the classroom. Where problem-solving tasks often fall short is in their ability to deeply and authentically engage students in the mathematics of our world. Take, for example, the classic locker task, where students open and close lockers in a unique pattern.

I have given this engaging task with a unique solution to my middle school students; however, to what purpose? Who actually opens and closes lockers in such a pattern?

Imagine there is an endless string of lockers in your school.

Person 1 starts at locker 1 and opens every locker.

Person 2 starts at locker 2 and closes every 2nd locker.

Person 3 starts at locker 3 and closes every 3rd locker.

Person 4 starts at locker 4 and closes every 4th locker.

Person x starts at locker x and closes every xth locker.

Which locker doors will be open when the process is complete?

If my purpose is for students to explore Mathematical Habits of Mind like Search for Patterns or Communicate Mathematically, then this is a quality task. It invites dialogue, helping students establish the mindset of a mathematician. However, if my goal is for students to see mathematics as a skill applied in their own lives—whether that is to create something or critique society—then a problem-solving task in and of itself may not go far enough.

This is where PBL comes into play. Through projects, students apply their mathematical skills and abilities to authentic contexts, embodying the role of a professional who uses mathematics. For example, students may assume the role of an engineer when designing a spacecraft or an architect when creating scale blueprints. Students may act as a sports statistician analyzing data to determine the peak performance levels of an athlete or an environmentalist using mathematics to persuade politicians to tackle tough issues. Moving from problem solver in a mathematics classroom to problem solver as an engineer, architect, statistician, or environmentalist elevates the dynamics of the classroom environment.

ALIGNMENT TO EQUITY-BASED TEACHING PRACTICES

Another reason I ensure PBL plays a central role in my classroom centers on my commitment to equity-based mathematics teaching practices. When using a problem-solving task or even a performance task, students may or may not experience all five equity-based mathematics teaching practices as well as the PBL equity levers described in Chapter 2. However, in a PBL experience, students almost always engage in these practices. Figure 3.2 highlights whether each equity-based mathematics teaching practice and equity lever is met on the scale of Rarely–Sometimes–Often–Always.

Figure 3-2 • Examination of Meeting Equity Levers

Equity-Based Teaching Practice [PBLWorks Equity Lever]	Problem-Solving Task	Performance Task	Project-Based Learning
Going Deep With Mathematics [Cognitive Demand]	Always A problem-solving task of high cognitive demand provides students with multiple solution pathways and representations. Problem-solving tasks support students in analyzing, comparing, justifying, and proving solutions.	Always A performance task of high cognitive demand is open-ended, allowing for multiple solution pathways and representations. Students work collaboratively in teams to analyze, compare, justify, and prove solutions.	Always A PBL experience of high cognitive demand is naturally open-ended, allowing for multiple solution pathways and representations. Students work collaboratively in teams to analyze, compare, justify, and prove solutions. Especially leveraged in a project is the opportunity for presentation and critique, leading to greater opportunities for comparison, justification, and communication of solution pathways.
Leveraging Multiple Mathematical Competencies [Knowledge of Students and Cognitive Demand]	Sometimes A problem-solving task may or may not allow for effective structured collaboration where students with varying content and success skills can contribute to complex problems. Due to the short-term nature of a problem-solving task, student collaboration is limited, perhaps not allowing all students to contribute meaningfully.	Always A performance task by its nature is collaborative. Effective structuring of a task allows students with varying content and success skills to contribute to complex problems.	Always A PBL experience by its nature is collaborative. Effective structuring of a PBL experience allows students with varying content and success skills to contribute to complex problems. In a PBL experience, our knowledge of students is heightened as we intentionally team students for long-term collaboration, allowing each student to effectively contribute through application of content knowledge or success skill.

(Continued)

(*Continued*)

Equity-Based Teaching Practice [PBLWorks Equity Lever]	Problem-Solving Task	Performance Task	Project-Based Learning
Affirming Mathematics Learners' Identities [Knowledge of Students]	Sometimes Problem-solving tasks promote student persistence and reasoning, leading to a growth mindset where mistakes are seen as opportunities for growth. Problem-solving tasks in and of themselves often do not recognize or lift up the multifaceted nature of mathematical identities. Reflection sometimes occurs on mathematical identity after a problem-solving task.	Often Performance tasks promote student persistence and reasoning, leading to a growth mindset where mistakes are seen as opportunities for growth. Because students have a longer amount of time in a performance task, opportunities for iteration to learn from mistakes are more prevalent. A performance task centered on an authentic context often allows for exploration of students' multifaceted mathematical identity. Reflection often occurs on mathematical identity at the conclusion of a performance task.	Always A PBL experience promotes student persistence and reasoning, leading to a growth mindset where mistakes are seen as opportunities for growth. An essential part of the project process is to critique and revise products, meaning opportunities for iteration to learn from mistakes are inherent in PBL. A PBL experience centered on an authentic context always allows for deep exploration of students' multifaceted mathematical identity. Reflection always occurs on mathematical identity both throughout and at the conclusion of a project.

Equity-Based Teaching Practice [PBLWorks Equity Lever]	Problem-Solving Task	Performance Task	Project-Based Learning
Challenging Spaces of Marginality [Shared Power]	Rarely Problem-solving tasks rarely center on students' lived experiences with racism or discrimination. In a problem-solving task, students rarely use mathematics to address societal injustices within the school or community. Problem-solving tasks sometimes are structured to leverage students as a source of expertise. Problem-solving tasks rarely allow students to generate math-based questions to explore an unjust situation. Note: Ongoing work in this area is directly addressed in *Engaging in Culturally Relevant Math Tasks* (Matthews et al., 2022a, 2022b).	Sometimes Performance tasks sometimes center on students' lived experiences with racism or discrimination. In a performance task, students sometimes use mathematics to address societal injustices within the school or community. Performance tasks often are structured to leverage students as a source of expertise. Performance tasks sometimes allow students to generate mathematics-based questions to explore an unjust situation.	Often A PBL experience often has a connection to students' lived experiences with racism or discrimination, whether that connection is at the center of a project or a part of the project. In a project, students often use mathematics to address societal injustices within the school or community. Projects are always structured to leverage students as a source of expertise, whether that expertise is content knowledge or a success skill, especially during peer-to-peer critique and revision opportunities. Projects often allow students to generate mathematics-based questions to explore an unjust situation. Projects always lift up mathematics-based questions based in authentic contexts during the gathering of Need to Know questions.

(*Continued*)

(*Continued*)

Equity-Based Teaching Practice [PBLWorks Equity Lever]	Problem-Solving Task	Performance Task	Project-Based Learning
Drawing on Multiple Resources of Knowledge [Literacy]	Rarely Problem-solving tasks rarely make connections to multiple resources outside of the task itself. Problem-solving tasks pose limited opportunities to connect school mathematics with the mathematics of the home and community. Problem-solving tasks sometimes allow students to reexamine their historical identity as a mathematics student, if students engage in targeted reflection on that topic.	Sometimes Performance tasks sometimes make connections to resources and research outside of the task. A performance task often connects school mathematics with the mathematics of the home and community. Performance tasks sometimes allow students to reexamine their historical identity as a mathematics student, if students embrace a mathematical role in the performance task and engage in reflection on that role.	Always A PBL experience always makes connections to resources and research, often leveraging experts in the field and primary sources to enhance learning. A PBL experience always connects school mathematics with the mathematics of the home and community. By embracing a role throughout the course of the project, students continually reexamine their historical identity as a mathematics student as they build a new, positive identity. This reexamination is especially lifted up during opportunities for reflection both throughout and at the conclusion of a project.

THE TWOFOLD PRESSURE OF TIME

After discussing PBL as an equitable teaching practice, mathematics educators are still often hesitant to dive into PBL because of the time factor, as initially addressed in Chapter 1. Time is a real pressure. I'm not going to deny that. Yet time can be a blessing. When looking at a problem-solving task, time plays a small role as tasks can often be completed in less than one class period. With such a small amount of time, students can choose to engage or not engage, knowing the short duration of that task. Even with the best effort to structure a problem-solving task for engagement by all, a student may be sick that day or have an emotional or behavioral need taking them away from class. Within a PBL experience, students are engaging with mathematics over a longer period of time, providing students multiple opportunities to deeply explore the content in an authentic manner and reflect upon their growth as a learner and mathematician. This is yet another reason I ensure my classroom practice includes PBL.

Another pressure is the time it takes to design a PBL mathematics experience. Most traditional curricula do not include the scaffolds and materials to be fully prepared to implement a project. Again, time becomes a factor. However, I have found the amount of time I spend designing and preparing a project decreases as I become more adept at my skills as a PBL practitioner. I continue to see increased engagement and appreciation of mathematics in my students during a project, making the reward of PBL much more tangible. Furthermore, one of my goals is to help fill the void of quality, ready-made projects that teachers can use and adapt for their classroom. To see several examples of PBL mathematics experiences, check out the companion website at https://qrs.ly/56ensfy.

Additional Resources

Additional resources can be found online at PBLWorks (www.pblworks.org) as well as in two series of books:

*   *Project-Based Learning in the Math Classroom* (K–2, 3–5, and 6–10 editions; Fancher & Norfar, 2019; Norfar & Fancher, 2022a, 2022b)

*   *Rigor, Relevance, and Relationships: Making Mathematics Come Alive With Project-Based Learning* (Lee & Galindo, 2018) and *Project-Based Learning in Elementary Classrooms: Making Mathematics Come Alive* (Lee & Galindo, 2021)

WEAVING TASKS AND PROJECTS TOGETHER

Looking back at my journey in my mathematics curriculum, I recognize that my pathway took me from traditional textbook problems to problem-solving tasks, then on to performance tasks and ultimately PBL mathematics experiences. Personally, I use a combination of all problem-solving tasks, performance tasks, and PBL mathematics experiences in my classroom, depending on my mathematical goals, my curriculum, my standards, and my students. In my work with other educators, I also encourage them to consider using these various teaching and learning strategies to effectively engage all students throughout the course of the school year.

In coaching high school mathematics teacher Josh Wilke, we worked through two units in his Algebra II classroom (Unit 7: Exponential Functions and Unit 8: Logarithmic Functions), paying particular attention to his use of problem-solving tasks, performance tasks, and PBL mathematics experiences. Josh already had a favorite problem-solving task he wanted to use where he asked students to determine if the "average worker" could ever make as much money as Jeff Bezos. Normally, Josh gave this task after students learned the various compound interest formulas. However, to boost intrigue for the upcoming unit as well as provide more opportunity for productive struggle, we decided to give the initial part of the task to students at the beginning of the unit, circling back to the task halfway through the unit. This provided students a reason to keep engaging with the material, to eventually solve the Jeff Bezos task.

Josh knew he wanted to create a project that helped students model data using linear, exponential, and/or logarithmic functions. While discussing potential real-world applications of these topics, Josh commented that one of his favorite professors studied modeling of a zombie apocalypse. We both really liked this idea and knew it would be a fun hook for students; however, in exploring the ability to sustain this topic and ultimately connect it authentically to a public audience, we decided the zombie apocalypse would make a strong performance task for students. This performance task along with a traditional chapter test would comprise his summative assessments for Unit 7 of his textbook on exponential functions.

Still in search of a project topic, Josh was watching his local news that shared a story about the rise in drug overdoses due to fentanyl. Intrigued to know more, he explored data surrounding the opioid crisis in America, recognizing that a lot of the data used exponential or logarithmic data in its modeling. These data became the basis of his project called the *Campaign Against Opioid Addiction*. We decided to weave this project throughout Unit 8 of his textbook on logarithmic functions, adding in a problem-solving task specifically modeling the half-life of a drug in the body system. This project allowed students to apply knowledge gained about exponential functions as well as logarithmic functions while using the mathematics to inform the public through social media campaigns. Figure 3.3 is a calendar snapshot of Josh's two units that highlights his use of problem-solving tasks, a performance task, and a PBL mathematics experience.

Figure 3-3 • Calendar Snapshot

Monday	Tuesday	Wednesday	Thursday	Friday
Problem-Solving Task: Jeff Bezos Part I	7.1 Intro to Exponential Functions	7.2 Zero & Negative Exponents Workshop	7.3 Fractional Exponents Workshop	Quiz & 7.4 Exponential Graphs
7.4 Exponential Graphs cont...	Problem-Solving Task: Jeff Bezos Part II	7.5 Solving Exponential Equations	7.5 Solving Exponential Equations cont...	7.6 Linear vs. Exponential Fuctions
Performance Task: Zombie Apocalypse	Performance Task: Zombie Apocalypse	Performance Task Presentations	Reflection on Performance Task & Review Ch. 7	Summative Test
Launch, Driving Question & NTKs	Form Teams, Research & Data Gathering	8.1 Intro to Log Functions	8.2 Logs & Exponential Functions	Problem-Solving Task: Drugs in the Blood
Share Out Problem-Solving Task & Work Time	8.3 & 8.4 Log Relationships	Work Time & 8.5-Natural Log Workshop I	Work Time & 8.5-Natural Log Workshop II	Quiz & Team Work Time
Expert Zoom	Work Time-Draft of Social Media Campaign	See-A-B Critique & 8.6 Log Equations	Finish 8.6 Log Equations & Work Time	Model Equations & Work Time
Gallery Walk Critique Protocol	Final Work Time & Quiz	Culminating Event: Launch Social Media Campaigns	Reflection & Self-Assessment	*[Extra Day]*

online resources The project featured in this vignette is available for download at **https://qrs.ly/56ensfy**.

TURNING TEXTBOOK PROBLEMS INTO PROBLEM-SOLVING TASKS, PERFORMANCE TASKS, AND PROJECTS

As previously noted, time plays an important factor in our role as educators. Because of this, I purposefully explore my mathematics curriculum with the lens of spiraling textbook problems into problem-solving tasks or even performance tasks. In other words, I don't add on to my textbook problems with other tasks and projects; I transform them *into* tasks and projects that suit my purposes and my students' needs. How exactly does this happen? I often work with other mathematics education colleagues to come up with the best ideas, modeling the process of working collaboratively. Let's look at an example where I worked with my colleague Jenn Kosiak on the sixth-grade geometry goal of understanding when and how to apply the volume formula with rectangular prisms.

As we sat in a coffee shop together, Jenn opened up her textbook and found the following problem:

What is the volume of a rectangular prism with dimensions of 10 inches by 6 inches by 3 inches?

Using this problem as the base of our conversation, Jenn and I talked about how this textbook problem leads to limited strategy use by students and one very concrete answer.

Problem-Solving Tasks

To create a more dynamic problem leading to deeper engagement, Jenn and I rewrote this into a problem-solving task:

Given a volume of 180 inches cubed, what could be the dimensions of a right rectangular prism?

YOUR TURN

Pick a problem from your textbook and practice rewriting it as a problem-solving task in the space provided.

Textbook Problem:	Problem-Solving Task:

Performance Tasks

As we continued to dialogue about the concept of volume, the conversation turned from purely mathematical to a look at society. Where is volume used in our world? What jobs might need to apply the concept of volume? How can we use volume to solve authentic issues in our society? To make the previous problem-solving task more authentic, we decided to create a performance task. Given that students engage in a performance task over a few days, these types of tasks emphasize success skills such as cooperation, problem solving, and authentic, hands-on learning while de-emphasizing memorization or rote mathematics.

Jenn had recently read a news story about Meals on Wheels, a community-based program that delivers meals to people who are older or home-bound. Part of that news story focused on the incredible role Meals on Wheels plays in our society, especially during the height of the COVID-19 pandemic when this organization started a new program delivering to children from low-income families, called Meals 4 Kids. However, the main part of the story highlighted the first ever "green energy" Meals on Wheels van, which had been retrofitted with an electric engine and a solar-powered refrigeration unit. We discussed how volume would play a key role in retrofitting that van, recognizing the volume of a refrigeration unit, a food storage unit, and a Meals on Wheels container would need to be examined. With that in mind, we set to work creating a performance task and a PBL mathematics experience that could be used in the middle school classroom.

We actually circled back to our problem-solving task and added some more context, turning it into a performance task.

Given a volume of 180 inches cubed, what could be the dimensions of a right rectangular prism?

You just learned the rectangular prism was used to store food. What dimensions make sense? Which ones do not make sense? Why? Explain your reasoning.

These additional questions focus on the same mathematics goal while also providing context for students to think about their solutions in an authentic scenario.

As Jenn and I thought about the news article, we determined the goal of the performance task to be the following:

Redesign the inside of a van to maximize the number of meals that could be delivered by the electric, solar-powered Meals on Wheels van.

Jenn tried out this performance task with a group of sixth graders (see Figure 3.4). Here is the process these students took after reading the initial article. Students began by asking several questions: "How big is the inside of the van? How much space would solar panels take up? How big is one meal? Are all the meals for seniors or kids? Are there different-sized meals? What sorts of items can we add to the van?"

Then, students conducted various tasks in order to complete the performance task:

- Conducted independent research
- Determined the size of the van highlighted in the article
- Reasoned mathematically about the size of a packaged meal
- Explored the dimensions and volume of a refrigeration unit and other food storage units
- Calculated number of meals that could fit in the van

- Created initial sketches and blueprints

- Designed a digital prototype

- Presented final prototype using mathematical arguments and research

This performance task was completed by small teams of two or three students whose strengths of content understanding and success skills complemented one another. For example, while one student excelled mathematically at understanding volume, another student used his design skills to create a three-dimensional model. Another student leveraged communication as a success skill, using public speaking and technology skills to weave together all the tasks into a seamless, multimedia presentation.

Figure 3-4 ◆ Sixth-Grade Students Engaging in the *Meals on Wheels* Performance Task

When exploring how this performance task meets our equity goals, students engaged deeply with mathematics content—using mathematics to problem-solve and find solutions. By working collaboratively and presenting their ideas, students affirmed their identity as doers of mathematics and literate mathematicians. Moreover, students engaged in shared power in the performance task as their voice and choice of how to redesign the vehicle and present their ideas was critical to the collaborative success of the team. Therefore, implementing a performance task provides great movement in the journey toward equitable teaching practices being enacted in the classroom.

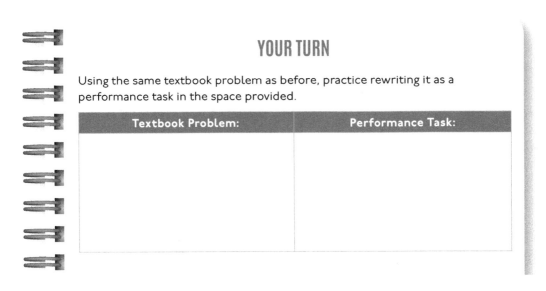

YOUR TURN

Using the same textbook problem as before, practice rewriting it as a performance task in the space provided.

Textbook Problem:	Performance Task:

online resources

The performance task featured in this vignette is available for download at **https://qrs.ly/56ensfy**.

PBL Mathematics Experiences

Lastly, Jenn and I explored what this could look like as a PBL mathematics experience as Meals on Wheels provides a strong community connection as well as mathematics connection. As compared to a performance task, the goal is to engage students over a sustained time period that goes deeply into multiple content standards—mathematics and otherwise—while emotionally engaging the student. We used our implementation of the performance task to support the creation of a PBL mathematics experience. Jenn and I implemented the PBL mathematics experience, launching the project by inviting a coordinator from Meals on Wheels to speak to her students. We then revealed the driving question, "How can we support older adults who face food insecurities?"

What's important to note about the difference between the performance task and the PBL mathematics experience is the introduction of the project through a driving question that leads to the cyclical nature of the PBL experience, cycles that perhaps look like mini performance tasks expertly strung together.

For example, in the Meals on Wheels project, students posed many "need to know" questions (see Figure 3.5). These questions provide a basis for the investigation. Various mathematical ideas present themselves from these student questions, including investigating the cost per meal, dimensions of a meal container, rate of delivery, budget of food, and percentage of older people who need food. These "need to knows" form the basis of future investigations that weave together content standards with the Mathematical Habits of Mind and success skills critical to a PBL mathematics experience.

Figure 3-5 • Student Need to Know Questions for *Meals on Wheels* Project

Meals on Wheels
How can we support older people who face food insecurities?

i wanna help
what can we do as kids

is the food good

Who pays for the food?

is the food hot or cold

Why do they need food?

i want to know
how many older
people need food...

how big is a meal container?

How many old people need
food? Do they need it every
day or just once a wk?

why are they hungry?

Who delivers the food?

i know my grandma gets
food but i dont know if
it is from meals on
whiels

Do they drive to each house?

who is eligible
like do you have to
be a certain age

Why do we let older
people go hungry?

how are meals
delivered and how
many each day

what types of food
do they get?

How much does it
cost for a meal?

Why are they hungry?

is the food like our
school lunch?
do they get options?
does it have each
food group?

My Question
Who cooks the meals?

My Question
How do we get food
to older people in
need?

How often are meals
delivered?

Note: This figure is a reproduction of student work; spelling errors have been left in for authenticity.

Source: money image by iStock.com/Maksym Kapiluk; house icon by iStock.com/rambo189; meals image by iStock.com/carlofranco; child eating image by iStock.com/kool990

YOUR TURN

Using the same textbook problem as before, brainstorm in the space provided how you might create a PBL mathematics experience inspired by the problem.

Textbook Problem:	Ideas for PBL Experience:

CONCLUDING THOUGHTS

I recently finished what we call "student-led conferences," a twist on traditional parent–teacher conferences where students lead their parents, guardians, and family members through a review of their academic learning and personal growth to date. At the conclusion of the conference, family members and teachers are invited to ask questions or share comments. After Lionel, a quiet, sixth-grade mathematics student, shared his learning, his younger, more vivacious sister asked if she could now present her learning. Visibly confused, I tried to redirect the conference back to Lionel. However, this younger sister proudly pulled some sheets of paper out of her backpack to display her redesign of the Meals on Wheels vehicle. Lionel then proceeded to tell me that his sister begs him daily to "play school." Lionel used the *Meals on Wheels* performance task as part of their daily playtime. Lionel's parents shared that even though he may be quiet in my classroom, at home, he plays the patient teacher to his sister.

After Lionel's conference, I reflected on that adage that "a teacher affects eternity; he can never tell where his influence stops" (Adams, 1918). I certainly never expected this performance task to be used at home as part of playtime between a brother and sister. Just as playtime is a daily experience for Lionel and his sister, my goal is to create engaging, authentic experiences for my students. As such, that is why I am passionate about incorporating performance tasks and PBL mathematics experiences regularly in my classroom.

PBL POINTS TO PONDER: CIRCLE OF VIEWPOINTS

Consider these two different viewpoints: student with a positive mathematical identity; student who struggles with mathematics. Use the following script (numbers 1–3) to consider what it would be like to engage in a problem-solving task, a performance task, and a project. Then proceed to Wrap-Up.

1. I am thinking of engaging in a . . . [problem-solving task, performance task, project] . . . from the point of view of . . .

2. I think . . . [*describe the topic from your viewpoint; take on the character of your viewpoint*]

3. A question I have from this viewpoint is . . . [*ask a question from this viewpoint*]

Wrap-Up: What new ideas do you have about the topic that you didn't have before? What new questions do you have?

The What

Section II explores the *what* of project-based learning (PBL) mathematics.

In this section, you will explore the Six Essential Attributes of a PBL mathematics classroom introduced in Chapter 1. As you peruse them, you may notice that each of these attributes can already be found in the mathematics classroom. This is exactly true! The essential attributes of PBL mathematics are not completely foreign to mathematics educators. PBL mathematics exploits these attributes to *deepen* the classroom practice of each of them.

Six Essential Attributes of the PBL Mathematics Classroom

- Growth Through Reflection
- Rigorous Content
- Productive Inquiry
- Identity & Agency
- Meaningful Assessment
- Authentic Connections

For example, all mathematics teachers boast rigorous content. So how does a PBL experience deepen this attribute? Chapter 4 explores how PBL reaches the highest level of Bloom's taxonomy or the deepest level in Webb's Depth of Knowledge (Bloom et al., 1956; Webb, 1997). Chapter 5 addresses productive inquiry, centering on how students—not teachers—take the lead during inquiry practices. Chapter 6 looks at identity and agency in the mathematics classroom.

Chapter 7 focuses on authenticity in the classroom and how authentic connections engage students. Chapter 8 looks at the purpose of formative and summative assessment in PBL mathematics, specifically questioning who finds assessment meaningful. Lastly, Chapter 9 highlights student growth through ongoing reflection and feedback.

Each of the Six Essential Attributes contributes to a robust PBL mathematics classroom. Taken collectively, they work to address the Driving Question of this book: "How can I bring project-based learning [PBL] to life in the mathematics classroom?"

CHAPTER 4

Rigorous Content

"When Mateo measured his bee hotel, he used feet because his is big, but mine is little, so I'm using inches," explained second grader Raine as she grabbed a ruler. Miss Allie Graumann's second-grade class was buzzing with activity as seventeen little bodies worked to create blueprints of their bee hotels aided by a class of preservice educators from the local university. These preservice educators were asked to serve as mathematical experts to help the young students translate a three-dimensional prototype of a bee hotel into two-dimensional blueprints that would be given to a volunteer woodworker who would physically build the bee hotel.

Need to Knows

- What does rigor mean?
- What does rigor look like in the project-based learning mathematics classroom?
- How can students reach deep levels of knowledge and apply mathematics knowledge in authentic contexts?

Raine continued to measure and chatter away about her bee hotel. "I wanted the bees to have a place to relax, so I built them a couch and a TV," she giggled. "I also put this water dish here because I learned bees need water like all living creatures."

While measuring and recording her bee hotel dimensions, the preservice teacher serving as Raine's mathematical expert prompted her with questions like "Why did you round up in this measurement?"; "How do you know this shape is a square?"; and "What units should we use for this quadrilateral?"

Nearby, Hazeem diligently measured his bee hotel, switching between using a yardstick and a ruler. His mathematical expert, a preservice educator, was helping Hazeem measure in inches while recognizing that one foot equals twelve inches. Laying down three rulers, Hazeem counted two feet, three inches as 10 inches + 10 inches + 2 inches + 2 inches + 3 inches = 27 inches. He then checked his calculations using a yardstick. Meanwhile, Hazeem's classmate wondered if the blueprints had to be in inches or if he could write measurements in both feet and inches. The two boys discussed what would be best for the bee hotel woodworker, deciding to keep the measurements in inches.

Over on the rug, a pair of second graders compared their blueprints to the example. The students asked whether they had to show both sides of their bee hotel because the two sides were the same. Aubrey pointed out that the example blueprint did not show both sides of the bee hotel, but her partner Matt countered that the woodworker might think the other side was a big hole if they didn't draw the blueprints. "We can't have a big hole because a bird or a squirrel could get into the hole and kill the bees and steal the honey," Matt shared. So, the students decided to draw both sides of their bee hotel on the blueprint.

In Miss Allie's classroom, these second graders engaged in rigorous content while exploring the driving question, "How can we attract pollinators to our community?"

Previously, they participated in measurement activities by using standard tools like rulers and yardsticks as well as non-standard measurement tools like blocks, paper clips, and hands. As students gained knowledge about measurement, they moved from surface-level to deep understanding, eventually transferring this knowledge by applying it in their project (Hattie et al., 2017). Let's look more closely at rigorous content in the project-based learning (PBL) mathematics classroom.

 The project featured in this vignette is available for download at **https://qrs.ly/56ensfy**.

RIGOROUS CONTENT DEFINED

Before defining rigorous content, let's look at what it is not. As a high school student, I recall night after night of homework in my mathematics classroom, being assigned something like problems 1–31, with problems 32–34 as extra credit points. Section A contained problems 1–14, which were similar to the examples completed in class. In Section B, problems 15–27 were a few steps harder, adding a slight twist on the original problem. Then came the dreaded Section C, problems 28–31 featuring those pesky word problems. And, the really daring or grade-oriented students always tried the extra credit problems.

See, rigor in this case, and in many classrooms, traditionally has been defined as *more* and *faster*; often teachers increase the number and difficulty of problems to point to rigor in their classroom. Specific to mathematics, rigor has often been seen as giving students hard-to-learn mathematics from a higher grade level simply for the sake of "increasing rigor." A shift in this definition occurred as the Common Core State Standards (National Governors Association Center for Best Practices & Council of Chief State School Officers, 2010) focused on rigor as a three-legged stool, balancing conceptual knowledge, procedural skills and fluency, and application. This balance helped open the door to redefine rigor in the mathematics classroom.

Since this redefinition, educators have focused on what learning looks like in a rigorous mathematics classroom. Gojak (2013) recognizes that "a rigorous lesson embraces the messiness of a good mathematics task and the deep learning that it has the potential to achieve." This focus moves closer to the ideal for the PBL mathematics classroom as it connects messy, nonlinear mathematics with deep content learning. Yet, without knowing if the tasks are connected to authentic situations, this notion still falls short for PBL mathematics classrooms. Building off the ideas of Sztabnik (2015), I prefer to define rigor as challenging students to apply conceptual and procedural content knowledge in new ways while connecting to authentic contexts. Rigor uses student curiosities and questions to explore content that reaches to the far edges of a student's learning zone, where more questions arise and invite wonder.

Rigor: is challenging students to apply conceptual and procedural content knowledge in new ways while connecting to authentic contexts, using student curiosities and questions to explore content that reaches to the far edges of a student's learning zone.

Defining rigor as content that challenges student thinking in new and unique ways, problem-solving tasks, performance tasks, and PBL mathematics experiences provide students the opportunity to do just that. During tasks and projects, students engage in nonroutine problems with multiple entry points, pathways, and potential solution outcomes, promoting divergent thinking. The degree to which these tasks apply to authentic situations varies as explored in Chapter 3. What makes rigor especially meaningful in a project, however, is use of student questions and curiosities to drive sustained learning.

In their work on visible learning in the mathematics classroom, Hattie et al. (2017) look at three levels of knowledge—surface, deep, and transfer—each leading to increasing complexity. Extending this work in the PBL classroom, McDowell (2017) contends that the role of the PBL educator is to help students transfer their knowledge of surface and deep content learning found in the academic world to the real-world applications called for in PBL, further enhancing mathematical content knowledge as well as the Mathematical Habits of Mind. In the PBL mathematics classroom, the application to real-world situations heightens, as addressed by the essential attribute of authentic connections (see Chapter 7).

As mathematics educators, we may be familiar with Webb's Depths of Knowledge, which move from lower levels of recall as well as skills and concepts to higher levels of strategic thinking and extended thinking. Webb (1997) contends that complexity comes from higher cognitive demand and application of multiple concepts, not simply harder problems. McDowell's (2017) three levels align to Webb's Depth of Knowledge levels (see Figure 4.1), creating a robust view of levels of knowledge that can be specifically applied to the mathematics classroom.

In order to reach the transfer level of rigorous content, students must engage in both surface and deep learning of mathematics. Mathematical content knowledge taught through high-quality problem-solving tasks and engaging inquiry is foundational for all students. Likewise, rigorous content knowledge through application can and should be used in the mathematics classroom, regardless of whether students are engaging in PBL or not. All students, regardless of race, culture, and/or identity, deserve opportunities to engage in rigorous, complex mathematics.

Figure 4-1 • Intersection of McDowell's Levels of Knowledge and Webb's Depths of Knowledge in Mathematics

McDowell's (2017) Levels of Knowledge	Webb's (1997) Depths of Knowledge (DOK)	Characteristics Written as "I Can" Statements for Students
Surface Level	DOK 1: Recall DOK 2: Skills and Concepts	I can . . . • define mathematical concepts • use mathematical skills to answer problems • follow a set of procedures • apply a formula • organize and display data in charts, graphs, or tables
Deep Level	DOK 3: Strategic Thinking	I can . . . • explain and justify my response • relate ideas and connect skills • develop an argument and reason complexly • flexibly choose an efficient, effective method
Transfer Level	DOK 4: Extended Thinking	I can . . . • connect my mathematical knowledge to new contexts, solving practical or abstract situations • apply complex reasoning and skills to real-world applications over extended periods of time • design multiple solution pathways • critique the reasoning of others

Where PBL mathematics thrives, however, is in authentically leading students to the deepest depth of knowledge or the call for transfer learning.

We examine more about authentic contexts in Chapter 7; however, it's imperative to note that for rigorous content to flourish, the application and depth of content must invite students to inquire about themselves and their society through empowering means. When students engage in a mathematics project by asking questions and constructing answers, they recognize that mathematics does not just live in a textbook, but rather can be used as a powerful tool in our society.

RIGOROUS CONTENT ILLUSTRATED IN PBL

Every student can and should engage in transfer learning through PBL mathematics. However, to reach this level, students must engage in surface and deep learning to solidify content knowledge and skills. This does not mean surface and deep learning must occur first. In fact, in PBL mathematics, sometimes launching a project with a problem that needs transfer learning will spark the realization that students must engage in surface and deep learning first.

For example, in a high school project called *GeoPhoto*, students viewed an image of a bridge with lots of parallel lines. The teacher, Katy Weber, posed successive questions: "How many sets of parallel lines are in this photograph? How do you know?" As students began debating whether two lines were parallel, many concluded the lines were parallel simply because they "looked" parallel or were believed to be parallel in real life. However, Katy was not satisfied with that answer. She had established a classroom culture where proving something mathematically was the expectation. This spurred the need for students to engage in surface- and deep-level learning, with the knowledge this learning would be applied to the task at hand as well as future photography moments.

Featuring projects that have been or will be explored throughout this book, let's examine what the three levels of rigorous content look like at the elementary, middle, and high school levels.

 These projects and the performance task are available for download at **https://qrs.ly/56ensfy**.

Elementary School

Exploring the concept of measurement in second grade, Miss Allie's students, profiled in the story at the start of this chapter, engaged in rigorous content exploration. This began with surface- and deep-level mathematics knowledge before engaging in transfer learning.

Surface	Students initially learned how to measure using a ruler. Students measured lines on paper, switching between centimeters and inches.
Deep	Students explored measuring objects in the classroom using both standard and nonstandard measurement tools. Students debated whether rulers were a better choice of tool than paper clips. Students used rulers and yardsticks, determining whether to measure objects using centimeters, inches, or feet.
Transfer	Students connected their understanding of measurement tools to determine which tool to use when measuring their 3D prototypes of a bee hotel. Students applied their knowledge of measurement by deciding which unit to use when creating their 2D blueprints. Students justified their reasoning for choosing the specific unit, especially when needing to round to the nearest whole unit.

Middle School

Looking back at Chapter 3, let's explore how a textbook question moved from surface-level learning in a traditional textbook question to deep learning through a problem-solving task. The same concept was then developed into a performance task, leading to transfer knowledge.

Surface	Students answered the textbook question: *What is the volume of a rectangular prism with dimensions of 10 inches by 6 inches by 3 inches?* Students followed a set of procedures by using the standard formula for volume.
Deep	Students engaged in the problem-solving task: *Given a volume of 180 inches cubed, what could be the dimensions of a right rectangular prism?* Students reasoned about different dimensions options, justifying their responses through visual pictures and mathematical operations.
Transfer	To transfer knowledge, students used surface- and deep-level understanding of volume to complete the performance task: *Redesign the inside of a van to maximize the number of meals that could be delivered by the electric, solar-powered Meals on Wheels van.* Students drew pictures, debated design options, created 3D models, and refined solutions. Students reasoned complexly as they proposed solutions to one another over three class periods.

High School

In the project called *GeoPhoto*, high school students explored how geometric concepts such as lines, angles, transformations, and symmetry affect a photograph. Students engaged in geometric photography by applying geometric concepts to their photography and analyzing the impact of that concept on the photograph.

Surface	Students conducted a card sort of vocabulary terms using words, numbers, and pictures to define key vocabulary. Students explored how parallel lines cut by a transversal line form congruent corresponding angles and congruent alternate interior angles through conjecture and hands-on activities.
Deep	Students formally proved two lines are parallel using postulates and theorems previously explored.
Transfer	Students took geometric photos showing parallel lines cut by a transversal, such as beams on a steel bridge, wooden planks on a dock, or beams on railroad tracks. They captured images from various angles and vantage points to see how parallel and transversal lines impact a photograph. Students imported images into the Desmos Graphing Calculator, drawing lines overtop the photograph to prove whether the lines were parallel or not.

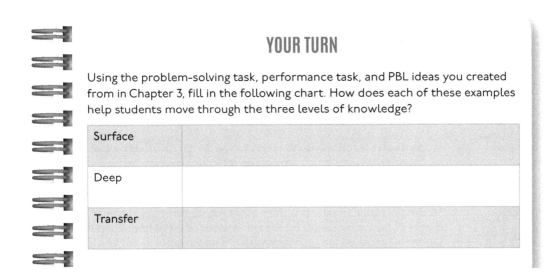

YOUR TURN

Using the problem-solving task, performance task, and PBL ideas you created from in Chapter 3, fill in the following chart. How does each of these examples help students move through the three levels of knowledge?

Surface	
Deep	
Transfer	

MAKING MOVES TO INCREASE RIGOR IN THE PBL MATHEMATICS CLASSROOM

There are many ways to increase rigor in the mathematics classroom, but specific to enhancing PBL mathematics, let's look at three moves that can happen anytime in the curriculum, inside and outside of a project:

1. Encourage risk-taking through creative solutions.

2. Design open-ended problem-solving tasks and performance tasks.

3. Connect Mathematical Habits of Mind with authentic situations.

Encourage Risk-Taking Through Creative Solutions

Mathematics is often seen as a discipline with one right answer. Because of this, students struggle when they arrive at an answer or solution pathway that is seen as different or creative. However, this is exactly the type of divergent thinking needed when applying mathematics to real-world tasks in PBL. Zager (2017) recognizes mathematicians need to take risks, "to be bold enough to try novel approaches, including far-fetched ones that have a high likelihood of failure, because new thinking is what's needed to solve a problem that's been stumping everybody else" (p. 31). As PBL mathematics experiences center on problems with multiple correct answers and solution pathways, encouraging risk-taking in mathematics is critical to successful PBL implementation.

One easy yet powerful routine that encourages creativity is a dot talk where teachers show a picture of dots and ask, "How many dots do you see? How did you see them?" In Figure 4.2, consider those same questions.

Figure 4-2 • Dot Talk

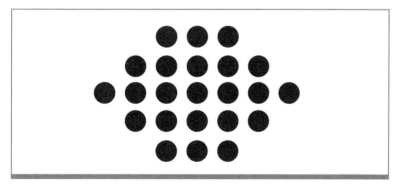

As an educator, I first confirm how many dots everyone sees, in this case twenty-three dots. If a student sees something different, I provide a few strategies to confirm there are twenty-three dots. Once verified, I prompt students to share creative solutions, eliminating the fear of being wrong. Students either verbally explain their reasoning or draw circles around groups of dots to share their thinking. Some fifth-grade student responses include the following:

> "I began with nine dots in the center making a square. Then I saw three dots on the outside of each square, making twelve more, so twenty-one. Then I added the two dots on the left and right, making twenty-three."

> "I saw a rectangle that would be five by five if the corners were filled in, so that is twenty-five. Then I thought all four corners were missing, except I could move two dots into the corners, so I am only missing two corners, which means I have twenty-three dots."

This routine can occur at the beginning of any mathematics class to encourage creative thinking. I've seen this exact same image used in a third-grade classroom as well as a high school classroom. For younger students, simpler dot visuals can be used as early as kindergarten. For older students, consider asking them to make dot talks to present to their classmates. What's important is this routine serves as a springboard for educators to continue encouraging creative thinking and risk-taking.

Another routine to encourage creative risk-taking many educators use is Estimation180 (estimation180.com). This site provides over 200 opportunities for students to engage in taking a creative risk through estimating and justifying an answer. My students particularly enjoy Days 206–210 where they estimate how many cheeseballs fit on a plate or in a container. To facilitate this routine, I begin by asking students to estimate their "highest" low estimate and their "lowest" high estimate. By doing this, I ensure students do not give me estimates from "zero" cheeseballs fit on a plate to "one billion" cheeseballs fit on a plate. It's a greater risk to come up with a "highest" low and a "lowest" high estimate.

Incorporating these creative risk-taking problems establishes a classroom culture conducive to PBL mathematics. It's important to help students transfer this kind of risk-taking mindset into their work in a project. In a high school Algebra II project called the *Campaign Against Opioid Addiction*, students examined data relating to the opioid crisis in America. Using their mathematical skills, students modeled the data, yet needed to take risks in determining what kind of function best represented the data—linear, exponential, logarithmic, or some combination. As teams debated which function best fit the data, their teacher, Josh Wilke, reassured his students his focus was on the justification of their answer, emphasizing the fact that most real-world data do not fit perfectly into one type of function. Josh encouraged creative risk-taking, prompting students to clearly justify their reasoning visually and algorithmically. To see the full breakdown of the *Campaign Against Opioid Addiction* project, check out the companion website at https://qrs.ly/56ensfy.

YOUR TURN

How do you encourage creative risk-taking in your mathematics classroom?

_____

_____

Design Open-Ended Problem-Solving Tasks and Performance Tasks

While routines like a dot talk or Estimation180 promote divergent thinking and creative risk-taking, they do so only to the surface level of knowledge. Problem-solving tasks and performance tasks promote creative risk-taking that moves surface-level knowledge into deep and possibly transfer levels. When exploring what makes a strong problem-solving or performance task, Krall (2018) highlights five design elements, stating that a quality task will do each of the following:

• Spark curiosity and foster engagement.

• Yield creativity and lead to new ideas.

• Promote access for all students in the classroom.

• Require and convey deep, crucial mathematical content.

• Connect and extend content.

Chapter 3 highlighted these types of tasks and ways to spiral one content idea from a problem-solving task to a performance task to a full PBL mathematics experience. Let's explore once again how to spiral a textbook problem into a problem-solving task, analyzing the task for the five design elements.

A second-grade textbook problem centered on counting coins showed a picture of two quarters, two dimes, and two nickels, asking students to simply write the sum of the money shown. In and of itself, this surface-level problem does not spark curiosity or foster engagement with students, the first design element of a quality task. There is no opportunity to show creative, strategic thinking or to highlight deep mathematical thinking. Spiraling this into a problem-solving task, a different version might ask a second grader the following (adapted from the 2016 Illustrative Mathematics "Jamir's Penny Jar" task):

LuLu has a jar of coins at home. She pulls out two quarters, two dimes, and two nickels.

- How would you help LuLu count the coins? Can you come up with at least two different ways?

- Write a number sentence representing the total value of the coins.

- LuLu's friend Pierce pulled a handful of coins out of the jar that totaled the same amount as LuLu but did not contain any quarters. Draw a picture of the coins Pierce might have pulled out.

Source: iStock.com/TokenPhoto

In spiraling a task from a textbook to a problem-solving task, notice how the design elements that Krall (2018) defined come alive. Additionally, notice how student thinking moved from surface- to deep-level thinking, increasing the rigor yet allowing all students the opportunity to engage in the task. Student engagement, then, is heightened with the opportunity to create multiple solution pathways. With the addition of manipulatives and other scaffolds, all students can access the problem that requires deep mathematical content. Students can connect their previous understanding of money and extend it throughout the series of prompts.

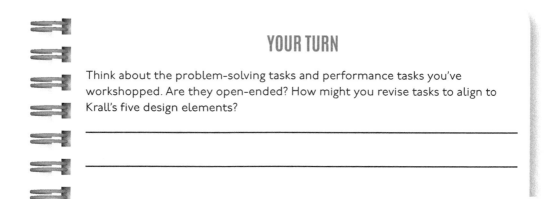

YOUR TURN

Think about the problem-solving tasks and performance tasks you've workshopped. Are they open-ended? How might you revise tasks to align to Krall's five design elements?

_____

_____

Connect Mathematical Habits of Mind With Authentic Situations

In order to transfer knowledge from surface- and deep-level understanding, students need to regularly see mathematics in authentic contexts; otherwise, the ability to apply mathematics to a real-world context may seem useful only during projects. One way I make content connections is through a think-aloud where I reflect upon how I saw mathematics during my day. For example, I recently started my sixth-grade class with two receipts showing a purchase for the exact same amount of fuel only one week apart. The difference in the two prices was approximately $10 due to a sudden increase in fuel costs. I asked students what they thought about the two prices, challenging them to hypothesize what would happen over the next few weeks and months and how that would impact my fuel costs.

As a mathematics educator, I know finding authentic connections can be difficult, so I have leaned upon a few "go to" sources for ideas, from Global Math Stories by Mathkind to social justice mathematics books (see Chapter 1 for a list of authentic resources). When linking mathematics to an authentic context, I work to intentionally name how students are transferring their knowledge of surface- or deep-level content.

Additional Resources

In addition to the resources cited in Chapter I, other sources for authentic mathematical inspiration include the following:

1. RealWorldMath.org: This website provides a collection of mathematics tasks centered on using Google Earth; resources range from tasks to projects; all resources are free.

2. CitizenMath.com: Thought-provoking mathematics lessons at this website are centered on an authentic question; very few free resources are available, but potential ideas can be sparked.

3. Math in the Real World (EconEdLink.org): This website connects economics and personal finance topics to mathematics for K–12 students. Lessons include "Price Elasticity: From Tires to Toothpicks" and "How Many Jeans Can I Buy?" and range in time from ten minutes to an hour; all resources are free.

4. Daily news! Check out the local, national, and global news stories for graphs, charts, or data that can be examined in the classroom. *USA Today* Snapshots usually provide a graphic students can examine in the classroom.

YOUR TURN

Explore these recommended resources or other resources that inspire authentic mathematical connections. List tasks you want to incorporate in your classroom. Then, list the content connection to each task and how your students might engage in surface-, deep-, or transfer-level learning.

Task	Content Connection	Surface, Deep, Transfer

PBL PLUS TIPS

- ☐ Model creative risk-taking.
  - Before giving your students a problem-solving task, try the task yourself using at least three different approaches.
  - Share your most creative approach with your students.
- ☐ Start with a rich task or problem!
  - Don't wait for students to learn the content in order to be able to solve the problem. Begin with the problem, allow for productive struggle, and provide just-in-time teaching for students to learn the content needed to solve the problem.
- ☐ Monitor the level of rigor.
  - Are your students engaging in rigorous tasks throughout a unit or only at the end?
  - Are you providing too many scaffolds that lessen productive struggle?

CONCLUDING THOUGHTS

Defining rigor in the mathematics classroom as challenging student thinking in new ways while connecting to authentic applications certainly contradicted my personal mathematical experiences in school. However, as I reflect upon the mathematics of my childhood such as building a Ferris wheel out of K'Nex, building sets for the school musical, or grocery shopping on a budget with my dad, I realize the mathematics of my lived experience more closely matched this definition of rigor. As you reflect upon this definition and its implications for the classroom, consider your own experiences with mathematics in and outside of school. What mathematics challenged your own thinking in novel ways? How did that mathematics apply to your own life?

PBL POINTS TO PONDER: BE SURE TO . . .

Use this thinking routine to envision how you will continue to grow as a mathematics educator.

☐ Reflecting upon this chapter, what is one idea you want to be sure to incorporate into your teaching and learning practice?

☐ Connecting the ideas of this chapter with your own practice, what is one idea you want to be sure to avoid in the future?

CHAPTER 5

Productive Inquiry

"How much should I scale this unicorn head down to get a small bubble?" Mai Li, an introspective student, asked her team members Teague and Delaney, all seventh-grade designers in my project called *3D Printing for the Community*. The project centered on creating three-dimensional printed bubble wands for clients, in this case toddlers and young children, who visit the Children's Museum in our city. In this mathematics and economics project, students explored the concepts of area of composite shapes and scale.

Need to Knows

- What is productive inquiry?
- How does just-in-time learning enhance productive inquiry?
- What does the iterative process of questioning, exploring, and reflecting look like in the project-based learning mathematics classroom?

During an initial investigation, students in the project classified bubbles created by bubble wands as small, medium, and large. Students then found the corresponding shapes and areas of the bubble wands to determine a range of areas that made each size of bubble. Mai Li's client, a three-year-old girl, wanted a unicorn bubble wand. Mai Li worked hard to satisfy her client's design needs. Working with her design team of Teague and Delaney, Mai Li shared a first draft of her unicorn bubble wand.

"What is the approximate area of your unicorn head right now? Is it making a large or medium bubble?" asked Teague.

Mai Li replied, "I think it would make a large bubble. If I scaled it down by a factor of four, I could get a small bubble, but then the unicorn horn would be a tiny line. I want the horn to be a triangle and still be able to hold bubbles in it."

"I wonder if you have to scale both sides down by the same factor. Like, can you reduce the vertical side by a factor of four and the horizontal side by a factor of two or three? Wouldn't that still be scaling it down?" Delaney postured.

"Maybe," started Mai Li. "Let me try."

INQUIRY DEFINED

As I shared my ideas for essential components of a project-based learning (PBL) mathematics classroom, a colleague paused when I mentioned productive inquiry. She shared, "I know what it means to be productive. I know what inquiry is. I don't know how productive inquiry is different from just regular inquiry." As my colleague noted, taken apart, the two terms are both familiar, but together they take on a deeper meaning.

Productive inquiry: is situated in a context where learning occurs both broadly and deeply over a span of time.

The original notion comes from the work of John Dewey, who defined **productive inquiry** as seeking knowledge specifically needed to complete a particular, situated task. The word *situated* here is critical to this definition. To Dewey (1938), a situated task is one that has an "environing experienced world" (p. 67). *Isn't it so Dewey-like to clarify his definition with even more nebulous definitions?* Perhaps Brown (2017) unpacks Dewey's idea best here: *Situated* means having "breadth and depth . . . [while including] elements distant in space and time" (p. 11). Basically, productive inquiry is situated in a context where learning occurs both broadly and deeply over a span of time.

So, how does productive inquiry differ from direct instruction as well as the directed inquiry that usually occurs in a traditional, non-PBL mathematics classroom? First, let me define these ideas, knowing each of these three instructional models has a place in the PBL mathematics classroom. I envision *direct instruction* as the approach of "I do, we do, you do," where the teacher leads students step-by-step through a concept. Direct instruction can be effective when used intentionally to solidify conceptual or procedural knowledge after students have had opportunities to develop initial understandings through exploration and collaborative construction of knowledge.

Direct instruction may or may not be needed depending on how students engage in inquiry—either directed or productive. *Directed inquiry* is a lesson or series of lessons where "teachers provide students with specified resources one by one, providing challenging questions and clear outcomes" (Discovery Education, n.d.). In directed inquiry, students actively construct knowledge through guided exploration and critical questioning, led by the teacher.

Unlike directed inquiry, *productive inquiry* focuses on just-in-time learning versus just-in-case learning. In directed inquiry, teachers provide the main source of questions to move mathematical ideas forward; yet, in productive inquiry, student questions take center stage. Lastly, productive inquiry leads to an iterative process of questioning, exploring, and reflecting, all with the intent of completing a task. Through analysis and reflection, students continue to question, reigniting the inquiry process until the particular task is completed.

Productive Inquiry Checklist (Yes/No Questions)

☐ Is learning occurring just in time, responding to the needs of the particular task?

☐ Are students taking the lead as critical questioners in order to engage in the iterative process of questioning, exploring, and reflecting?

PRODUCTIVE INQUIRY ILLUSTRATED: DIRECTED INQUIRY VERSUS PRODUCTIVE INQUIRY

To examine the differences in directed inquiry versus productive inquiry (PBL), let's explore the concept of scale and how it is taught when students engage in a PBL mathematics setting versus a directed inquiry setting.

Directed Inquiry in a Mathematics Classroom

I had the opportunity to observe seventh-grade mathematics educator Thomas Ruiz explore the concept of scale factor with his students. Groups of three or four students began with a card sort, matching images of two figures that had been scaled with a corresponding scale factor. Groups of students discussed and debated scaled figures that ranged from shapes like triangles, rectangles, and trapezoids to capital letters like *E* and *K*. When groups completed that task, Thomas conducted a whole-class discussion centered on what students noticed about the figures and the corresponding scale factor. Students pointed out that scale factor makes letters or shapes bigger or smaller depending on whether the scale factor is less than or greater than one.

For the whole-class activity, Thomas provided rulers and grid paper to each student, directing students to draw the first letter of their name in an outlined five-by-five unit corner of the grid. Then, Thomas tasked students with drawing that same letter using a scale factor of three. As students worked on scaling their letter, Thomas circled the room, providing individual assistance and cheering student success. Thomas asked two students whose name started with the letter *M* to share their work to the entire class, noting how their scaled letters looked slightly different based on the original size of their letter. Wrapping up the class, Thomas directed students to pull out their mathematics notebooks. Students taped or glued the letters of their name in their notebook. Thomas then prompted students to reflect on the question, "Without calculating anything, how do you think scale factor impacts area and perimeter?"

In this classroom example, Thomas successfully engaged his students in directed inquiry. Rather than a direct instruction approach of telling students the definition of scale factor, lecturing about how to scale objects, and providing students a myriad of examples to mimic, Thomas engaged students in inquiry by creating opportunities for students to think critically about the topic, engage in exploration, and consider the implications of scale factor on area and perimeter. Thomas's approach laid a foundation for inquiry, but did not engage students in *productive* inquiry. In this example, students learned the concept of scale just in case, with no connection to a larger situation or context, which would be indicative of productive inquiry.

MAKING MOVES TO INCREASE PRODUCTIVE INQUIRY IN YOUR CLASSROOM

The Driving Question of this book asks, "How can I bring project-based learning [PBL] to life in the mathematics classroom?" As highlighted by the Productive Inquiry Checklist, productive inquiry focuses on sustaining engagement in the mathematics classroom through just-in-time learning, where students act as questioners and engage in an iterative learning process. These notions can occur in the mathematics classroom whether in a project or not. Increasing these characteristics to heighten productive inquiry benefits students and the classroom experience throughout the year. So, let's look at how to increase these characteristics of productive inquiry.

Productive Inquiry Checklist (Yes/No Questions)

- ☐ Is learning occurring just in time, responding to the needs of the particular task?

- ☐ Are students taking the lead as critical questioners in order to engage in the iterative process of questioning, exploring, and reflecting?

Just-in-Time Learning

I spent over two hours watching YouTube videos on how to cut men's hair before ever picking up the electric hair clippers. I knew I needed to prepare as thoroughly as possible before ever giving my first (and only) client a haircut. It was April 2020. My husband and I had been in quarantine for over two weeks, and he needed a haircut before going back to the office as an essential worker.

As adults, we engage in just-in-time learning regularly. Think of all the questions you google on a regular basis. How do I use clippers to cut men's hair? What ingredients make the fluffiest pancakes? Does Gilligan ever get rescued from his island? How do I make more money while doing less work?

Just like in real life, opportunities to engage in just-in-time learning occur naturally in the project process, but can also be intentionally scaffolded into lessons throughout the year. One way to increase this teaching and learning technique is through a flipped classroom. Consider asking students to watch a short video, listen to a podcast, or engage in a web-based investigation on a topic before class begins, either at the conclusion of the previous class period or for homework depending on your classroom composition and school culture. At the conclusion of the flipped classroom learning, provide opportunities for students to engage in a series of practice questions, activities, or a problem-solving task with your assistance. What was traditionally considered "homework" is now the heart of the in-class work.

After teaching a new concept, ask each student to reflect upon their Clearest Concept (the concept the student understands the best) and Muddiest Point (the concept the student is most unclear about). Analyze student responses for patterns in order to provide just-in-time learning opportunities to clarify Muddiest Points. One way to address these Muddiest Points is to create mathematics stations. Mathematics stations may take the form of hands-on manipulative tasks, QR (quick response) codes to videos clarifying a misconception, card sorts, problem-solving tasks, or a teacher-led mini lesson. Partner students who have opposite Muddiest Points and Clearest Concepts; this opposite partnership empowers students to further develop their identity as a mathematician as they can take the lead in helping their partner better understand the mathematics at hand.

Students as Critical Questioners

The saying goes that there are no stupid questions. Although I know many teachers who might beg to differ, let's presume that the questions I am writing about are asked with the goal of productive inquiry. Let's also create a new saying: "All questions are not created equally." Questioning is an art form, not something innately understood by all students; questioning is also a skill, something to be taught, learned, and practiced.

To create the conditions necessary for students to engage in productive inquiry, I begin by modeling and explicitly teaching how to ask questions through a think-aloud strategy. I use this strategy to scaffold student learning throughout a problem-solving task or performance task in addition to projects. Using this strategy, I vocalize my questions out loud to students at various stages of inquiry. For example, when initially faced with a problem-solving task or performance task, I may pause and ask students to think of questions they posed upon receiving the task. I then share some questions I have, noting I am only sharing a few of my questions. This think-aloud strategy invites students to engage with the information at hand, gather their own thoughts, then listen to detect if my thinking converges or diverges from their own, prompting conversation and debate.

In addition to the think-aloud strategy, I regularly provide students with a list of questions before engaging in a problem-solving or performance task. I categorize these questions to correspond with the iterative process of questioning, exploring, and reflecting. As most of my problem-solving and performance tasks are completed with partners or small groups, the questions are written in plural form. This helps students do two things: (1) internally reflect upon their own work throughout the inquiry process and (2) voice questions aloud to a peer.

Taken as a complete list, these questions can be overwhelming, so I suggest having students practice their questioning skills with a trimmed-down version of this list. Many of the questions in Figure 5.1 have been adapted from a list of 100 questions to promote mathematics discourse (Kersaint, 2015).

Figure 5-1 • Question Stems to Promote Iteration

Stage of Iterative Process	Goal of Question	Question Examples
Questioning	Making Sense of the Task	• What is the task all about? • What is the context of the task? What do we know about that context? • How can we restate the goal of this problem in simpler terms? • Is there a limit we need to define for this task? • Are there assumptions we need to make? • Is there missing information? Is there information we can eliminate? • Have we ever solved a problem like this before? If so, what strategy worked?
	Estimating or Predicting a Solution	• What is a reasonable estimate or answer to this task? • What estimate or answer is too high? Too low? • What units or labels will my solution include?
Exploring	Planning a Solution Pathway	• What are two different ways we could start this problem? • What would happen if _____? • What will we do if we can't move forward with a certain pathway? • How will we know we are on the right pathway?
	Engaging in the Exploration	Do our steps seem appropriate so far, given the context? • Do our units make sense at this point in the process? • How can we organize our thinking? (table, chart, graph, picture) • Would a diagram or a sketch help clarify our work? • Have we made any assumptions? How have those assumptions impacted our work?

Stage of Iterative Process	Goal of Question	Question Examples
Reflecting	Analyzing a Solution	• Is our solution reasonable, given the context? • How is our solution method similar to or different from _____'s method? • Is there another possible solution? • How does our solution compare to our original prediction? • What mathematical concepts did we use during our exploration? • What mathematical skills did we use during our exploration? (problem solving, reasoning, mathematical communication, etc.) • What are our next steps? • What kinds of problems might use a similar strategy? • What knowledge or skills do we need to take as next steps in our inquiry process?

As students engage in a problem-solving or performance task, promoting questioning skills between peers is vital to moving students toward productive inquiry. To promote this skill, I work to establish the classroom culture within which questioning and seeking resources occurs among peers before students invite me into the conversation. I have heard other teachers use a "three before me" rule, meaning a student asks three peers a question before asking the teacher. In my classroom, I give students question coins. This corresponds to the number of questions a student can ask me in a class period. At the beginning of the year, students may begin with two or three coins a day. By the end of the year, I provide my sixth-grade partners with only one coin and teams of three with only two coins. Teams can earn more questioning coins if I see them providing assistance to other teams. Creating a classroom culture of questioning requires intentional time and practice along with deep knowledge of students. See Chapter 10 for more about classroom culture.

YOUR TURN

Think about the tasks and PBL ideas you brainstormed in Chapter 3. What question stems from the list would you provide to your students? Are there any you would add?

_____

_____

PRODUCTIVE INQUIRY IN THE PBL MATHEMATICS CLASSROOM

Let's return to this chapter's opening story of Mai Li to see productive inquiry in action in the PBL mathematics classroom. After talking to her classmates, Mai Li decided to try different scaling techniques. First, she scaled the original unicorn head down by four, or a scale factor of one-fourth. Mai Li didn't like the look of this scale factor because the unicorn horn was too small. She wanted to see the area inside of the unicorn horn. So, Mai Li tried to scale the unicorn horn using her peer's suggestion of using two different scale factors (see Figure 5.2).

Figure 5-2 ◆ Mai Li's Scale Example

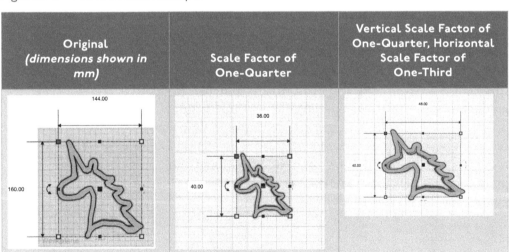

Source: Workplane

Mai Li shared her new unicorn design with Delaney and Teague. "I like how you can see the area under the horn, but it looks different than my original design."

"I don't think using two scale factors is really scaling, then," interjected Teague. "I think the video said that scaling should keep the image the same. Your new unicorn head looks fatter than the original."

At this point, the students reviewed the video lesson on scaling. They confirmed that scaling should be by only one factor. They also learned scaling an image down by a factor of four was the same as multiplying by a scale factor of one-fourth. There was some confusion about multiplying by a fraction versus dividing not only in that design team but in other teams as well. As the teacher, I proposed conducting a mini lesson on that topic to the teams who needed it.

Returning to the unicorn head task, Delaney asked, "Could you scale just the unicorn head down? Then, once the head has an area that makes a small bubble, you could add the unicorn horn on like how you want it. Does that seem reasonable?"

Teague also added his idea: "I wonder if the unicorn horn is actually too tall. It might break off when printed. Maybe make it shorter?"

"Those are both good suggestions. Let me try that," Mai Li responded. Mai Li continued to refine her unicorn design through multiple iterations, receiving ongoing feedback from her design team members and other design teams. She eventually shortened the unicorn horn and added more hair to the mane of the unicorn. See her final design, with the wand, in Figure 5.3.

Figure 5-3 • Mai Li's Final Design

Source: Workplane

Productive Inquiry Checklist (Yes/No Questions)

☑ Is learning occurring just in time, responding to the needs of the particular task?

☑ Are students taking the lead as critical questioners in order to engage in the iterative process of questioning, exploring, and reflecting?

In exploring the Productive Inquiry Checklist, we see that productive inquiry occurred throughout this project, as exemplified by the design team of Mai Li, Teague, and Delaney. Learning occurred just in time as students experienced an immediate need to understand scale, scale factor, and how scale impacts the area of a shape. When confusion arose, students participated in a formal lesson to solidify learning and clarify misconceptions. As Mai Li and her team discussed scaling as "scaling down" by a certain factor, they reviewed a video lesson where they encountered the idea that scaling down and a scale factor of a fraction less than one were mathematically the same.

Students worked in design teams with the project norm that questions were posed within the team before consulting the teacher. As students engaged in inquiry, new ideas arose, like scaling by two different factors or re-creating the unicorn horn after scaling the head down. Even if these ideas did not work, students actively followed an iterative process of posing critical questions, exploring their ideas through either trial and error or researching information, and reflecting on their actions. For example, after Delaney posed the idea of scaling the unicorn head down by two factors, Mai Li explored this idea by implementing the suggestion. Upon completion, the design team reflected on the result, critically analyzing whether a figure could be scaled using two different scale factors. This resulted in the need for continued questions and exploration, leading to more engagement in the inquiry cycle.

CONCLUDING THOUGHTS

Mai Li's unicorn bubble wand went to a three-year-old girl, but what this young girl did not know was the hours of problem solving, thought, and attention to detail Mai Li and her design team spent on that single bubble wand. As Mai Li, Teague, and Delaney engaged in productive inquiry, they took ownership over the process and final product, leading to increased identity as mathematicians. The skills of questioning, exploring, and reflecting not only enhance the PBL mathematics classroom experience but, more importantly, impact the life skills these students need to be successful individuals in our society. If more individuals learn to question the critical issues facing our world, explore possible solutions, and reflect upon the knowledge gained, our future will be in good hands.

PBL PLUS TIPS

- ☐ Create a short video or podcast of an important lesson.
  - ● Use websites or apps like Explain Everything (explaineverything.com) where you can talk and draw simultaneously.
  - ● Videos or podcasts created in your voice help students to access familiar material to navigate just-in-time learning.
  - ● Digital lessons allow you to direct students back to the material for remediation or clarification of misconceptions.
- ☐ Promote students taking the lead of critical questioners.
  - ● Create question stem table tents or "cheat sheets" for students to use when working in teams.
  - ● Model question asking through think-aloud strategies.
  - ● Foster question creation through protocols like the Question Formulation Technique (Right Question Institute, 2022).

PBL POINTS TO PONDER: ESP+I

Use this thinking routine to identify key areas that moved your understanding of productive struggle forward as well as questions (puzzles) and struggles that remain.

- ☐ **Experience:** What is your current experience engaging students as questioners during productive inquiry?
- ☐ **Struggles:** What struggles have you had or might you encounter engaging students as questioners during productive inquiry?
- ☐ **Puzzles:** What new questions or "puzzlings" do you have about productive inquiry?
- ☐ **+Insights:** At this point, what new or additional insights do you have about productive inquiry?

CHAPTER 6

Identity and Agency

I'm sitting in an Algebra I classroom filled with high school freshmen who are in the beginning stages of a performance task called the *Wage Gap*, looking at the disparity of earnings between white men and various other demographic groups including white women, Black men and women, and Hispanic men and women. Also included are data comparing the pay rates between "traditional workers" and workers who identify as LGBTQ+. These students are grappling with the driving question, "When will all workers in the United States achieve equal pay?" As students share their thoughts about the problem of fair pay, I can't help but reflect on how mathematical identities and agency are flourishing throughout this heated conversation.

"I just don't think we're ever going to get equal pay. I mean, even if we pass laws, people will just find ways to keep us down. And by people, I mean men, white men," quips Ellie, a curly, blonde-haired student, as she elbows a white male seated next to her.

Need to Knows

- How does project-based learning mathematics increase individual mathematical identity?

- How does project-based learning mathematics engage students in change agency?

- How does increased identity and agency benefit students?

Heron, a nonbinary student, continues the conversation by sharing, "My parents don't want me to get screened for autism because there are loopholes in some policies where employers can pay people with disabilities less money, and I don't think that's fair." Several heads nod in agreement. The teacher thanks Heron for vulnerably adding to the discussion.

"And don't get me started on pay for LGBTQ+ people. It says here that the pay is lower than a 'traditional worker,' but who are they calling 'traditional'? If I'm not 'traditional,' am I 'untraditional'? Why can't I just be me, a worker?" questions Oakley. The conversation about fair pay continues to grow, with each student sharing bits and pieces about the inequity of the wage gap, and many students believing Americans will never reach equal pay.

 The performance task featured in this vignette is available for download at **https://qrs.ly/56ensfy**.

IDENTITY AND AGENCY DEFINED

Identity: is a learner's positive disposition as a mathematician who can engage in complex problems through critical thinking and mathematical reasoning across a range of contexts in their life.

As we continue to center our instruction on the diverse learners in our classrooms, educators have become particularly focused on mathematical identity and agency, as initially highlighted by the equity levers discussed in Chapter 2. Specific to the mathematics classroom, **identity** is a learner's positive disposition as a mathematician who can engage in complex problems through critical thinking and mathematical reasoning across a range of contexts in their life. Furthermore, a student's identity highlights how a learner would like to be perceived by their community, including both home and school communities.

Agency: refers to a learner's ability not only to comprehend the mathematics of our world but also to impact our world using mathematics as a tool for societal change.

Ritchhart (2015) recognizes agency as a learner's "ability to make choices and direct activity based on one's own resourcefulness and enterprise. This entails thinking about the world not as something that unfolds separate and apart from us but as a field of action that we can potentially direct and influence" (p. 77). Here, Ritchhart links a learner's identity in the classroom with their change agency. **Agency** refers to a learner's ability not only to comprehend the mathematics of our world but also to impact our world using mathematics as a tool for societal change. Simply put, agency is identity in action (Aguirre et al., 2013).

As Aguirre et al. (2013) contend, "Teaching involves not only developing important skills and conceptual understanding in mathematics but also supporting students' coming to see themselves as legitimate and powerful doers of mathematics" (p. 14). I want to emphasize the idea of being a *legitimate* and *powerful* mathematician. This image of a learner goes beyond doing mathematics in the traditional sense, such as completing worksheets or solving the word problems of my childhood. *I mean, who goes to the store to buy twenty-five watermelons anyway?*

To become this kind of doer of mathematics requires educators to create the authentic contexts for students to use mathematics in ways that are meaningful to them, to their school, or to the community. To enhance the identity and agency of a student, the *context* of mathematical learning—not the content—drives how students see themselves as mathematicians. This is supported by Aguirre et al. (2013) who assert that the mathematical context of learning reflects "a sense of oneself as a competent performer who is able to do mathematics or as the kind of person who is unable to do mathematics" (p. 14). Thus, being a *legitimate* and *powerful* mathematician is someone who uses rigorous mathematics to augment awareness or advocate for change in society, a mathematical change agent.

IDENTITY AND AGENCY ILLUSTRATED

Telling one's story is a powerful way for students to express their mathematical identity as it relates to change agency. Let's explore the ideas of identity and agency through the voices of students.

Identity

I interviewed a vivacious seventh-grade student, Aaliyah, about her identity as a mathematician. Aaliyah is a student I have known for two years, who learns in a project-based school where she completes projects originated by her teachers as well as individual projects she designs. In the story, Aaliyah shares her struggle to identify as a mathematician.

{Tell me about yourself.}

I'm an African American twelve-year-old female. People say I have a lot of spirit. I'm a daughter, a sister, a friend, a cousin, a basketball player, a dancer, and a student. Sometimes, I'm a mother to my little sisters.

{Do you consider yourself a mathematician? Why or why not?}

I'm not a mathematician because I don't like math.

{Tell me about using mathematics in your personal project.}

When I planned my dance studio, I had to figure out prices and square feet and schedules. That was a lot of math. I had to budget all the furniture and dance bars and mirrors. I used my iPad app to lay out all of the items, and sometimes when they didn't fit, I had to change the layout or number of items I planned to put in each room, which changed my budget because I had a price per square foot. So I used a lot of math to figure out how much it cost to start my own dance studio.

{Sounds like you used a lot of mathematics in your project. How is that different from school?}

I just don't like to do school math. It's different. It doesn't make sense because it's just . . . [*long pause*] there. Like in school. The math is just on worksheets or on the board, and you just do it. It doesn't make sense. I mean, sometimes it does, but not always. So, I like the math I need for my projects. I like to use math, but not do math.

{What I heard is that you like mathematics in your projects, but not in school. I'm curious. Does that make you somewhat of a mathematician?}

I guess I'm a project mathematician, not a school mathematician.

Aaliyah's Identity

Herein, Aaliyah voiced examples of her identity as a legitimate and powerful user of mathematics, even though she personally struggled to define herself as a mathematician. She acutely distinguished between using mathematics and doing mathematics. To her, using mathematics for something meaningful and relevant (designing and budgeting her own dance studio) equated to being a mathematician, which she described as a "project mathematician." This was in stark contrast to being a "school mathematician," which to her meant worksheets.

As I think of Aaliyah's identity, I recognize Aaliyah possesses the ability to engage in complex mathematical thinking and reasoning in contexts that make sense to her, namely situated in projects. I wonder what transformations in her educational career need to occur for her to merge the identities of school mathematics and real-world mathematics, and if those messages needed to occur earlier than when she entered middle school and began learning in a project-based setting.

YOUR TURN

Aaliyah was asked, "Do you consider yourself a mathematician? Why or why not?" How would you answer this question?

_____

_____

CHALLENGE

Engage students in conversation using this question as a prompt. Listen to understand student experiences.

Agency

Exploring the idea of agency, I chatted with Oakley, a freshman in high school participating in the *Wage Gap* performance task. I have known Oakley for four years, since he was a student in my sixth-grade classroom. Like Aaliyah, Oakley attends a project-based school where learning through teacher-led projects and creating personal projects is part of the curriculum. Here are some highlights of our conversation.

{Tell me about yourself.}

My name is Oakley. I am a son, a friend, a brother. I love reading. I love doing art. I love being with my family. I love to help make a difference.

{What does it mean to have agency?}

Especially over the pandemic and the rise of Black Lives Matter, seeing people oppressed and hurt and murdered because of their skin color, that was a huge thing for me. As a child growing up reading *I Am Malala* [Yousafzai, 2013] and learning about girls not being able to go to school, these world events are a big eye opener that expose me to new forms of injustice. So, agency is seeing those injustices and doing something about it.

{Tell me about a time where you made a difference in the community or world.}

My most notable time when I made a difference was last year. I had seen a YouTube video on how unhoused women don't get the proper products for feminine hygiene. In eighth grade, I created holiday cards like Merry Christmas, Happy Hanukkah, and Happy Kwanzaa, and I sold them at small businesses around town. I charged $15 for a five-pack. All the profits I made went toward profits to the Women's Fund, which is a nonprofit grants organization, which helped distribute grants to people and places that wanted to put feminine hygiene items in schools and other public places. I donated over $750 last year.

{*How did mathematics play a role in that project?*}

A big thing for that project was keeping everything organized. I kept tables and graphs and charts of inventory being sold, how much inventory I needed to order, how much time it took to make this, what's a reasonable price to sell things for to make a profit. That was a big thing for me, to keep these tables and charts to keep me organized. So, the $750 was the profit, with the net worth being much more, but I needed to take away supply costs. The cool thing was that the lady who runs the nonprofit is the mom of some students I went to elementary school with.

{Tell me about the *Wage Gap* performance task. What are you learning?}

The data definitely show we are getting closer. We used to be absolutely terrible. We are closing the gap as a country, but a big thing I have been looking at is how reliable these predictions are. I like to graph these out to see what might happen. Some students are looking at the data and just using the rate of change as a constant, but I'm looking at our world knowing how much it changes, and wondering, "Will there be a sudden drop or increase due to passing laws or things like this pandemic?" The math is just telling one part of the story, a critical part of the story, but we need to keep examining what happens around the math to get the complete picture.

{What role does mathematics play in our society?}

Math is a huge part of our society. I can't think of a single project that doesn't require some math. In order to comprehend how to make a big change, you need to comprehend the little changes that need to happen. And math is a huge part of analyzing that in our society, especially if we want to make change. Like I said before, we need math to tell the story because some people really only believe numbers, whereas other people believe pictures or videos or testimonials. So, if we want to make a difference, we need math.

Oakley's Agency

Throughout the conversation, I was intrigued by how Oakley recognized mathematics is needed to tell a story, yet he acknowledged the story cannot exclusively be told with mathematics. Oakley described how he used mathematics as a tool both to bring awareness to an issue—like the *wage gap*—and to impact society—donating money to the Women's Fund. Oakley proved through his words and his mathematics that he is a legitimate and powerful mathematician using mathematics as a tool for agency.

Oakley's agency took on the form of both awareness and action. In the *Wage Gap* performance task, Oakley brought awareness of the issue to the forefront through mathematical modeling. When Oakley described needing to examine the wage gap data in the context of what was happening in our society, he was connecting mathematics to the lived reality of the data, recognizing that true mathematics is messy and cannot be taken at face value. Modeling with mathematics helps students make sense of our society, which in this case allowed Oakley to bring awareness to the issue of unequal pay in the United States and the length of time it will take for pay to become equal between demographic groups.

Oakley also initiated change in the community by using mathematics as a tool in his personal project, selling cards to fundraise for a local nonprofit. Oakley recognized his need to use mathematics as a tool for organization and communication. Using visual representations like tables, charts, and graphs helped Oakley actualize his goal of donating money.

As a young adult, Oakley realized he can make a difference in society, that mathematics is a needed skill to impact our world for the better.

MAKING MOVES TO INCREASE IDENTITY AND AGENCY

Let's look back at our Driving Question for this book: "How can I bring project-based learning [PBL] to life in the mathematics classroom?" When examining this question through the lens of developing identity and agency, the PBL mathematics classroom provides ripe conditions for students to enhance their mathematical identity and build change agency. At its core, "PBL is an important instructional approach that enables students to master academic skills and content knowledge, develop skills necessary for future success, and build the personal agency needed to tackle life's and the world's challenges" (HQPBL, 2018). In order to achieve these goals, we must reimagine the mathematics classroom experience.

In this reimagination, our first step as educators is to reconceptualize our classroom goals. No longer should we focus on teaching our students how to *do* mathematics; rather, we should empower and inspire students to *be* legitimate and powerful mathematicians—mathematicians who use mathematics in authentic, personal, culturally relevant ways—like Aaliyah. Embracing that identity of a mathematician, as first addressed in Chapter 1, inherently changes how we speak and act in the classroom. By incorporating project-based learning (PBL), we bring forward multiple opportunities to embrace an authentic role in the classroom. For example, students in a fourth-grade classroom took on the role of being architects whereas students in an eighth-grade classroom became scouts for a sporting team. These roles help students embrace the identity of a mathematician, not simply doing mathematics in a school classroom.

In our instructional practice, we must navigate students to have more freedom to inquire into the beautiful and complex nature of mathematics. Too often, educators conclude a unit with a problem-solving task during which students apply the mathematical skills they have just learned. Instead of ending with such a task, consider beginning mathematical explorations with authentic contexts situated in real-world scenarios. "Exploring meaningful and important concepts that are connected to the world often means students want to take action. Providing opportunities and structures for them to do so encourages students' agency and power while making the learning relevant" (Ritchhart, 2015, p. 8). When we begin a project with a rich, juicy problem that inherently needs mathematics as part of the solution pathway, students recognize the need to learn and engage in the content at hand so they can take action.

In the PBL mathematics classroom, centering a project on the wonder, joy, and beauty of mathematics might mean beginning a project knowing students do not have the skills necessary to come up with a solution . . . yet! As students develop questions and overcome roadblocks, we can provide just-in-time instruction on the mathematical concepts necessary to help students find solutions. (See more about student questions in Chapters 13 and 14.)

To develop mathematical identity in the PBL mathematics classroom, anticipate students will make mistakes, fail, and learn from those failures by persevering to find new solution pathways. As educators, we can create the conditions for students to productively struggle. Inherent in the struggle is our role as educators to provide students with the right tools to navigate the struggle and persevere in their problem-solving efforts. Additionally, we must link this notion of mistake making and perseverance to that of being a legitimate mathematician, as all mathematicians make mistakes. "By challenging [students] and supporting them through the struggle . . . you empower them to see that they are in control rather than reliant on someone for their learning" (SanGionvanni et al., 2020, p. 16). This intentional connection develops a resilient mathematical identity in our students.

YOUR TURN

Think about a time you struggled. What did it feel like? How did you overcome your struggle?

_____

_____

CHALLENGE

Share this story with your students to normalize productive struggle.

In the PBL mathematics classroom, our goal at times is to guide students toward becoming community change agents, using mathematics to impact their community. At some point, the need to correct mistakes in order to achieve accurate solutions is critical, especially when the mathematics solves a real-world problem or connects to an authentic outcome, such as sharing financial reports with a nonprofit like Oakley did or, as students did in Chapter 4, developing the blueprints to a bee hotel to be constructed by an expert. By crafting a public product to be shared with an authentic audience, students recognize accuracy in their mathematics is the same as spelling everything correctly in a formal letter. Mathematics, when needed to make a difference in society, is used as a language, a way to communicate and tell a story, like Oakley shared. What a gift to our future if all students viewed mathematics this way!

Students can also develop agency by voicing input into the goals and direction of a project. While brainstorming, designing, and implementing a project, consider forming a project leadership team of students. This team should incorporate students who have varied interests and expertise—mathematics and other—including artistically inclined students, readers, technology enthusiasts, activists, multilingual students, and physically active students. Invite this leadership team to meet with you before or after school, over lunch, or during a prep period, recess, or homeroom. Pose your project idea to the students. Ask students to provide feedback and input into the project; ensure every student has an equal voice. Here are some questions that could guide your conversation:

Prior to Starting a Project

- How does this project topic connect to your life/our community/our world?

- What knowledge do you bring to this topic?

- What music/movies/TV shows/celebrities are connected to this project?

- Where do you see the mathematics connections in this project?

- What jobs or careers would be engaged in this project?

- How would you like to show your learning? What kind of products can you create? (Show a product list such as the one in Chapter 15.)

During a Project

- Share one "high" and one "low" of the project so far.

- What is going well with the project process?

- What can I do to support the project process?

- What mathematics concepts do you find challenging? How can I scaffold your learning of the mathematics?

- What connections do you see to other subject areas or to our world?

- What can I do to support your learning of ___ [other interdisciplinary concepts]?

- If you could describe the perfect "showcase" or "culminating event" to this project, what would it look like? Sound like? Feel like? How can we make this a reality?

After a Project

- Describe the project as a whole using one word.

- Share a highlight of the entire project.

- What is one thing that frustrated you during the project?

- What roadblocks did you face? How did you persevere through them?

- As we look to assess this project, what should I keep in mind?

- If I were to run this project again, what changes would you make? Why?

PBL PLUS TIPS

- ☐ Name students as "mathematicians," "problem solvers," "math rock stars," or "change agents."

  - Instead of saying, "Good morning, students," say, "Good morning, mathematicians!"

  - Consider including a role, like "architects" or "statisticians," in the driving question of the project.

- ☐ Share stories about our world or problems in society enhanced with mathematics.

  - Talk about current events. Use mathematics to illustrate what is happening or elaborate on the issue.

  - Consider finding statistics, graphs, charts, or detailed drawings with measurements.

  - Use data to highlight if the problem is getting worse, getting better, or staying the same. Ask students to guess what will happen based on the data shared.

- ☐ Create and implement a project leadership team.

  - Invite students from a variety of backgrounds to create a balanced group of leaders. Try new groups for each new project.

CONCLUDING THOUGHTS

As we shift our instructional practice to incorporate PBL, we change how students view the nature of mathematics. No longer will students view mathematics as a set of prescribed steps to memorize and mimic in pursuit of answers; rather, students will see mathematics as the vehicle for exploration into the problems of our society as well as a pathway for solutionary answers to employ as change agents. Perhaps, with this kind of instruction, students like Aaliyah will no longer distinguish between school mathematics and project mathematics.

PBL POINTS TO PONDER: WORD-PHRASE-SENTENCE

Use this thinking routine to distill the essence of this chapter into something small and manageable to share.

☐ Reflecting upon this chapter, what is one word that captured your attention or struck you as powerful?

☐ What is one phrase that moved, engaged, or provoked you?

☐ What is one sentence that was meaningful to you, or that you felt captures the core idea of this chapter?

CHAPTER 7

Authentic Connections

Need to Knows

- How do I answer the age-old question, "When am I ever going to use this?"

- What is authenticity in the project-based learning mathematics classroom?

- How can I increase authentic connections in the project-based learning mathematics classroom?

Growing up, I would often ask my mathematics teachers, "When am I ever going to use this?" Those words were said when I was frustrated. Those words were said when I was bored. Those words were said when numbers and letters came together in seeming randomness with no application to my very important middle school social life of talking on the phone and going to the mall.

Let's be honest. Nearly every mathematics teacher has heard a student or two or ten (*thousand*) hurl those words at them in frustration, anger, boredom, cheekiness, or defensiveness. How, as a mathematics field, have we attempted to answer this age-old question? One of the first responses, and the one I remember the most, is "You'll need it next year when you . . ." or some variation of needing mathematics for a future class. Teachers would also talk about careers that needed mathematics. More recently, posters showing how mathematics is used in these careers have appeared, especially in middle and high school classrooms.

A mathematics teacher addressed this same question in his blog. He wrote about all the times we use mathematics in our daily lives, concluding that although we may "never need to know the relationships of the angles in an isosceles triangle after high school . . . these are the skills that prepare your brain for real world problems" (DiNoia, 2021). As an adult, I can appreciate this sentiment. However, our students are in our classrooms now. Right now. They want a more immediate answer than some nebulous future of real-world problems. The problems they face are immediate to them. As student-centered practitioners, our call is to center our work on the lived experiences of our students now, not five or ten or twenty years from now.

Authenticity, then, is a key tenet to unlock student engagement in the project-based learning (PBL) mathematics classroom. Take, for example, Destiny, a seventh-grade girl in my classroom. When I asked her about her feelings toward mathematics in elementary school, she said:

> I didn't hate math in elementary school. I didn't love it either. I just did it because I had to. We did all these worksheets, and . . . we would use blocks and circles to do fractions and stuff. It made sense, but I just didn't care.

The apathy with which Destiny spoke about mathematics made me sad. Here is a bright, talented student who simply did mathematics because it was expected of her. I also asked Destiny about other classes, such as science, English, social studies, art, and gym. For almost every other class, Destiny shared a specific memory, such as a favorite book that inspired her class to plant a school garden or a field trip she took to collect water samples. Her engagement through these authentic connections in her other classes sparkled in her voice and eyes and mind.

AUTHENTIC CONNECTIONS DEFINED

Destiny spoke of authentic connections in her elementary school experience as highlights of her learning. Our charge as educators is to make movements toward more authenticity in our classrooms to engage our learners. Authenticity is a critical component of the PBL classroom and the mathematics classroom, making it an essential attribute of PBL mathematics. Both the high-quality PBL framework (HQPBL, 2018) and the PBLWorks (n.d.) design elements highlight authenticity as an essential criterion in PBL. **Authentic connections** relate to those situations directly connected to our students' lives and the real issues they face in their communities (Larmer, 2012). Authenticity highlights the need for students to work on projects relevant to their lives, cultures, and personal interests, perhaps even leading to student agency where students directly impact their community or world. Authentic connections also naturally elevate the need for a public product, a component of the HQPBL framework and the PBLWorks design elements. A public product brings the authentic nature of the project to the forefront, asking students to show evidence of learning to an audience beyond the teacher.

Authentic PBL mathematics experiences should do all of the following:

1. Aim to solve realistic problems using rigorous mathematics.

2. Provide multiple avenues for solution pathways.

3. Connect to students' lives outside of the classroom.

4. Reveal knowledge that should be shared publicly.

In *Principles to Actions* (National Council of Teachers of Mathematics [NCTM], 2014), the authors highlight that "an excellent mathematics program requires effective teaching that engages students in *meaningful learning* through individual and collaborative experiences that promote their ability to make sense of mathematical ideas and reason mathematically" (p. 7, emphasis added). Further elaborating on an excellent mathematics program as one that focuses on access and equity for all students, the authors include that students should have the opportunity and "ability to use mathematics in authentic contexts" (NCTM, 2014, p. 60). The Standards for Mathematical Practice include "model with mathematics," describing mathematically proficient students as able to "apply the mathematics they know to solve problems arising in

> **Authentic connections:** relate to those situations directly connected to our students' lives and the real issues they face in their communities.

everyday life, society, and the workplace" (National Governors Association Center for Best Practices & Council of Chief State School Officers [NGA & CCSSO], 2010, p. 7).

This need to bridge mathematics to authentic connections is seen in revisions to state standards, including the Common Core State Standards for Mathematics, which include this popular phrase in many standards: "real-world and mathematical problems" (NGA & CCSSO, 2010). That phrase, or a variation of it, appears thirteen times in the sixth-grade standards alone! Obviously, the intent to apply mathematics to the "real world" is just that—*real*!

Realistic Versus Authentic

Now, some problems in the classroom may be considered realistic but would not be considered authentic. Take, for example, the following problem:

> *Our school is going on a field trip. We need to figure out how many buses to take. Each bus can comfortably seat 56 people. With 240 students and 8 teachers, how many buses should we order?*

Yes, students can visualize this problem. In fact, it might even be a realistic situation. However, will students feel more connected to mathematics because of this problem? Will they develop a deeper appreciation for the mathematics needed to analyze and critique society? Not likely.

Determining what is authentic ties directly to the practice of developing a strong relationship with students. Are your students interested in sports? If so, which ones? What about the environment, animals, or nature? How about paranormal beings or extraterrestrial life? Cell phones? Photography? Art? Video games? Fashion? Health? Reading? Collect these interests through a get-to-know-you survey or via ongoing conversation.

I know it can feel daunting to try to learn about the interests of every student in every class, especially if the goal is to develop a lasting relationship. So, I challenge myself to do something manageable each week for each classroom. I call it my 2 × 5 (two-by-five) challenge. Here's how it works. I choose two students to engage in a short conversation for each of the five days of the school week (or however many class days there are that week). Depending on your situation, you may choose only two students because you see the same group all day, or you may choose two students from every class. The brief conversation usually begins with a short greeting and a question or prompt, such as, "Hey, Leah! So glad to have you in class today. Watched any good YouTube videos lately?" If I hadn't asked Leah this quick question, I would never have learned about Mothman, a paranormal, humanoid creature—part man, part winged being. (*I'm currently working on a performance task for that class to coincide with this fascinating hobby of exploring paranormal creatures.*)

Other go-to questions or conversation prompts include these:

- Tell me about your pets. If you could have any animal as a pet, what would you choose?

- Do you prefer sweet or spicy foods?

- What would you do if you were invisible for twenty-four hours?

- It's storming outside. The power goes out. What will you do inside with no electricity?

- If you could live inside the world of a book or movie, what book or movie would you choose?

As I learn about the hobbies and passions of my students, I purposefully search for ways I can incorporate these interests into problem-solving tasks, performance tasks, and projects. So, let's explore how a team of teachers developed authentic connections in a problem-solving task and PBL mathematics experiences.

YOUR TURN

Consider engaging in a 2 × 5 challenge to get to know your students better. Plan your 2 × 5 here!

Student 1:

Student 2:

Day 1 Question	Day 2 Question	Day 3 Question	Day 4 Question	Day 5 Question

AUTHENTIC CONNECTIONS ILLUSTRATED

When working with a sixth-grade mathematics team in Texas, I asked the classroom teachers to show me a rich task they use from an upcoming unit on rates and ratios. The team chose a problem using rates similar to the following:

> Aesop's fable has come to life. The tortoise and the hare are running a race. The tortoise runs at 2 miles per hour while the hare runs at 6 miles per hour.

- How many 5-minute naps can the hare take along the way to tie the race?

- If the tortoise had a 10-minute head start, what is the slowest the hare could run and still win?

- Let's say the hare starts at a rate of 6 miles per hour, then reduces the rate to 1 mile per hour at some point during the race to end in a tie with the tortoise. At what point in the race does the hare reduce its rate?

Using this example, let's explore a checklist for questions to ask about authentic connections in the PBL mathematics classroom.

Authentic Connections Checklist (Yes/No Questions)

- ☐ In the real world, would students solve this problem using *rigorous* mathematics?

- ☑ Is the mathematics needed for this situation open-ended with multiple pathways to solutions?

- ☐ Would students care about this outside of the classroom?

- ☐ Would students share their knowledge through a public product?

Even though this problem-solving task could be solved in multiple ways by students, looking at the Authentic Connections Checklist, I'm sure many of you—like my students—are quick to critique this problem. In the real world, the actual speed of the fastest tortoise, according to the Guinness World Records (2022), belongs to Bertie at 0.63 miles per hour, while a brown hare can reach speeds of about 45 miles per hour. Regardless of this tidbit of trivia, in the end, a tortoise and a hare would never actually be racing in the real world, students don't care about who wins, and no one would create a product to share with the public.

Continuing with this mathematics team in Texas, we revised the problem to center on a real-world situation involving unit rates. The teachers shared how drought and water scarcity was an issue many students faced, so they decided to look at the topic of global water inequities, thus creating a problem-solving task situated in an authentic context. Students were prompted to read the stories of Cheru and Kamama, a pair of five-year-olds from Kenya who spend part of their day walking to get water (Reid, 2017). After reading stories about each child, students considered various questions, including these:

- Roundtrip, Cheru walks a total of 6.88 kilometers in 3 hours and 32 minutes.

- How far does Cheru walk to the waterhole in meters?

- Approximately how far can Cheru walk in 1 hour in kilometers? Meters?

- Do you think Cheru walks at the same pace *to* the waterhole and *from* the waterhole? Why or why not? How does your answer impact the previous question?

• Roundtrip, Kamama walks 252 yards, or 0.14 miles, to the well for a total of 6 minutes and 49 seconds.

- Approximately how far does Kamama walk to the well in meters?

- If Kamama had to walk to the waterhole, what would Kamama's rate be? What units did you choose? Why?

- Who walks faster: Kamama or Cheru? How do you know? What assumptions did you make?

Authentic Connections Checklist (Yes/No Questions)

☑ In the real world, would students solve this problem using *rigorous* mathematics?

☑ Is the mathematics needed for this situation open-ended with multiple pathways to solutions?

☑ Would students care about this outside of the classroom?

☐ Would students share their knowledge through a public product?

Looking at the Authentic Connections Checklist, we see three of the four questions are checked yes. Collectively, the first three questions in the checklist identify a strong, authentic problem-solving task. The Texas teachers continued to focus on unit rates, but also added in metric conversions to create a rigorous mathematics task to solve. Various pathways exist for students to solve these problems, from visual representations to algorithmic approaches. Situated in the story of two young children, most students would empathize with this real-world situation. This problem-solving task is a step in the right direction to increasing authenticity in the classroom. The question remains: Would students share their knowledge publicly?

In this instance, students created a poster of their mathematics to show their teacher and peers; however, no authentic audience outside of the classroom existed. The Texas teachers made a strong movement in authenticity. This movement helped these educators see how authentic problem-solving tasks can lead to a classroom conducive to PBL.

FROM AUTHENTIC TASK TO AUTHENTIC PROJECT

Moving beyond a problem-solving task into creating a project became the next step for these Texas educators. Specifically, they questioned, "How can we engage students in authentic problems or situations that lead to a public product in the mathematics classroom?" When I personally consider this question, I pose more questions to myself:

- Is there an issue faced by our local, national, or global society that students can analyze with mathematics?

- What are topics students care about that have mathematical connections?

- What need can be fulfilled by my students using mathematics?

- Who uses this mathematics in their profession or daily life?

Access to clean water is an issue faced by our global society and a topic for which students can feel empathy given Cheru and Kamama are little children, younger than the Texas middle school students. We brainstormed several ideas to engage students authentically in a final product. One idea was for students to create a map of a country in Africa such as Ethiopia or Mali where access to clean water is greatly needed. On this map, students could show distances and approximate walking rates where children and families have to walk to water, creating a key of whether that water is from a well or a natural source. Students could use their maps to advocate for the location of a new well. Students could develop and implement a social media campaign to raise funds for clean water or create a budget for a fundraising event.

After much conversation, the Texas teachers decided on a student-created fundraiser, specifically a walk-a-thon mimicking the walk that Cheru needed to take to retrieve water every day. Students planned the walk and accompanying events, such as stops along the way where student posters and maps, like the ones described earlier, shared information about the need for access to clean water. Students used rates and ratio understanding to create a budget detailing how much bottled water to purchase for the walkers and the sale price of each bottle of water. Students wrapped each bottle of water with a unique label including a QR (quick response) code to their website, showing maps of their city displaying routes between known locations that approximated the daily walks by Cheru and Kamama, further highlighting the need to raise funds for building wells.

This event merged a real issue faced in the world with students' mathematical skills and desire to create change, making for an authentic product to share with the community. Beyond that, students enhanced their agency by using mathematics to directly impact their local and global community. Students knew their work was valuable and headed somewhere beyond the teacher's desk, providing students the opportunity to showcase their best work. When looking back at the Authentic Connections Checklist, we can see this project met all the criteria for authenticity.

Authentic Connections Checklist (Yes/No Questions)

☑ In the real world, would students solve this problem using *rigorous* mathematics?

☑ Is the mathematics needed for this situation open-ended with multiple pathways to solutions?

☑ Would students care about this outside of the classroom?

☑ Would students share their knowledge through a public product?

YOUR TURN

Look back at the tasks and PBL ideas you brainstormed in Chapter 3. Evaluate your initial brainstorming for authentic connections. How could you create authentic connections in the tasks or PBL mathematics experiences?

_____

_____

AUTHENTIC EXPERTS

In considering authenticity in the PBL mathematics classroom, let's consider how the mathematics topics we explore with students are used in the real world by people in careers within our society. I often invite people in the community to be an expert in my classroom regarding a specific topic connected to a PBL mathematics experience. Yes, this takes time and some sweet talking, but the payoff is well worth it. I vividly remember calling a marketing professional to ask if he would come speak to my middle school students. The first thing he said was "I hated middle school," followed quickly by "and I'm not good at math." I explained the goals I had in mind for this presentation, only to be posed one more critical question: "How do you stand the constant smell of BO?"

After assuring the professional we would be in a well-ventilated classroom and his experience would be positive, he agreed to speak. Not only did he bring PopSockets to the students (which were newly popular and made him an instant hit), but he seemed to thoroughly enjoy his time in middle school. Two days later, he followed up with an email saying he wished he had a mathematics classroom experience where professionals or "experts" spoke about how mathematics was used in their careers. He ended by thanking me for helping him see he was good at the mathematics of his job, mathematics my students now recognized was used in a popular profession. No, we aren't called to change the minds of all the mathematics haters in the world, but this was an added bonus that impacted my students and one person's view of mathematics education.

Experts can also boost authenticity in the product creation. During a project when students were creating a blueprint for an accessible park, the students often referred to the architect we invited to speak to our class. I would hear comments like "Remember, the architect said we need a fall zone of at least four feet" or "Don't forget the architect mentioned we need to be precise in our measurements because an error of one foot could cost thousands of dollars." Students take to heart the rules and guidelines set forth by a professional. Instead of me, as the teacher, creating the parameters for a task or public product, the parameters have been set by the expert, allowing the process to align more strategically with real-world needs.

Lastly, we can create authentic connections for students to present their public products to outside experts. When working on a project about who makes the ideal athlete, students were first introduced to the topic by the head and assistant soccer coaches from our local university. The coaches asked students to conduct quantitative research, informing students that a team of coaches and mathematicians were interested in the findings. The soccer coaches, then, became our client. Throughout the project, students knew they would be presenting their statistical findings to these experts. This heightened the authenticity of the project, empowering students to own their mathematical identity needed to address the needs of their client.

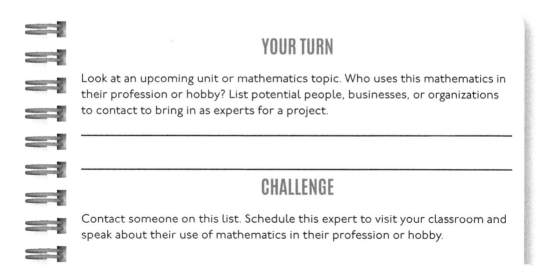

YOUR TURN

Look at an upcoming unit or mathematics topic. Who uses this mathematics in their profession or hobby? List potential people, businesses, or organizations to contact to bring in as experts for a project.

_____

_____

CHALLENGE

Contact someone on this list. Schedule this expert to visit your classroom and speak about their use of mathematics in their profession or hobby.

PBL PLUS TIPS

- ☐ Change a task to include an authentic context. Use exact or approximate numbers from the real world to promote mathematical modeling and problem solving.

- ☐ Develop an authentic product that uses deep mathematical knowledge, something students would see created by professionals or enthusiasts.

  - ● Examine the list of ideas in Chapter 16.

  - ● Try creating the product yourself! What mathematical knowledge did you use?

  - ● Share your process with your students, showing sketches and highlighting mistakes that led to learning opportunities.

- ☐ Invite community members to speak about how mathematics is used in their profession. Consider industry leaders, government officials, nonprofit organizers, community activists, small business owners, medical workers, and higher education faculty.

- ☐ Create opportunities for students to develop products for authentic clients.

- ☐ Invite a panel of experts to provide feedback at a critique opportunity or culminating event.

- ☐ Use authentic physical or digital tools that experts use for construction or creation of products.

CONCLUDING THOUGHTS

Authentic, public products enhanced by community experts heighten the relevancy of a project. Additionally, authentic projects build each student's positive identity and agency as a mathematician, an important equity lever and essential attribute of the PBL mathematics classroom. As you think about ways to increase the authentic connections to mathematics in your classroom, consider what mathematics is used on a regular basis in our society. Align that to your content standards as well as Mathematical Habits of Mind. How can the mathematics of your community become the central focus of a project?

PBL POINTS TO PONDER: SAY WHAT?

Brainstorm a list of authentic problems or situations in your local or global community. Analyze the problem or situation using the four *what* questions:

- ☐ What is my authentic problem or situation?
- ☐ What mathematics is needed to solve this?
- ☐ What audience would care about solving this?
- ☐ What can my students create to publicly share their solution?

CHAPTER 8

Meaningful Assessment

Need to Knows

- What does meaningful assessment look like in the project-based learning mathematics classroom?

- How is meaningful assessment used by both teachers and students?

- How does assessing a public product elevate student identity and agency in the project-based learning classroom?

- How can public products highlight each of the Six Essential Attributes of a PBL mathematics classroom?

I remember the first time I failed a mathematics test. I was crushed. No, I was more than crushed. I felt debilitated and questioned my entire future. This test was in Calculus III in college. I remember that the test was one big question separated into individual parts. I made one mistake on the first page, which led to the entire "solution" deemed incorrect. To this day, I don't recall a single concept from that test. I do remember exactly where I sat in the classroom, who sat next to me, and how I felt receiving that failing grade. I remember questioning whether I would pass the class, then spiraling to thoughts of a plummeting grade point average, leading to an inability to graduate with a mathematics degree, wrecking my entire teaching career. (*I'm a bit dramatic, I know.*)

Being the ever-vigilant student, I went to my professor's office hours. I carefully explained my error and pleaded my case for a retake. I vividly remember my heart pounding as I waited for my professor's response. Deliberately, he said, "I can see you actually knew the content. I'm sorry your knowledge didn't show up better on the test." Crushed. A second time.

ASSESSMENT IN THE MATHEMATICS CLASSROOM

My failing that calculus test didn't stop my mathematics education career. However, that memory sticks with me each and every time my students need to take a test, whether in a mathematics class or not. In my own classroom, I work toward creating assessment opportunities that mirror the call for the high-quality mathematics teaching practice of "elicit and use evidence of student thinking" brought forward by *Principles to Actions: Ensuring Mathematical Success for All* (National Council of Teachers of Mathematics [NCTM], 2014). This teaching practice recognizes that student *thinking* and *progress toward mathematical understanding* is critical for successful implementation of rigorous academic standards. NCTM (2014) further supports assessment as a tool directly linked to instruction, citing that assessment should inform a teacher's instructional decisions. Lastly, high-quality assessment practices include students monitoring their progress and recognizing high-quality mathematical thinking and reasoning within their own work.

In the mathematics classroom, traditional assessment practices center on tests and quizzes. However, ongoing attention to formative assessment has brought to the forefront use of formative assessment opportunities like mathematics notebooks, exit tickets, written reflection, observations, and interviews. (See Chapter 16 for more formative assessment ideas for the project-based learning [PBL] mathematics classroom.)

MEANINGFUL ASSESSMENT DEFINED

Meaningful assessment: in PBL relates to the creation of public products that have relevance, significance, and purpose.

As I grow as a PBL mathematics educator, I recognize one big difference in my practice centers on **meaningful assessment**. For something to be meaningful, it must have relevance, significance, purpose—basically, it must provide a *why*. In terms of assessment in PBL, this connects to the creation of a public product that answers the *why*. Why am I learning this content? Why am I showing my learning through this assessment? Although a test or quiz may have the purpose to help students progress mathematically or to solidify content needed for the next unit, in the end moving on to the next unit or next grade is not inherently meaningful to the majority of our students.

To align with equitable teaching practices, calls in the Catalyzing Change series from NCTM (2018, 2020a, 2020b) highlight the need for varied and ongoing assessments that not only measure but moreover advance learning. This is where PBL mathematics experiences have the potential to deepen our assessment practices and align to equitable teaching practices. Actively engaging with the driving question, student "need to know" questions naturally provide a *why* for mathematical learning and assessment, as elaborated upon in the subsequent story of a fourth-grade classroom. As students move toward creating a public product, they accrue multiple formative assessments that highlight evidence of learning. The public product itself, along with the culminating event, is considered the summative assessment, which assumes a larger purpose and audience beyond the classroom, further providing a *why* for student learning of mathematical concepts.

It's important to note that in PBL, all assessment completed prior to the public product is considered formative assessment. As students inquire and engage in learning, the activities, investigations, tasks, quizzes, and reflections coalesce formatively to provide ongoing feedback and support decision making about next steps. Students learn through the project process, where making mistakes is a natural and valued part of the process. Formative assessments, then, are used as informational tools in classroom teaching and learning practices.

Students gain insight into their learning progress through formative assessments while educators reflect on their practice through formative assessments, finding ways to help students deeply engage with the content.

Meaningful assessment should do all of the following:

1. Be linked to the project learning goals and "need to know" questions.

2. Inform teaching and learning practices.

3. Be meaningful to your classroom and students.

4. Be meaningful to the community.

5. Enhance student identity and agency.

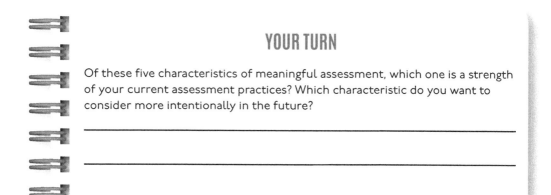

YOUR TURN

Of these five characteristics of meaningful assessment, which one is a strength of your current assessment practices? Which characteristic do you want to consider more intentionally in the future?

_____

_____

These five characteristics of meaningful assessment in a PBL mathematics experience are highlighted by the Meaningful Assessment Checklist. You can use this checklist to examine assessment in problem-solving and performance tasks as well. Making moves to alter traditional assessment practices by utilizing more problem-solving tasks and performance tasks often leads to more meaningful assessment practices. Problem-solving tasks do not include creating a full "need to know" list; however, both types of tasks inform our teaching and learning practices and could enhance student identity and agency. Let's look at these five characteristics exemplified throughout a project used in a fourth-grade classroom.

Meaningful Assessment Checklist (Yes/No Questions)

☐ Is the content being assessed directly linked to the project learning goals and "need to know" questions?

☐ Is the assessment being used to inform teaching and learning practices?

☐ Do students believe in the *why* behind the assessment practice?

☐ Is the assessment meaningful to a public audience beyond the teacher or classroom?

☐ Does the assessment enhance student identity and agency?

MEANINGFUL ASSESSMENT ILLUSTRATED

Fourth-grade teacher Jasmine Valentine designed a project during which her students created blueprints for their dream school. In her school district, plans to consolidate two schools and build one new school were being discussed. Therefore, this project authentically linked to a current community need. Jasmine launched the project by giving her students mystery blueprints to examine. As Jasmine listened to her students ponder each blueprint, she heard her students use rich mathematical vocabulary like *right angles, feet, inches,* and *area*. After revealing the driving question and providing students with a project summary, Jasmine continued to hear vocabulary like *obtuse angle, protractor, parallel,* and *perpendicular* as students wrote their "need to know" questions. Jasmine recognized she could use this activity to formatively assess her students' background knowledge.

When students shared their "need to know" questions, Jasmine paused at times to ask the whole class a question. After a student posed, "Can we build a room with obtuse angles?," Jasmine turned to the whole class, asking, "Who knows how to find the exact measure of an obtuse angle?" When only one hand went up, Jasmine smiled and shared, "That will be one of our goals as a whole class, then." Throughout the "need to know" process, Jasmine continued to pose preassessment questions, discovering the majority of her students could describe a ninety-degree angle while only one of her students knew how to use a protractor to determine the exact measure of an angle, one of the project's major learning goals. These quick checks for understanding enabled Jasmine to naturally preassess her students' knowledge, providing her insight into her next steps for teaching.

 The project featured in this vignette is available for download at **https://qrs.ly/56ensfy**.

Productive Inquiry as Formative Assessment

After gathering "need to know" questions, Jasmine grouped the questions together to facilitate learning. Some of these questions that guided exploration included "How many students are in one classroom?"; "How big does a classroom need to be?"; and "Do classrooms have to be rectangular, or can they be other shapes?" To answer these questions, students needed to explore the concept of area and angle measurements. Now, instead of learning area because "You'll need to know it next year" or linking area to growing a garden, tiling a floor, or painting a room, learning how to calculate area held an immediate need for the students. Similarly, angles were not simply drawn on paper and classified as acute, obtuse, or right. Angles became meaningful and essential to the project.

To answer these questions, students first conducted an investigation into the dimensions of their own classroom, which was shaped like a trapezoid. Students used protractors specific to measuring a physical room with unique angles and tape measures, diagramming their classroom and classifying angles. Before finding the area of their classroom, students explored the concept of area through multiple activities using hands-on manipulatives. As their classroom is shaped like a trapezoid, students determined the area of their classroom through various techniques—including estimation, breaking the shape apart, physically cutting a trapezoid apart to create a rectangle, and drawing the trapezoid on grid paper to count the squares—before submitting their work for assessment.

While constructing knowledge about angles and area, students knew exactly why these concepts were critical to learn. As one fourth-grade girl shared, "I want my dream school to be unique like our classroom. Rectangular rooms are sort of boring. I want big classrooms with lots of windows and a circular library. Mrs. Valentine said she'd help me learn about the area of a circle because I don't know how to find that." Not only did this student recognize why area and angles were important; she also naturally pushed herself academically, desiring to learn more about area of a circle because it authentically connected to her project goals.

Through formative assessment, we can see two of the five questions are addressed. However, in order to actualize all the goals of meaningful assessment, we need to explore what summative assessment looks like in the PBL mathematics classroom.

Meaningful Assessment Checklist (Yes/No Questions)

- ☑ Is the content being assessed directly linked to the project learning goals and "need to know" questions?
- ☑ Is the assessment being used to inform teaching and learning practices?
- ☐ Do students believe in the *why* behind the assessment practice?
- ☐ Is the assessment meaningful to a public audience beyond the teacher or classroom?
- ☐ Does the assessment enhance student identity and agency?

Student-Led Feedback as Assessment

As educators, we often assume the majority share of giving feedback; however, in the PBL mathematics classroom, empowering students to assess their growth, either independently or in teams, leads to independent, reflective learners. Students can assess their mathematical progress through the use of checklists, rubrics, and daily logs. In the *Dream School* project, the project manager led a daily team progress assessment report briefing at the end of each class period. With five minutes left of class, the project manager would record what the team accomplished and what steps needed to be taken in the subsequent class work times. Teams used the project rubric to assess progress toward achieving their blueprint goals.

Checklists are another valuable tool to use as a formative assessment. Individuals can use a checklist of questions to assess their mathematical knowledge whether in a project or in a unit of study. Checklist questions might range from "I can plot a point in Quadrant III of the coordinate plane" for a middle school student to "I can describe how the vertex is used in business applications" for a high school student.

Peers can also provide constructive feedback to their classmates. In the *Dream School* project, prior to formal presentations in front of a panel, teams partnered to practice presentations and to give and receive feedback on their blueprints. Students provided verbal feedback to one another through the use of an "I like/I wonder" protocol. After each practice presentation, peers who listened to the presentation each shared one "I like" and one "I wonder" statement. For example, one boy shared the following: "I like how you made a key to label features like the water fountains, doors, and stairs. I wonder if you could create a label for acute and obtuse angles because I don't see any labels or measurements." This feedback, coming from a peer, helped the team immensely as they spent the remainder of class measuring and labeling angles on their blueprint. (See Chapter 17 for more about peer critique and assessment protocols.)

YOUR TURN

Think about an upcoming unit or project. Plan for each of the following assessment options. What could it look like? Sound like?

Students Assess Individual Progress	Teams Assess Their Collaborative Progress	Peers Assess Individual or Team Progress

CHALLENGE

Design an opportunity for student-led assessment in an upcoming unit, even if it is not a project.

Summative Assessment Through a Culminating Experience Illustrated

Dressed in suit jackets, sweaters, dresses, and button-down shirts, the fourth graders in Jasmine Valentine's classroom were ready to present their blueprints and formal slideshow presentation at their culminating experience. After weeks of work, the morning came for each young architectural group to embody their roles of project manager, designer, mathematician, and lead speaker. Teams presented their blueprints to a panel of experts, including mathematicians, designers, and administrators who would make decisions about the potential new community high school.

While presenting, each team member explained how they contributed to the overall project. Teams shared ideas about creating spaces inclusive to all students, including gender-neutral bathrooms and locker rooms, as well as having multiple languages offered from Spanish to Hmong to Japanese. Some teams showed an emphasis on bringing nature into the design, adding outdoor seating, koi ponds, and large fountains to their blueprints. One team even cited the science that natural light increases students' emotional and physical well-being. Blueprints included everything from an administrative office shaped like Batman to a three-story aquarium at the heart of the school.

Using a rubric co-created with the students, panelists asked questions about angle measurements, total area of the dream school, unique design elements, research conducted, and collaboration efforts. At the conclusion of the presentations, panelists shared concluding thoughts, where evident collaboration and thoughtful design was an ongoing theme. Mathematically, the experts highlighted the professional look of each blueprint that labeled angle measurements, used rulers and graph paper to make straight lines, and showed calculations for dimensions and area. As the panelists spoke, students smiled at one another, pointing at their blueprints when a positive attribute was shared. These students embraced their identities as mathematicians, recognizing the panelists appreciated their detailed efforts.

Before everyone left, one little girl whose role was the designer approached two of the panelist experts, the superintendent and associate superintendent. She curiously asked, "If the new school is built, will one design be chosen? Or, will the architects use ideas from all of us to create the new school?"

Taken slightly aback, they asked this fourth grader what she would like to see happen, to which she replied, "Well, I think everyone had good ideas. I would be happy to talk to the architect and make sure the best ideas are included." This student fully embraced her role as a designer. She recognized her work had value outside of the classroom and wanted to honor the work of her peers.

Beaming from ear to ear after the presentations, Jasmine reflected upon the experience, noting her biggest takeaway: "Often, in assessments, the students who understood the material versus the students who struggled is very apparent. Today, every kid shone brightly. They all did so fantastic and spoke with such confidence and pride in their work."

Through this experience, Jasmine realized that meaningful assessment not only increased each student's positive identity in her mathematics classroom, but also created an equitable environment wherein all students could—and did—succeed.

Meaningful Assessment Checklist (Yes/No Questions)

- ☑ Is the content being assessed directly linked to the project learning goals and "need to know" questions?
- ☑ Is the assessment being used to inform teaching and learning practices?
- ☑ Do students believe in the *why* behind the assessment practice?
- ☑ Is the assessment meaningful to a public audience beyond the teacher or classroom?
- ☑ Does the assessment enhance student identity and agency?

ESSENTIAL ATTRIBUTES HIGHLIGHTED BY PUBLIC PRODUCT

As mathematics educators, PBL teaching practices encourage us to create formative and summative assessments beyond traditional tests and quizzes. Don't get me wrong. Tests and quizzes still have their place in the mathematics classroom, including in the PBL mathematics classroom. However, a true summative assessment in the PBL mathematics classroom incorporates meaningful assessment as previously illustrated.

When designing a summative assessment for a project, each of the Six Essential Attributes of a PBL mathematics classroom can be explored through a critical question:

- Will students show deep, **rigorous content** knowledge transferred into the public product?

- Will formative assessments and iterations of the public product highlight **productive inquiry**?

- Will students enhance their **identity and agency** by sharing or presenting the product?

- Will the public product be valued by an **authentic** audience through a culminating experience?

- Will the public product be used as a **reflective** tool for mathematical knowledge and **growth**?

These questions can help guide the process of choosing a public product that aligns to the content standards, Mathematical Habits of Mind, and success skills as well as the authentic situation or problem. In Figure 8.1, let's look at each question with the product of the *Dream School* blueprints and presentation.

Remember PBL focuses on learning throughout the project. Students transfer their surface and deep knowledge, showing evidence of learning through formative assessments and iterations of the public product; the emphasis in PBL should not be solely on the end product (Eisberg, 2018). In the PBL mathematics classroom, formative assessments may include quizzes, common assessments, exit tickets, and high-quality problem-solving tasks aligned to learning goals. All of these modalities highlight productive inquiry and inform the assessment of the public product.

Figure 8-I • Essential Attributes Exemplified via Meaningful Assessment

Essential Attribute Question	Explanation
Will students show deep, rigorous content knowledge transferred into the public product?	Blueprints highlighted ability to label and measure acute, obtuse, and right angles. Blueprints showed dimensions of rectangular spaces with appropriate labels. Additional work showed calculations of area.
Will formative assessments and iterations of the public product highlight productive inquiry?	Formative assessments and public product iterations included: • Creating a diagram of the classroom, which was hexagonal in shape, with labels of angles and dimensions • Creating a diagram of rectangular hallways and classrooms with labels of angles and dimensions • Exit tickets finding area of rectangles and composite shapes that could be decomposed into rectangles • Initial sketches of classroom designs • Daily logs of team accomplishments and goals
Will students enhance their identity and/or agency by sharing or presenting the product?	Students embraced their roles throughout the project and team presentations, developing their identity as mathematicians who can apply mathematics to a real-world context.
Will the public product be valued by an authentic audience through a culminating experience?	The public product was shared to a panel of experts who were interested in the design of the school as well as the mathematics used to create the blueprints.
Will the public product be used as a reflective tool for mathematical knowledge and growth?	Daily, students reflected on their accomplishments and set goals for the following work time, as facilitated by the project manager. After team presentations, students reflected individually on their mathematical and personal growth.

Let's explore this idea in the *Dream School* project where not every blueprint included angle measurements or area calculations. For example, one team labeled angles as acute or obtuse but did not use a protractor to specifically measure the angles. During the presentation, the mathematician of the group reflected she spent so much time on calculating the area of the classrooms she did not have time to measure the angles, so she quickly labeled them based on visual understanding. The project manager then shared she could have helped measure angles but did not realize the mathematician needed assistance. This accurate, sincere reflection by both team members directed the attention of the panelists toward what the team did accomplish, recognizing that although the angle measurements were lacking, the reason was due not to lack of understanding but more so to lack of time. As their teacher, Jasmine recognized that she would need to use formative assessments to gauge understanding of angle measurements; additionally, she could provide the team time to finalize their blueprint angle measurements.

Lastly, public products can and should be displayed or implemented outside of the classroom through a culminating experience (see Chapter 18). Consider a group of high school students learning statistics who explored population trends for cities across their state. Instead of a test, students wrote detailed letters to the city council members describing their analyses and recommending actions each city could take. For example, one analysis showed a steady increase in birth rates in a city, highlighting the action item to build more parks or attract more child care centers. This public product delivered through the culminating experience of mailing letters to the city council elevated the meaningful learning experience for students.

Additional Resources

For more about both formative and summative assessment, check out the following resources:

- *The Formative 5: Everyday Assessment Techniques for Every Math Classroom* (Fennell et al., 2017)

- *Mathematics Formative Assessment, Volume I: 75 Practical Strategies for Linking Assessment, Instruction, and Learning* (Keeley & Tobey, 2011)

- "Resource List: Assessment in PBL" (PBLWorks, 2018)

- "A Rubric Masterclass" for mathematics educators (Krall, 2021)

PBL PLUS TIPS

☐ Engage students in taking the lead on assessment.

- Co-create a rubric with students.

- Teach students how to use a rubric through individual assessment.

- Engage in protocols such as "I like/I wonder" to intentionally teach peer-to-peer critique and assessment.

☐ Create a space in your classroom or school to display public products.

- Empty a few bookshelves or a "trophy" case to display public products.

- Highlight all evidence of learning that led to the public product by making a binder or portfolio to accompany the public products.

☐ Consider inviting experts or invested audience members to the classroom to aid in assessment at the culminating experience.

- Provide experts with copies of the rubric or a simplified checklist to assess students.

- Make sure students create thank-you notes or a thank-you video to send to experts or audience members who provide feedback.

CONCLUDING THOUGHTS

Let's examine our Driving Question for this book in terms of assessment: "How can I bring project-based learning [PBL] to life in the mathematics classroom?" Assessment opportunities, when used as an ongoing process to provide feedback to students, work to engage students in rich mathematical learning. Elevating assessment practices to include meaningful public products highlighted during a culminating experience lead to increasing student identity and agency. By creating a public product as a summative assessment, students will find relevance in formative assessments and assignments that align to their "need to know" questions. More about assessment, including ideas for rubric creation, meaningful formative and summative assessment practices, and culminating experience ideas, will be highlighted in Section III.

PBL POINTS TO PONDER: "I USED TO THINK . . . NOW I THINK . . ."

Given your background knowledge and ongoing understanding of PBL mathematics, complete the following sentence stems regarding the notion of meaningful assessment in the classroom.

☐   I used to think . . . Now I think . . .

CHAPTER 9

Growth Through Reflection

At the conclusion of the *Wage Gap* performance task, initially highlighted in Chapter 6, Algebra I students spent time in reflection. Using the prompt, "Thinking back on my math journey during the *Wage Gap* task, a big aha for me was . . ., " students were asked to share their thoughts with no right or wrong answers. Their reflections proved to be both extremely honest and insightful both to the students and to their teacher.

Need to Knows

- How is reflection different in the project-based learning mathematics classroom?
- How is reflection tied to critique and revision?

"Math is about more than getting the right answer. A lot of what we did in our math task was to explain our thoughts and ideas and reasons behind what we did and how we did it. Sometimes other people had a different idea, and that was okay as long as you explained your ideas. It was nice to not always have to get the right answer. Less pressure to be perfect and more opportunities to just explore ideas." (*Rigorous Content, Productive Inquiry*)

"Math can be really useful to look at our world. Until we did the *Wage Gap* task, I thought math was only for measuring and counting, like only engineers, construction workers and bankers used math. Now I realize that math can help lots of people in lots of jobs look at really important information. I want a career in marketing, and I'm starting to see how math might help me in my future job." (*Authentic Connections, Identity & Agency, Growth Through Reflection*)

"I like math tasks and hate math tests. I'm not good at tests, and I don't really care about tests. I liked the *Wage Gap* task because the graphs told a story and had a purpose and a meaning, unlike a test. I think I did well on the math task because I could take my time and work with my friends. I do better with a group because they keep me focused because my ADHD [attention deficit hyperactivity disorder] makes me easily distracted." (*Authentic Connections, Meaningful Assessment*)

Upon reading student reflections, I noticed each of the essential attributes of an ideal project-based learning (PBL) mathematics classroom were illuminated in their responses. Although these six attributes were not explicitly taught to students, the fact that each one manifested during reflection reinforced how they contribute to a successful PBL mathematics classroom.

GROWTH THROUGH REFLECTION DEFINED

Growth through reflection: refers to the metacognitive ability of students to establish a mindset that learning is ongoing and that struggle is a normal part of the process.

Growth mindset. Productive struggle. These two ideas continue to impact the educational system. Productive struggle in the mathematics classroom focuses on students developing grit and perseverance in the face of tackling problems they don't immediately know how to solve. Productive struggle can lead to incredible growth in student learning; this learning is deepened and solidified when students reflect upon the ways they struggled and the actions they took to persevere through the struggle. Reflection is one of the most powerful means to achieving growth in the classroom. Growth through reflection, then, refers to the metacognitive ability of students to establish a mindset that learning is ongoing and that struggle is a normal part of the process. Boaler et al. (2018) write that engaging students in reflection helps "move the focus from performance to learning" (p. 6). Intentional reflection in the classroom should lead to action, whether that action is revising work in progress or making changes for future work.

Much has been written about growth mindset and productive struggle. In the mathematics classroom, reflection provides opportunities for students to grow both in their understanding of content and in their Mathematical Habits of Mind, fostering a growth mindset. In the PBL mathematics classroom, another key focus of reflection is on the success skills that students utilized throughout the project. What can unlock this potential student growth are the times and ways we help students reflect.

Additional Resources

Learn more about growth mindset and productive struggle in the mathematics classroom through these sources:

* *Mathematical Mindsets* (Boaler, 2015)

* *Productive Math Struggle: A 6-Point Action Plan for Fostering Perseverance* (SanGiovanni et al., 2020)

GROWTH THROUGH REFLECTION ILLUSTRATED

Let me reflect upon my own experiences as an early-career educator to share how I have grown in my use of reflection.

In my early years of teaching, I often felt the pressure to wrap up one unit of study to quickly move to the next, leaving little to no room for transformative reflective moments. As I grew in my understanding of the importance of reflection, I provided opportunities for my students to reflect on their learning, but often those reflection moments occurred only after a unit of study was completed. With a growing understanding of reflection, I recognized it was important for students to reflect often, throughout the entirety of the project. Yet, this activated my curiosity to explore the goals of reflection. If I wanted my students to learn and grow from reflection, doesn't that mean students would have to act upon that reflection? How does reflecting throughout the process lead to action?

At its core, reflection means to give thought or serious consideration to something, which does not inherently seem active; yet, in order to grow from reflection, I needed to shift my thinking toward reflection being an active, dynamic process that is cyclical in nature. Some prepositions used with reflection help distinguish the opportunities for growth and action. As an educator, am I asking students, and myself, to reflect *on* action, meaning a past event or learning opportunity? Are students reflecting *in* action, pausing at a learning opportunity to recalibrate thinking and learning with an immediate change? Or, are students reflecting *for* action, considering future actions with the goal to change or improve learning opportunities?

The most natural type of reflection is to reflect *on* action. This is how I initially engaged my students in reflection. At the conclusion of a unit or project, I would ask my students to reflect upon what they had learned and how they had grown. However, this did not always lead to immediate, implementable action. Therefore, as I grew to include reflection throughout a project or mathematical unit of study, I started considering how to help students reflect *in* action and reflect *for* action. Helping students reflect *in* action meant I needed to focus on varying my reflection techniques between formal, preplanned opportunities and informal, in-the-moment opportunities to pause and think about learning. This also meant I needed to focus my questioning techniques to aid in-the-moment reflection by students throughout the project.

Reflection *for* action should be occurring throughout a project; this type of reflection leads students to pause in order to think about future actions they need to take in the project. Teachers need to guide students to consider the skills they have developed and how those skills could be enacted throughout the rest of the project. This means that reflection should occur on more than just content understanding, including reflection on the Mathematical Habits of Mind and success skills.

Lastly, I realized that my default reflection technique as a young educator was to pose a question and ask students to respond in writing. Just as we work to provide opportunities for students to engage through various techniques of written, verbal, and visual representations, reflection should occur in various formats as well—written, oral, visual, independently, or collaboratively. When I realized that writing was actually the barrier to reflection for some of my mathematics students, I began to encourage verbal reflection, then reflective drawings, then partner reflections, and so on. This paved the way to my recognition that reflection can and will lead to growth if I provide options for my students to reflect. By varying reflection techniques, teachers provide students more opportunity to maximize growth through reflection.

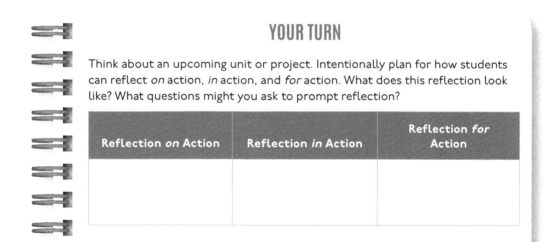

YOUR TURN

Think about an upcoming unit or project. Intentionally plan for how students can reflect *on* action, *in* action, and *for* action. What does this reflection look like? What questions might you ask to prompt reflection?

Reflection *on* Action	Reflection *in* Action	Reflection *for* Action

REFLECTION LEADING TO CRITIQUE AND REVISION

As students engage in reflection throughout a project, opportunities for critique and revision naturally exist. Reflection connects to the experience of learning throughout the entire process, whereas critique and revision focus deeply on the product being created and a student's ability to enhance the product.

When I hear the word *revision*, I automatically think of the writing process. However, helping students revise their mathematical thinking and their public products in the PBL mathematics classroom continues to foster a growth mindset, de-emphasizing the notion that mathematics needs to be completed correctly the first time. As a young mathematics educator, I was not prepared to help students think of revision in the mathematics classroom. Redoing an incorrect problem to correct work and find the right solution was the extent of my understanding of revision in the mathematics classroom.

Similarly, I was not prepared to invite students to critique mathematics. I thought, *Math is either correct or incorrect. What is there to critique?* Through ongoing professional development, I recognized how nuanced mathematical thinking and learning can be, especially as we invite students to share their mathematical reasoning. With the Mathematical Habit of Mind to critique the mathematical reasoning of others, this notion of critique has become more prominent in my personal teaching and learning practice. While critiquing reasoning and critiquing a product are slightly different in the outcome, the premise of reflecting critically on someone else's work and providing constructive feedback weaves a common thread through the PBL mathematics classroom experience.

REFLECTION ILLUSTRATED

Reflection looks vastly different at the elementary, middle, and high school levels. More about how to engage students in reflection at each level will be explored in Chapter 17. To illustrate reflection, let's explore a sixth-grade project called the *Accessible Park*. The Reflection Checklist can help guide our understanding of reflection in action.

Reflection Checklist (Yes/No Questions)

☐ Are students reflecting formally and informally throughout the project process?

☐ Are students reflecting *on* action, *in* action, and *for* action?

☐ Does reflection lead to critique and revision opportunities?

☐ Is reflection centered on multiple facets of learning including content, Mathematical Habits of Mind, and success skills?

In my sixth-grade classroom, I worked closely with my motivated, vibrant student teacher Megan Steffen to implement a project called the *Accessible Park*. When I initially created this project, I invited students to design an accessible playground that had yet to be built in our community. Since that time, an accessible playground has been built, yet students continue to enjoy designing not just playgrounds but amusement parks, waterparks, zoos, nature reserves, and spas, dreaming big about how our community can accommodate the needs of all people.

For this project, students created bird's-eye view blueprints of their parks and play areas, learning about the coordinate plane, positive and negative integers, scale, and scaled area along the way. Previously learned concepts such as area, fractions on a number line, fraction multiplication, decimal addition, and unit rate were all revisited during the project as students created elaborate blueprints on their coordinate planes and budgets for their park.

online resources ⟶ The project featured in this vignette is available for download at **https://qrs.ly/56ensfy**.

Working with Megan, we planned opportunities for students to reflect *in* action, *on* action, and *for* action. These happened both formally and informally throughout the duration of the project. Informal reflection *in* action occurred often, such as when a team had a dispute among its members. Megan and I gently stepped into the situation, asking students to refer to their team contracts highlighting how decisions were to be made, guiding students to reflect upon how their team could work together productively moving forward. These short conversations occur naturally in our PBL mathematics classroom as we take on the managing role of the project.

Helping students reflect *for* action means to consider future opportunities for growth. One day we observed Thomas, a student who struggled with social interaction, explaining how he chose his scale of two feet in real life equaling one centimeter in scale because he noticed most of his dimensions in real life were even. When Thomas finished the conversation, Megan sat by him and asked, "When you shared your mathematical thinking with another student, how did it make you feel?"

"It felt great. I really felt like I could speak confidently to help them with the scale for their project. I think I convinced them to choose my scale, because it's easy," Thomas replied with a big grin on his face.

Guiding Thomas to consider future opportunities to share his learning, Megan questioned, "I wonder, what could we do if another student is struggling with scale?"

Thomas jumped right in: "I could help! Maybe we can put my name on the board with a message like, 'See Thomas if you want to learn about scale.' Then they'll just know they can come and don't have to ask."

Megan responded, "That's an awesome idea. We'll do that for sure. Now, I know you sometimes struggle to talk to your peers in advisory. What have you learned about communication that can help you?"

Thomas paused, his face getting visibly upset. "I just don't always think they'll listen to me. I guess today they listened because I could help."

"Okay. Well, let's look for more ways we can have you be the helper in class, then, so you can talk more to your peers."

Here, Megan engaged Thomas to reflect *for* action, leading to an outcome that benefited multiple parties. Thomas enhanced his mathematical identity and practiced positive social interaction with his peers. Megan and I elevated the strengths of a struggling learner. Lastly, the entire class benefited as they had a peer expert willing to share his thinking.

In addition to informal moments of reflection, formal reflection occurred throughout the project both individually and as teams of students. Before intentionally being placed in teams, individuals were asked to reflect upon their strengths and struggles. Students wrote down one strength they could bring to the team, with descriptors ranging from leadership skills, to artistic talent, to mathematical knowledge, to humor. Students also reflected on potential struggle areas; content-specific topics like graphing points or calculating area often topped the list, yet other success skills like focus and organization showed up as well. This moment of reflection prior to forming a team provided students the opportunity to recognize that everyone brings a strength to the team, yet everyone benefits from having other team members who can share their strengths in service of the team.

About halfway through the blueprint creation, teams paused to complete a plus/minus/delta reflection chart (see Figure 9.1). Using this chart, students reflected on what was going well (*plus*), what academic topics or team dynamics had led to struggles (*minus*), and what changes needed to be made moving forward (*delta*). One sixth-grade team used the chart and reflected, "We need to change the shape of the overall design. Since we have so much we want to add we need more space and the original circle design isn't space efficient." Through this reflection, students were able to revise their collaborative thinking in order to create a stronger final product.

Before completing the final product, students engaged in a critique protocol called See-A-B (see Chapter 17). Prior to starting the protocol, as a whole class we reviewed the rubric for the project, highlighting potential ideas for feedback. Megan and I then asked two students to model one round of the See-A-B protocol. While modeling, we highlighted aspects of the protocol we wanted students to be particularly attentive to, such as listening when receiving feedback and not responding immediately.

Figure 9-1 • Plus/Minus/Delta Reflection Chart: Student Example

Accessible Park + - Δ

As you are in the midst of creating your Accessible Park, consider the following questions. Reflect honestly and accurately with your team as this will help you make changes and adjustments moving forward.

Plus (+)	Minus (–)	Delta (Δ)
a "plus" is something you are doing well as a team; consider what is going well academically and what is going well as a team of mathematicians	a "minus" is something that is not going well as a team; consider if there are academic misconceptions or group dynamics that have caused your team to struggle	a "delta" is something you want to change as a team; consider both academic and design changes as well as changes to team decision-making structures
We are doing a great job as a team having a steady workflow. We are on track to get finished in time if we work hard.	Some of us on Fridays are losing valued work time for volunteer hours.	We need to change the shape of the overall design. Since we have so much we want to add we need more space and the original circle design isn't space efficient.

Students were then randomly partnered and spread out throughout the room. Partners shared their designs for an accessible park, receiving verbal feedback using the following sentence stems:

- Good: "One *good* aspect of this design is . . ."

- Better: "Something that would make this design *better* is . . ."

- Best: "To make this design the *best* it can be, consider . . ."

One sixth grader shared this feedback with Thomas, who continued to work on social interactions. "One *good* aspect of your design is that you correctly labeled all four quadrants. Something that would make this design *better* is drawing shapes other than squares and rectangles. You might want to add curving pathways or a pond. To make this design the *best* it can be, consider adding more items than the minimum required and adding color." Thomas listened intently during this critique protocol, although his face showed he was struggling to not jump or get upset.

Afterward, when students were prompted to write one or two goals based on the feedback they received, Thomas wrote, "I plan to add a splash pad that will be in Quadrants II and III." Thomas successfully completed the protocol due in large part to our classroom culture of growing and learning from one another, highlighted by the intentional modeling of the protocol. By having two students demonstrate the protocol to the whole class, expectations were clearly established, and students—especially students like Thomas—felt safe academically and emotionally during a vulnerable time of feedback.

After completing the project, students worked on final, individual reflections. The individual reflections used sentence stems as prompts, such as "I struggled the most mathematically with . . ." and "As a mathematician, I grew in my ability to . . ." Although many students chose to write or type their responses, a few students used the option to reflect verbally via voice memos. Since the goal was to help students reflect, taking away the barrier of writing and providing options proved to eliminate barriers for some students.

REFLECTION EXAMINED

This project checks each of the boxes on the Reflection Checklist. Student reflections occurred informally, such as when my student teacher Megan Steffen questioned Thomas about his role as a scale expert, as well as formally through the plus/minus/delta chart and individual final reflection sheet. Reflection happened strategically at major points of the project, such as halfway through the blueprint creation. These reflections allowed students to purposefully make changes by enhancing the blueprint creation and tweaking team decision-making protocols, a type of reflection *in* action. Both types of changes, academic and interpersonal, were critical to teams successfully navigating to the end of the project. Students engaged in a critique protocol, providing them the opportunity to reflect upon the feedback received and engage in revision of their work.

Students reflected on multiple facets of the project learning goals. The individual final reflection highlights reflection on content, Mathematical Habits of Mind, and success skills. When asked to complete the sentence stem, "I struggled the most mathematically with . . . ," students mainly shared a content topic that remained a struggle, many citing multiplying fractions when calculating the area of scaled shapes. Students shared a Mathematical Habit of Mind when responding to the question, "As a mathematician, I grew in my ability to . . ." For this question, I brought up our list of Mathematical Habits of Mind to help students reflect specifically in that avenue. Lastly, projects in the mathematics classroom should also lift up the success skills that students considered in response to "Personally, I grew in my ability to . . ." Students cited ideas such as collaborating with others, thinking creatively in the mathematics classroom, problem solving when challenges arose, and organizing teammates.

Reflection Checklist (Yes/No Questions)

- ☑ Are students reflecting formally and informally throughout the project process?
- ☑ Are students reflecting *on* action, *in* action, and *for* action?
- ☑ Does reflection lead to critique and revision opportunities?
- ☑ Is reflection centered on multiple facets of learning including content, Mathematical Habits of Mind, and success skills?

YOUR TURN

Think about an upcoming unit or project. Craft a reflection question that would prompt your students to reflect upon each of the following: a content topic, a Mathematical Habit of Mind, and a success skill.

Question Prompt for Content	Question Prompt for Mathematical Habit of Mind	Question Prompt for Success Skill

PBL PLUS TIPS

- ☐ Begin at least one class period each week reflecting on prior learning.
- ☐ Connect reflection to the "need to know" questions of a PBL mathematics project.
  - Ask students to reflect on the progress of a project by noting which questions have been answered and which have yet to be explored.
- ☐ Purposefully teach students about productive struggle and growth mindset, enhancing the metacognitive abilities of your students.
- ☐ Vary reflection techniques.
  - Instead of written reflection, ask students to use a digital voice recorder like Voice Memos to share their thoughts.
  - Instead of sentences, ask students to draw a picture in response to a question accompanied by a short caption.
  - Instead of asking individuals, ask student teams to submit a group reflection.

CONCLUDING THOUGHTS

Reflection in and of itself does not lead to growth if not coupled with opportunities for action, including the action of revision. By using the Reflection Checklist, we can intentionally reflect upon our own classroom experiences and grow as practitioners. More about growth through reflection, specifically ideas for reflective practices at differing grade levels, will be highlighted in Chapter 18. Dewey (1933) states, "We do not learn from experience . . . we learn from reflecting on experience" (p. 78).

PBL POINTS TO PONDER: GLOWS AND GROWS

We often critique ourselves harshly without pausing to reflect on the good. Use this protocol to highlight the way you *glow* as an educator and areas to *grow* your practice.

☐ Glow: In what ways do I *glow* in my use of critique and reflection to support student learning?

☐ Grow: In what ways can I *grow* in my use of critique and reflection to better support student learning?

The How

Section III focuses on the *how*. How do we design a project for the mathematics classroom? This section starts by considering how to build a culture conducive to project-based learning (PBL) mathematics (Chapter 10) before exploring how the role of the teacher expands in the PBL classroom (Chapter 11). Creating PBL mathematics experiences may seem overwhelming at first, so Chapter 12 highlights how to become a PBL designer.

Chapters 13–17 move sequentially through the PBL process, from launch (Chapter 13) to planning milestones (Chapter 14), then on to how to manage the project (Chapter 15), assess the project (Chapter 16), and reflect upon the project experience (Chapter 17).

Chapter 18 brings all these ideas together, walking through the planning process using an example project from a seventh-grade mathematics classroom.

CHAPTER 10

Classroom Culture

Need to Knows

- What concrete strategies can I use to establish a classroom culture that fosters project-based learning mathematics?

- How does a project-based learning mathematics classroom focus on classroom culture all year long?

"What if the goats are too heavy for the bridge? They'll fall and the troll will get them!" cried four-year-old Piper while building a bridge.

"What if the troll eats all the goats?" replied DeSean, playing along.

"Let's just make a really tall bridge so the troll can't eat the goats! I'll use the rectangles!" Piper exclaimed.

"What if we make a trap for the troll?" DeSean wondered, gathering pieces to begin making the trap.

Piper jumped in excitedly, "Yeah! We can take out one of these triangles and put a popsicle stick over it, and then when the troll walks over it to get the goat, the troll will fall in!"

Piper and DeSean are two students in Stephanie Umberger's prekindergarten (PK) class. As someone who has spent my entire teaching career in secondary classes, the world of PK is a magical place to me. The students are engaging in a project on bridges, specifically designing a bridge for their indoor sensory path, which is a series of guided movements for students to follow as shown by markings on the wall. In Stephanie's school, the indoor sensory path has markings for frog hops, tip toes, and side-to-side jumps. However, a gap exists in one part of the pathway, which is where Stephanie's students plan to design a bridge. To engage in this mathematics project while connecting with literacy, Stephanie read *The Three Billy Goats Gruff* (Carpenter, 1998). Students then built bridges that could hold the three goats from the story while escaping the troll.

Every day I spent in Stephanie's PK classroom brought me joy and laughter; what I soon realized was that the classroom culture established at this very young age was exactly what I hoped all classrooms would feel like, a place filled with curiosity and play that values every member of the classroom and embraces the joy of learning together.

ESTABLISH A CLASSROOM CULTURE

As educators, we set the culture of our classroom. From get-to-know-you activities the first day of school to establishing the structures and routines of class, how we establish culture sets the tone for the remainder of the school year. In a positive classroom culture, students feel a sense of belonging and trust. That trust allows students to ask questions, make mistakes, tackle challenges, and take creative risks.

Classroom culture is not a one-and-done activity, though. As an early-career educator, I remember engaging in all sorts of activities at the beginning of the year to establish my classroom environment, only to move into "content" as quickly as possible, rarely reengaging in those culture-building activities. Now, I recognize the importance of continual engagement in fostering a classroom culture conducive to learning and growth.

As I have grown in my practice, I recognize some key culture-building steps that enhance the PBL mathematics classroom specifically. I value what Bergeron (2022) recognizes about PBL and community: "By its nature, project-based learning (PBL) has a reciprocal relationship with community building; PBL fosters community among learners, and a strong learning community is necessary for successfully implementing PBL."

Based on this reciprocal relationship between PBL and community, let's explore five ideas to not only build culture but also allow for PBL mathematics experiences to flourish in the classroom.

1. Develop community agreements.

2. Honor student identity and relationship to mathematics.

3. Embrace curiosity and wonderment.

4. Foster flexibility.

5. Value process over product.

DEVELOP COMMUNITY AGREEMENTS

Within the first few classes of a new school year, I work with my students to develop classroom norms or community agreements. These differ from classroom rules. A rule in my room is "Come prepared with a charged device." A rule is an expectation I set *for* the students; community agreements are developed *with* my students and express how we all agree to treat each other.

When working with sixth graders, here's how I develop community agreements. Consider how you may adjust this process for your classroom. I begin by posing questions such as "How would you like to feel in our classroom? What will help you to learn and grow? What will inspire and motivate you to be your very best?" Individually, students reflect on these questions; then they move into small groups to process their ideas. Collectively, we share answers to these questions, recording them on a whiteboard or poster paper.

Then, I purposefully direct a conversation about the difference between classroom rules and community agreements. I emphasize we are a community of learners; what we propose as agreements will guide how we interact with one another. Once students understand our goals, they return to small groups to propose a set of community agreements. Usually, I suggest they choose four or five community agreements; however, I remember one year a group of students only wanted the agreement of "Respect" as they felt everything would fall under that one word. Their passion persuaded the entire class!

Here are some potential community agreements specific to the mathematics classroom:

- Listen to everyone's ideas. Work to understand their thinking.

- Support one another in learning and growing.

- Take risks by sharing your thinking or trying new ideas.

- Celebrate learning from mistakes.

- Collaborate. Everyone has something to share.

There is a community agreement I add, which will be highlighted more in Chapter 17: "Critique the work, not the person." This community agreement is essential as students move deeper into the project process.

Once established, write or type the community agreements on a large classroom poster. I then ask every student to sign the community agreements, including myself, and hang them in the classroom.

All too often, this is where community agreements end. A poster lives on the wall, referenced only when a community agreement is broken. In the PBL mathematics classroom, ensuring community agreements are alive and vibrant is essential. Here are some ideas to foster continued engagement throughout the school year in the community agreements.

- As the teacher, reference when you engage in a community agreement. For example, when asking students to share their mathematical thinking, say, "I'm going to engage in the community agreement to listen to everyone's ideas. If I ask you to tell me more, it's because I want to understand your thinking."

- After a project or unit, ask students to reflect on what community agreement was most essential for their success. What did it look like, sound like, and feel like to engage in that community agreement?

- Before moving into tasks that require collaboration, ask three students to share a community agreement that would make group work successful.

- As students engage in a task, highlight students who are engaging in a specific community agreement. For example, if students are engaging in a problem-solving task, consider focusing on "take risks by sharing your thinking or trying new ideas." Write down names of students who actively live out that community agreement on a sticky note, then place it on the community agreement poster as you debrief the activity. This shows you value both the *what* and the *how*: What did students learn (content), and how did they learn it (community agreements)?

- Take pictures highlighting community agreements in action. Arrange these pictures around the community agreements poster. This not only celebrates students but also provides a visual to help all students clearly "see" the community agreement. I've taken photos of student work before and after a mistake was made. I love photos of group work where students are actively collaborating and listening to one another. Photos of messy work with solutions half started, then revised, highlight taking risks or trying new ideas.

YOUR TURN

What community agreement is essential for your students and classroom? How will you foster engagement in that community agreement throughout the school year?

_____

_____

HONOR STUDENT IDENTITY AND RELATIONSHIP TO MATHEMATICS

In the PBL mathematics classroom, we often ask students to embody the role of a mathematician, an emphasis in mathematics education highlighted in Chapter 1. This makes it critical to provide opportunities for students to embrace this identity. Chapters 1 and 6 highlighted some ideas to bring student identity and agency to the forefront of our work. Here is one more idea.

Students come to mathematics class with varied feelings and emotions, all too often centered on negativity or anxiety around mathematics. Recognizing and honoring these emotions is a first step to helping establish a classroom culture conducive to learning and growth. To help students explore their personal history with mathematics, consider scaffolding a learning experience around creating a Mathography.

To launch the creation of a Mathography, I begin by reading some children's books out loud to my students. There are a growing number of children's books about being a mathematician, including _The Girl With a Mind for Math: The Story of Raye Montague_ by Julia Finley Mosca (2018), _Counting on Katherine: How Katherine Johnson Saved Apollo 13_ by Helaine Becker (2018), and _The Boy Who Loved Math: The Improbable Life of Paul Erdos_ by Deborah Heiligman (2013). These books highlight stories of young children growing up to become mathematicians. After sharing these books, I share one more story: my personal Mathography.

Similar to an autobiography, a Mathography is a history of a person's relationship to mathematics. This activity is one where student voice and choice can be lifted up. Ask students to write a letter, record their thinking, develop a spoken-word piece, create a comic strip, or develop a bubble map. There is not a wrong way to create a Mathography! Here are some guiding questions:

- How do you feel about mathematics? Do you love it, like it, tolerate it, dislike it? Why?

- Consider your experiences in the mathematics classroom. What feelings and emotions come to mind? Why?

- Are there certain aspects or areas of mathematics you like better or worse? If so, tell me more.

- What is a vivid memory you have of the mathematics classroom (good or bad)?

- How do you experience mathematics outside of the classroom? What mathematical connections do you have through sports, hobbies, games, music? What about your family and friends—how do you engage in mathematics with them?

- What hopes do you have for mathematics class this upcoming year?

 Student examples of a Mathography are available for download at **https://qrs.ly/56ensfy**.

Additional Resources

Developing a sense of identity as a mathematician is an ongoing subject of books and articles, especially how identity and equity are interwoven. Explore more about this topic:

- *The Impact of Identity in K–8 Mathematics: Rethinking Equity-Based Practices* (Aguirre et al., 2013)

- Articles by mathematicians like Rochelle Gutiérrez, Imani Goffney, or Robert Q. Berry

EMBRACE CURIOSITY AND WONDERMENT

The Catalyzing Change series from the National Council of Teachers of Mathematics (NCTM, 2018, 2020a, 2020b) highlights the goal to broaden the purpose of mathematics, specifically by helping students experience the wonder, joy, and beauty of mathematics at every age and grade. This aligns with PBL mathematics, which builds upon students' wonderment and curiosity about our world, such as the PK classroom where students were in a continual state of wonder, joy, and beauty.

In 2019, neuroscientists from the University of California, Davis proved that curiosity boosts our ability to learn and retain information by preparing the brain and rewarding subsequent learning (Gruber & Ranganath, 2019). Curiosity is such an innate trait to us as humans, yet as educators, we may not know how to build this culture that embraces curiosity and wonderment. Here are two ideas to spark curiosity in your classroom:

1. Act like a four-year-old—question everything!

2. Follow the Curiosity Path.

Act Like a Four-Year-Old—Question Everything!

Yes, it might seem cliché to say that all four-year-olds question everything, but every four-year-old I have ever met seems to ask more questions than do anything else. Reignite that questioning in yourself and your students. Questioning is at the heart of PBL. Use the question stems of "What if . . . ?"; "How . . . ?"; and "Why . . . ?" Build curiosity by saying, "I wonder . . ." This idea of asking question upon question upon question brings curiosity to the forefront of the classroom, an essential PBL skill when developing "need to know" questions and following through with productive inquiry. Reread the opening story. Notice how often the students use "What if . . . ?" in their *Billy Goats Gruff* playtime.

Follow the Curiosity Path

When a colleague first introduced me to the idea of a Curiosity Path, I had visions of Alice in Wonderland following a white rabbit down a hole, then through tiny doors, and wandering around the Cheshire woods. Alas, no. This Curiosity Path is actually for mathematics educators. Developed by Orr and Pearce (2019), the Curiosity Path scaffolds a mathematical task to maximize student engagement through curiosity. Based on using 3-Act Math Tasks (Fletcher, n.d.; Meyer, n.d.; Pearce & Orr, n.d.; Wiernicki, n.d.), the four elements of the pathway are (1) Withhold Information, (2) Build Anticipation, (3) Notice and Wonder, and (4) Estimate. Collectively, these four steps spark curiosity in our students.

Within this pathway, Orr and Pearce highlight what has become a powerful routine in the mathematics world, that of Notice and Wonder (Ray-Riek, 2013). This routine asks students to share what they notice and wonder about a problem or context free of judgment, providing students the opportunity to view problems from multiple lenses while building self-confidence and reflective skills. The Notice and Wonder protocol can be used outside of the Curiosity Path, yet consider exploring more of that pathway, leveraging all four elements to maximize curiosity.

In the PK classroom, educator Stephanie Umberger used the Notice and Wonder routine to help students explore the shapes found in bridges. After showing a picture of a bridge, Stephanie asked students what they noticed and wondered, charting their responses on paper. As an experienced early childhood educator, Stephanie rephrased students' thoughts into complete sentences to aid language acquisition. For example, when sharing wonderings, a student intoned, "No circles?" to which Stephanie rephrased, "Why aren't there circles on the bridge?" Figure 10.1 presents some of the noticings and wonderings these four-year-olds shared.

 The project featured in this vignette is available for download at **https://qrs.ly/56ensfy**.

Figure 10-1 • Noticings and Wonderings of Prekindergarten Students

What We *Noticed*	What We *Wondered*
• The bridge is blue.	• How does the bridge stay up?
• The bridge is long.	• Will the bridge fall into the water?
• Cars are on the bridge.	• Why aren't there circles on the bridge?
• People are on the bridge.	• How heavy is the bridge?
• The bridge has arches.	• Who drives over the bridge?
• The bridge has rectangles.	• How long is the bridge?
• The bridge has triangles.	

FOSTER FLEXIBILITY

Have you ever reminded a student that it's important to be flexible, only for that student to respond, "I am!" while dropping down into the splits? If so, you probably teach middle school.

Of course, I was referring to the notion of flexibility and adaptability in the mathematics classroom, not the gymnastics floor. However, my student was not that far off. I am playing on the notion of flexibility here to mean two things—flexibility in mathematical thinking and flexibility in learning conditions. Although flexible mathematical thinking is vitally important to student success, in terms of building a classroom culture for a PBL mathematics experience to flourish, it's also important to embrace flexibility in how students learn, how students adapt to change, and how students react to the unexpected. How can we center our classroom culture on flexibility? Consider these two ideas:

1. Visibly random groups

2. Beautiful constraints

Visibly Random Groups

Liljedahl (2021) established fourteen practices to build thinking classrooms, one of which is *visibly random groups*. To help students embrace flexibility and increase collaboration skills, Liljedahl advocates teachers should randomize students into groups of three during work time. Importantly, these random groups must be made visible to students. This can be done using a technology tool like Picker Wheel (https://pickerwheel.com) or Random Lists (www.randomlists.com) as well as through hands-on means like giving students a numbered playing card as they walk into the room or choosing from a set of popsicle sticks with student names on them.

Within these random groups, Liljedahl advocates for a set of procedures to foster collaboration. Through practices like using vertical nonpermanent surfaces and visibly random groupings, student self-efficacy increased, reliance on the teacher decreased, and the classroom community gained greater trust, leading to the opportunity to critique work, a critical skill in PBL mathematics. Check out more of Liljedahl's work in his 2021 book *Building Thinking Classrooms in Mathematics*.

Using visibly random groups lays the foundation for establishing success skills like collaboration and Mathematical Habits of Mind like Communicate Mathematically. This also provides students the ability to learn from and with one another regularly. When engaging in a PBL mathematics experience, students eventually work in teams, yet at several points throughout the project, visibly random groups will aid cooperative learning and critique strategies.

Beautiful Constraints

Business consultants Morgan and Barden (2015) published the book *A Beautiful Constraint: How to Transform Your Limitations Into Advantages, and Why It's Everyone's Business*. The premise of this business-centered book is how to adapt when life throws you a curveball. The goal is to recognize that with every limitation, there is a silver lining. So, how do we use this idea to establish flexibility and adaptability in our students?

In Miss Allie Graumann's second-grade classroom, students practiced measurement using nonstandardized tools like paper clips, LEGO bricks, unit cubes, and their hands. One boy, Landon, became all out of sorts because he wanted to measure the entire length of the room, but he didn't have enough unit cubes. This was a natural constraint on his learning. Instead of fixing the problem, Miss Allie challenged Landon to think about how he could solve this problem. Together, they worked on the solution to lay down a pencil marking where he had fifty cubes in length; he would then pick up the cubes and begin counting again, starting at the pencil tip with fifty-one cubes. This beautiful constraint led Landon to become more flexible in his thinking and approach to problem solving.

Beautiful constraints happen naturally in the classroom, but we can also create constraints to lead our students toward more flexibility in their disposition. Here are some ideas for beautiful constraints:

- Limit the use of standardized tools like rulers or protractors, propelling students to think creatively about measurement.

- Ask students to redesign their product with a specific user in mind, such as a child with a physical disability or a working professional with a visual impairment.

- Focus on estimation over computation by limiting the use of calculators or formulas.

- Challenge students to a task with a twist, such as designing a floor plan without any ninety-degree angles or building the structure without any rectangles.

YOUR TURN

Think of a task you recently implemented with students. How might you craft a beautiful constraint to promote flexibility and adaptability in students? What impact would the beautiful constraint have on your students?

_____

_____

VALUE PROCESS OVER PRODUCT

PBL values process over product. Students learn through the process of research, exploration, and creation. Making the value of process over product visible to students ensures the classroom community centers on the growth of each student. Inherent in this value is promoting productive struggle and a growth mindset. This value also eases students' anxiety and potential negative views surrounding mathematics as honoring the process, and the thinking de-emphasizes getting a quick, correct answer.

As mathematics educators, we often verbally show our value of the process over the product (or solution) when we ask questions that explore student thinking. I remember marveling at expert teacher Katy Weber when she processed a mathematical modeling task. Geometry students discussed in depth the multiple entry points to the problem and their specific solution pathways. Katy then moved on to the next part of the lesson, only to be stopped by her students shouting at her, "But what's the right answer?" She didn't miss a beat when she replied, "You tell me!" She highlighted how groups of students justified their solution pathways. Because it was a modeling task, multiple solutions existed. In mathematics, the right answer matters, yet what Katy emphasized was her value on the process before the solution.

Classroom Fridge

I grew up in a household where A+ assignments and shiny gold star work were hung on the refrigerator door. Keeping in mind this is not the case for every student, my colleague Bri Larcom created a classroom fridge, tracing the outline of a refrigerator door on a large sheet of paper. To lift up every student and not just students who traditionally shine, Bri only hangs up work that highlights the process of learning and creating—no polished final pieces on this door!

As mathematics educators, we can highlight student processes on a classroom fridge door as well. When students work collaboratively on a problem-solving task, consider grabbing their messy work or taking a picture of the work if on a whiteboard to hang on the classroom fridge. Make a point to stick messy work on the classroom fridge door. Perhaps add a "gold star" to juicy mathematical work that shows creativity or risk-taking. If the work has a solution on it, consider eliminating that part to show you valued the process.

My Favorite "Not Yet"

I remember first hearing about the routine "My Favorite No" (Teaching Channel, 2015). In this routine, a teacher poses a question and asks students to respond on a notecard. After collecting the cards, the teacher sorts the answers into Yes (aka Correct) and No (aka Incorrect) piles. Then, the teacher chooses a "Favorite No," meaning a card that might show a common misconception or error to highlight to the class. From there, the class might correct the problem or explain why the misconception is incorrect.

I'd like to propose a twist on this routine, called "My Favorite Not Yet." As students are working on a problem-solving task, performance task, or project product, pause work time to share some of your favorite in-progress "Not Yets." These "Not Yets" could highlight errors or misconceptions. They could highlight points where students are "stuck" and need help recalibrating their thinking. They could even be creative pathways that are leading to novel solutions. By sharing your favorite "Not Yets," you continue to emphasize how you value the process over the product or solution.

Reward the Struggle

In their book *Productive Math Struggle: A 6-Point Action Plan for Fostering Perseverance*, SanGiovanni et al. (2020) highlight tangible actions that show valuing the process, specifically the struggle. In the book, they highlight Struggle Bucks, Shout-Outs, and Brag Tags.

I have used Shout-Outs before and feel they positively contribute to a strong PBL classroom culture as both the teacher and students can be the giver of Shout-Outs. Get creative in how you want to use them! I've made Shout-Outs on cardstock using a Shout-Out template (Figure 10.2). I've made them by using plain name tag stickers and writing *Shout-Out* at the top. When a student actively engages in the process of learning, write their name on the Shout-Out with a quick message. As students see you model this process, invite them to give Shout-Outs to classmates as well. Younger students can practice writing a classmate's name on a sticker, or you can assist them in the process.

Figure 10-2 • Shout-Out Template

PBL PLUS TIPS

Verbalize how you value the process over the product.

☐ Ask process-oriented questions.

- "What strategy did you use to find your solution?"

- "Is there another way you could solve the problem?"

- "Can you share your process with another student?"

☐ Use growth mindset phrases with students when they request assistance.

- "Thank you for calling me over. Asking for help is a sign of strength."

- If the question is one the student can solve, ask, "Whose brain do you want to grow today? Mine or yours?"

- ☐ Show excitement over learning from mistakes.
    - ● "Ooooh! This is a creative mistake. Can I please share this with the class?"
    - ● "Whoa!?! I just saw your brain grow from that mistake."

Show you value the process over the product through actions.

- ☐ Create problems or tasks where students only start the task.
    - ● Ask students to draw diagrams of the problem or situation without solving the task.
    - ● Direct students to identify a formula or visual model needed to solve the problem. Offer choice to continue solving the problem or not.
- ☐ Emphasize depth by de-emphasizing speed.
    - ● Assign fewer practice problems and more rich tasks for in-class work or homework.
    - ● Ask students to justify their answer to tasks or show two ways to find a solution.
- ☐ Replace practice problems with reflection questions that highlight growth in learning. Provide choice for students to respond in writing, in pictures, or verbally.
    - ● "What was something you struggled with in class today?"
    - ● "What was a mistake you made? What did you learn from that mistake?"
    - ● "What new ideas did you encounter today?"

CONCLUDING THOUGHTS

Developing classroom culture centered on these five ideas not only builds relationships with and among students but also strengthens students' beliefs about themselves as mathematicians. Focusing on classroom culture should be ongoing throughout the year. Our students need to feel that sense of belonging and safety in our classrooms to take risks, the risks needed to engage in a high-quality PBL mathematics experience.

PBL POINTS TO PONDER: WORD-PHRASE-SENTENCE

Use this thinking routine to distill the essence of this chapter into something small and manageable to share or convey. Share the *sentence* and your reflection with the world on social media using the hashtag #PBLmath.

☐   Reflecting upon this chapter, what is one word that captured your attention or struck you as powerful?

☐   What is one phrase that moved, engaged, or provoked you?

☐   What is one sentence that was meaningful to you that you felt captures the core idea of this chapter?

CHAPTER 11

Role of the PBL Mathematics Teacher

When I was in high school, I traveled to New Orleans for the first time. Talk about a world completely different from my small town in Wisconsin. From the swamp boat tour where the guide threw marshmallows to make the alligators surface to the blues-playing harmonica players on street corners, my eyes were constantly in thrall of something new.

Walking around the French Quarter one afternoon, my friends and I ducked into a hat shop. This was not your average souvenir baseball hat or even your Mardi Gras hat shop. This place had hats of every size, shape, variety, and occasion. Viking helmets, rainbow-striped propellor beanie hats, Mexican sombreros, fez hats with tassels, French berets, buccaneer hats, and two-toned court jester hats with bells. The colors and shapes and materials and sizes were endless. We had so much fun trying on the different hats.

> ## Need to Knows
>
> - How does my role as a teacher change throughout a project-based learning mathematics experience?
>
> - What do various teacher roles in the project-based learning mathematics classroom look like in action?

173

That memory of wearing multiple hats is one I hold dear as I think of my role as a project-based learning (PBL) mathematics educator. When I work with mathematics educators about to embark on their first PBL experience, some of the trepidation they feel is assuming new roles—wearing new hats, so to speak—in the mathematics classroom. Take, for example, Kaleo Peleke, a high school mathematics educator whose rural Hawaiian school district decided to implement PBL. Kaleo felt skeptical about PBL in his mathematics classroom. As we planned the major benchmarks of his project, Kaleo said, "I'm really excited by all of this, but I'm not just a math teacher during the project."

Curious, I asked Kaleo to elaborate on his statement. "Well, at the beginning, I'm sort of laying the groundwork for the whole project. Then they're posing their questions. Then they're researching and interviewing experts before we explore the math concepts. Then they're building their final products and presenting them. So, I feel like I'm more than a math teacher."

What Kaleo recognized was that PBL mathematics educators embrace roles beyond the traditional viewpoint of a mathematics educator. Kaleo would be wearing multiple hats during the project, hats he previously had not worn or considered. In talking with Kaleo, we realized he had previous experience with some of these roles, just not during a project. So, let's explore the roles, summarized in Figure 11.1, you may take on in a new context.

ACTIVATOR

An **activator** is someone who sits alongside the student as a partner in constructing knowledge, actively engaged as a learner with equal stakes in the outcome.

Say what? I never heard this word described in education until I engaged deeply in the work of PBL. Pieratt (2020) describes an **activator** as someone "who is deeply engaged with their students, rather than mere 'facilitators' of learning" (p. 11). Whereas a facilitator can create the conditions necessary for learning, then act as a guide along the way, an activator sits alongside the student as a partner in constructing knowledge, actively engaged as a learner with equal stakes in the outcome.

Although *activator* may be a new word, the role itself is not new to educators who have long realized that bringing about growth in a student requires intense, ongoing engagement. In a seventh-grade mathematics project where students designed three-dimensional printed mugs for local businesses, I could often be found at the computers alongside my students learning the new-to-me program of Tinkercad (www.tinkercad.com). As students ran across issues in their designs, I actively sought resources to help us learn together. I created my own mug, seeking feedback from students who became quickly adept at the online design software.

As students faced stumbling blocks during the project process, I quickly gauged the pulse of the class as I was deeply entrenched in the work with them. For example, when businesses asked for their mug to hold twelve, sixteen, or twenty ounces, I recognized students needed an investigative lab connecting volume in cubic inches and fluid ounces, finding a universally accepted ratio between these two measurements. This just-in-time response is critical during a project, as authentic learning means authentic barriers will present themselves. Likewise, authentic barriers create opportunity for authentic learning. Our role in the PBL mathematics classroom is to quickly and expertly address barriers to continue engaging students in productive inquiry.

PBL PLUS TIPS

- ☐ Pull up a chair while student teams work on their project.
  - ● Engage in conversation with wonderment, not answers.
- ☐ Complete portions of the project alongside your students.
  - ● Share your ongoing learning with students. Ask for feedback. Lift up your struggles and how you persevere through them.
- ☐ Create just-in-time learning experiences as you encounter areas of new learning that pose a struggle for your students (see Chapter 5).

QUESTIONER

"How would architects use shapes to create a bridge?" I listened as prekindergarten (PK) teacher Stephanie Umberger posed this question to her young learners. With pattern blocks and wooden shapes scattered across tables and floors, these curious minds explored shapes found in bridges. During this phase of her project, Stephanie embodied the role of questioner. "Why did you pick the rectangle to support the base of the bridge? It looks like your table partner chose triangles for the base. Which shape is going to best support our bridge? Which bridge would you choose to walk across?"

Questioning plays an integral role in the PBL mathematics classroom, moving from information gathering to probing questions, as shared in Chapter 5. Not only are questions needed to elicit student thinking about the mathematics content, but questions that connect to the authentic project at hand also must be posed. To that end, when teachers take on the role of questioner, they are investigating student thinking by listening to understand what the student knows, clarifying misconceptions, providing students the opportunity to take ownership of their learning, and propelling learning forward.

Effective educators naturally embody the role of questioner. What might be different in the PBL experience is linking questions to authentic roles as well as the project process. When Stephanie posed her question about shapes, she linked the need to use shapes with the role of architects. She continued her questions by reminding the student bridges are real structures people use to walk across. In the questioner role, we make connections between student learning and the authentic situation at hand, continually emphasizing why the learning is occurring and how experts use the mathematical concepts.

MANAGER

"I've got four teams on track, two teams well ahead of the game, and one team that's at least four days behind. I have no idea how that last group is going to finish or what to do to help them. They just aren't keeping up with the calendar." Tamari Bello is an eighth-grade mathematics teacher at a suburban academy for girls. As I met with her about her project, she was lamenting about her inability to motivate one group of girls to meet the project deadlines. In talking with Tamari, I visually saw she had a calendar of due dates on a bulletin board behind her with a big purple star on the presentation day. Curious, I asked Tamari how the straggling group responded to this calendar. "Oh, they just said since they are so far behind, they won't give a presentation. They plan on being sick that day."

In the PBL classroom, managing student teams as they complete the project at hand may be a new role for mathematics educators. Sure, we've had to manage classroom behaviors, but project management is a whole new ballgame! Being an effective manager means having clear communication about the project expectations, helping students establish goals and responsibilities among their team members, providing mini deadlines for students to meet project goals, and providing constructive feedback to guide teams forward. In Chapter 15, we'll focus heavily on what management looks like during a project, focusing on how to embody the role of manager to help all students, but especially struggling students, meet the deadlines of the project.

SAGE

We've all heard in education not to be the "sage on the stage." However, I advocate there are times where our knowledge and expertise as mathematicians is best provided in the form of the sage. Let's be honest. Most students would never come up with the quadratic formula on their own. We can lead them there through investigations and examples; however, formalizing algorithms often needs the assistance of the sage. This is a hat we can and should wear during the project process, albeit for a limited time. As the sage, we must recognize that our relationship with students should still center on being an active partner in the learning process.

A critical part to playing the role of a sage is the way wisdom is imparted. Think of your favorite sage from a movie or book, such as Mr. Miyagi from *The Karate Kid*, Dumbledore from

Harry Potter, The Oracle from *The Matrix*, or my favorite, Yoda from *Star Wars*. When imparting wisdom, these sages provide wisdom that is memorable and accessible to the learner. Who couldn't finish the quote and make the hand gestures for "Wax on, ____"? Can't we all live by the words of Dumbledore: "It is our choices, Harry, that show what we truly are, far more than our abilities"? Can we marvel at the simplicity of The Oracle's proclamation, "Everything that has a beginning has an end"? And who doesn't love Yoda's line delivered in Yoda speak, "Do. Or do not. There is no try"?

Sages are memorable. Sages make their wisdom easy to understand yet so powerful that the learner can linger on their words or ideas for minutes, hours, days, even weeks to come. The lessons keep unfolding. So, when acting as the sage, we must teach with intentionality. We must ensure our words and our wisdom are being imparted for long-term success in students' brains. In the mathematics classroom, students may not derive the quadratic formula, but after twenty-plus years, I can still sing the formula to the tune of "Pop Goes the Weasel."

LEAD LEARNER

"I'm worried because I've never designed a zip line course before. I'm going to have to do a lot of research to get this project ready, and that's time I don't have right now. I can do the math; I'm just not sure of all the applications of the math to zip lines."

A veteran high school teacher with more than twenty years of experience, Chase Frank worked at a school district that was revamping its approach to learning by implementing PBL. As I worked with Chase, he voiced his fear of not knowing enough about zip line courses before engaging in this Algebra I project. For most of his career, Chase has felt confident as an educator because he possesses the knowledge to answer his students' questions. However, applying the ideas of slope, rates of change, similar triangles, and the Pythagorean theorem to this design project brought forward Chase's hesitancy to implement PBL.

I reframed the idea to Chase, asking him, "What if you didn't know an answer to a math question? Let's say a former student who is now in a college calculus course asked you about partial derivatives, and you didn't know the answer. What would you do?"

Chase paused a beat. "I guess I'd sit down with them, look at their textbook, maybe google some ideas, and do the best I could. If I couldn't figure it out, I'd help them reach out to their professor or see if there was tutoring on campus."

"Exactly."

What Chase defined was how he would act as a learner—analyzing texts, conducting research, and seeking expert assistance. In the PBL mathematics classroom, we may embark on new pathways that stray from our comfort zone. Ideally, students pose critical, creative questions we readily can't answer. Our response is to act as the **lead learner**, as someone who models the process of learning for our students, who delights in not knowing answers and exemplifies how to find potential solutions. We must model what it looks like, sounds like, and feels like to be a learner through our words and actions. One way to do this is through a think-aloud, where you as the lead learner vocalize your internal thinking out loud when solving a problem. During a think-aloud, you would take the following steps:

A **lead learner** is someone who models the process of learning for students, who delights in not knowing answers and exemplifies how to find potential solutions.

- Explain what you initially notice in a problem.

- Ask questions that come up before, during, and after solving a problem.

- Describe decisions you make during the problem-solving process.

- Justify your solution and why you believe it is correct.

Validating feelings of anxiety, hesitancy, and frustration, as well as wonderment and elation, for learners becomes part of our everyday role when we act as the lead learner. As the lead learner, we embody a growth mindset attitude, recognizing that mistakes are an integral part of the learning process.

PBL PLUS TIPS

- ☐ Embrace the words, "I don't know!"
- ☐ Plan and conduct think-aloud protocols with your students.
- ☐ Model what it looks like to be a learner.
  - Share how you conduct research.
  - Make your reasoning and problem-solving strategies visible to students.
- ☐ Validate feelings of anxiety, frustration, stress, and elation.
  - Explain how you address those feelings within yourself. Provide opportunities for students to express their feelings when learning.
- ☐ Embody a growth mindset. Normalize mistakes by readily sharing them with your students.

YOUR TURN

Let's create an opportunity for you to exemplify the lead learner role, whether or not you are in a PBL mathematics classroom. Think of a problem in an upcoming unit or task where you could conduct a think-aloud. Write down what you might say to make your thinking visible.

Problem:	Initial Noticings:	Questions You Have:
	Decisions Made:	Solution Justification:

Figure II-I • Role of a PBL Mathematics Educator

Role	What the PBL Mathematics Educator Does	What the PBL Mathematics Educator Says
Activator	• Creates a learner-centered culture of inquiry • Sits alongside the student and actively engages in the process • Responds with just-in-time learning	• "Let's tackle this problem together." • "What do you already know about this that can help us move forward?" • "What resources can we use to help us with this problem?"
Questioner	• Models mathematical thinking through notice and wonder activities • Asks questions to probe student thinking • Values questioning as an integral part of the learning process • Purposefully links questioning to the project at hand	• "How does this concept help us move forward in our project?" • "How would architects use shapes to create a bridge?" • "If we viewed these data like a sports analyst, what patterns would we notice that we would want to report?" • "How did our expert use the math we are learning in their job?"
Manager	• Creates scaffolds to ensure all students can access the content • Provides checklists and deadlines to move the project forward • Assists students in working collaboratively	• "What support do you need to reach your goal?" • "How can you use your strengths as a team to solve this problem?"
Sage	• Provides just-in-time learning of critical mathematics concepts • Makes wisdom accessible and memorable	• "The mathematics you need is rooted in the concept of . . ." • "Mathematicians do this because . . ." • "Mathematics is a language. To communicate effectively in this language, let's . . ."
Lead Learner	• Models what the process of learning looks like • Uses protocols to make thinking visible • Validates emotional responses in the learning process • Practices growth mindset	• "I don't know, but let's find out!" • "In the past, this strategy has worked for me. I wonder if it could work here." • "When I feel stuck on a problem, I like to ask a friend how they might move forward from where I'm at. This helps me feel less anxious." • "After making that mistake, I realized I needed to . . ."

CONCLUDING THOUGHTS

Taking on new roles in the mathematics classroom may feel scary and unnatural at first. The first time I admitted to a student I didn't know an answer, I felt embarrassed, unsure, and less than competent. I lacked the tools to change my mindset from "less than competent teacher" to being the lead learner. No one prepared me to not know an answer as a teacher. In time, I have found letting students know I don't have all the answers is freeing. It allows me to more easily become the lead learner as well as a questioner and activator.

PBL POINTS TO PONDER: COMPASS POINTS

Reflect on your emotions when reading this chapter. Consider writing down your ideas in a journal, conversing with a colleague, or sharing your learning with the world on social media with the hashtag #PBLmath.

- ☐ **E = Excited:** What excites you about the various roles in the PBL mathematics classroom? What's the upside?

- ☐ **W = Worrisome:** What do you find worrisome about the various roles in the PBL mathematics classroom? What's the downside?

- ☐ **N = Need to Know:** What else do you need to know or find out about the various roles of PBL in the mathematics classroom? What additional information would help you to evaluate things?

- ☐ **S = Stance/Suggestion Moving Forward:** What is your current stance on PBL in the mathematics classroom? How might you move forward in your understanding of PBL in the mathematics classroom?

CHAPTER 12

Find Inspiration

The other day I chatted with my friend Sara who teaches kindergarten through a project-based learning (PBL) model. She described to me this incredible project she was tackling with her kindergarteners focused on creating sculptures out of LEGO bricks, which she developed after being inspired by the artist Nathan Sawaya and an exhibit called "The Art of the Brick" (https://artofthebrickexhibit.com). In this project, her kindergarteners created counting collections of their LEGO bricks, sorting them by size, by shape, and by color along the way, all with the goal to make LEGO brick sculptures.

Need to Knows

- Where do I find inspiration for a project-based learning mathematics experience?

- How can mathematics be used in a project to *analyze* a problem as well as to *solve* a problem?

Throughout our conversation, I recognized the authentic role of mathematics in the project. When asked how she conceptualized the mathematics of this project, Sara responded, "It's simple. I ask myself, 'Where's the math?'"

Often when I've worked with mathematics educators, a struggle teachers have is coming up with a project idea. Why? As educators, we have not necessarily been trained to become curriculum designers. Developing comprehensive projects can seem daunting; however, with time and practice, designing projects becomes a fun exploration of our society.

When designing PBL mathematics experiences, consider three sources for inspiration: our students, our world, and our standards. Each of these three sources should eventually become apparent within a project; however, one of them might serve as the initial inspiration for a project (see Figure 12.1).

Figure 12-1 • Sources of Inspiration

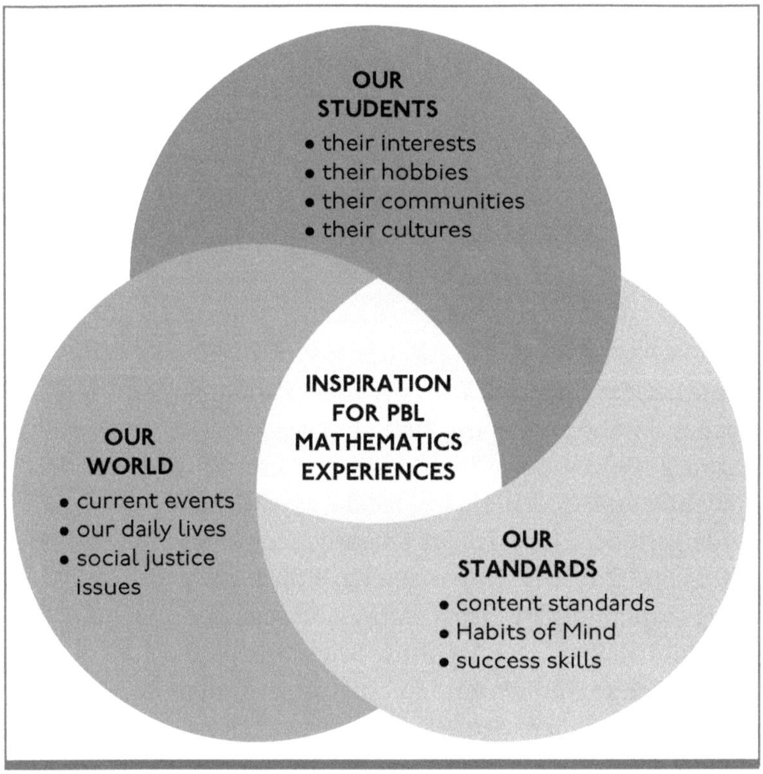

OUR STUDENTS AS INSPIRATION

"My students could do that!"

I just showed Mike Lawrence, a fifth-grade teacher, a video with a strong example of a PBL mathematics experience from PBLWorks (2019) called "The Tiny House Project." This video highlights a teacher and her third-grade classroom designing tiny homes for clients. Throughout the video, Mike's excitement visibly grew as he pointed to the screen and made comments connecting his prior knowledge to this idea of PBL mathematics. When the video ended, Mike desired to try a Tiny House Project in his classroom.

This is where I pushed Mike in his thinking. Yes, he could take the existing Tiny House Project, extend the mathematics to connect to the appropriate fifth-grade standards, and engage his students in meaningful learning. However, I asked Mike if his students were interested in tiny homes. Was there a reason to explore tiny homes in his community?

Admitting his students probably wouldn't connect with the tiny homes topic, we talked about what his students were passionate about. After rattling off a few ideas such as gardening, sports, and video games, Mike mentioned his students were especially connected to animals. Creating a spin-off of the tiny home idea, I asked Mike if his students could engage in geometry standards by designing a unique dog house or cat condo. Mike took that kernel of an idea and talked to his students.

Many of Mike's passionate young students come from low-income households. Their school has not only a Little Free Library but also a Little Free Food Pantry. Building off their passion for animals, these fifth-grade students decided to build a Little Free Animal Food Pantry to be placed at a local business, with proceeds going to the Humane Society.

Students are an immense source of inspiration. Not only will asking your students what they care about create projects with high engagement; it will also empower young people to see mathematics as useful and necessary, further solidifying their identity as a mathematician. To help gather student interests, try one of these ideas!

PBL PLUS TIPS

- ☐ Create a survey for your students to talk about their interests at a back-to-school night or the first week of school.

- ☐ Make an idea board and keep it posted in the room.

- ☐ Visit with incoming students at the end of the previous school year.

- ☐ Hold a morning, lunchtime, or after-school focus group.

- ☐ Empower older students to interview younger students for ideas.

- ☐ Ask the librarian what books students are borrowing regularly.

- ☐ Be entertained like your students—watch their movies/TV shows; read their books; listen to their music.

YOUR TURN

What project ideas come to mind when thinking about the lives and interests of your students?

1.

_____

2.

_____

3.

_____

OUR WORLD AS INSPIRATION

There are nights I get sucked into the swirling vortex of the online world, falling deep into a rabbit hole with no end in sight. You know what I mean? Those times where you say you are only going to check Facebook or Twitter or YouTube or Instagram or TikTok for ten minutes, but two hours later you have watched everything from a young dad styling his little girl's hair using a vacuum cleaner to a squirrel perfectly maneuvering a ninja warrior course someone set up in their backyard to a fourteen-year-old singer who is blind and autistic expertly belting out the national anthem at a Major League Baseball game, bringing tears to the eyes of baseball players and fans alike. I'm not crying. You're crying. But seriously, that squirrel was pretty amazing!

With technology, the adage of having the world at your fingertips becomes even more transparent as literally typing in a few keystrokes brings our global society into being. Because of this, I have tried to give myself a break whenever I find myself down the rabbit hole as I never know what projects may spring up. For example, scrolling through YouTube, I found a group of Portuguese artists creating T-shirts, sweatshirts, and tote bags by painting and inking the manhole covers around Europe, then pressing them onto their respective surfaces. The resulting pieces are sold to tourists and locals alike. This video got me thinking: *How could we honor our city through inking what is below our feet? Could my students create a similar business? How would students budget for materials before selling items? What sort of discount could we receive on items purchased in bulk? What would be the maximum profit students could make if they sold every item created?*

Our world is filled with opportunities to explore mathematical concepts. For me, these explorations begin in the form of questions. Whether the questions come about because of stories I read or see on the news, opportunities to travel and explore, or videos and pictures I see while mindlessly scrolling the internet, questioning is my first step.

When working with teachers, I often hear that science, social studies, and English have it "easy" because project ideas are more apparent. Just search for the latest stories from *National Geographic*, Newsela, the History channel, or the *Smithsonian*. As a mathematics educator, I have found these sources to be viable for finding strong mathematical connections as well, leading to rich interdisciplinary projects. Our challenge is to open our eyes to the fact that mathematics is all around us, if we ask the right questions!

Our world is full of problems that can be explored using a mathematical lens. Poverty, lack of housing, childhood obesity, overpopulation, gender inequality, racial discrimination, bullying, climate change . . . The list goes on and on. These social justice issues form the basis of powerful projects. When I think about one of these topics, I begin by grounding myself in the data. I look for statistics that will help me better understand the problem from a local, statewide, national, and global perspective. Adjusting my perspective like that of a camera lens, I zoom in and out on the issue, exploring how mathematics can shed light on the injustice from a micro to a macro lens.

Our Everyday World as Inspiration

Our everyday world also inspires authentic projects. Here's a snapshot of my day and how I ask mathematical questions:

Driving to school in the morning, I wait to go through road construction. *How many different routes could I take to get to school? Would a longer route without road construction get me to school faster than my normal route with road construction? If more people changed their route to avoid road construction, what would be the fastest route? Fines double in work zones; is that rate high enough to change behavior? How many accidents or fatalities have occurred in and around work construction zones? How did the pandemic and quarantine impact car accidents and fatalities?*

My middle school students spend time at recess outside at a local park across the street, built for elementary school children. *How does the area and spacing needed for elementary school playground equipment differ from young adult play equipment? What is the cost differential? How could we revamp the space given the current equipment and dedicated play area? What percentage of the time is the playground occupied by babies or toddlers, young children, or middle schoolers? What percentage of the time is the playground unoccupied? How does this compare to other local playgrounds?*

Right now, it's bitterly cold outside, and yet I see unhoused people putting up tents to brave the evening. *What percentage of our local population is unhoused? How many are unhoused veterans? Unhoused youth? What can we do to support the unhoused population, especially during the winter? Given the negative temperatures with even colder wind chill, what sorts of food, shelter, and clothing are most needed? How can we effectively distribute items of need?*

At night, I watch a commercial for electric vehicles. *Since I live in a rural part of Wisconsin and drive into a larger city, would an electric vehicle be a financially sound investment? Does the amount of fossil fuel needed to charge the electric vehicle offset the amount of gas I would use in a traditional gas-powered vehicle? Given the rate of gas price increases, at what point is an electric vehicle more financially viable than a comparable gas-powered vehicle?*

Our daily lives provide ample opportunities to explore topics with mathematical connections. So do our hobbies and interests. Students become passionate about a topic when we, as educators, are passionate. Personally, I had little to no interest in guitars in high school other than when my friends and I were jamming out with air guitars, but when a teacher hooked up his electric guitar and amp into a computer program that showed the wavelength of sound of different guitar strings, my interest piqued. I spent three weeks exploring the mathematics and physics of a guitar, everything from Pythagorean intervals to differential equations, and I ended up asking my parents to buy me a guitar for Christmas. One teacher's passion changed the way I looked at guitars for the rest of my life. (I didn't end up getting a guitar that Christmas, but I did end up attending a concert by Alan Jackson and enjoyed his country strumming!)

Project Types as Inspiration

As I think about centering PBL mathematics experiences on the authentic problems in our world and daily lives, I recognize mathematics can play specific roles in the project process: *mathematics as analysis* and/or *mathematics as solutionary*. In Chapter 9, I shared a story about high school Algebra I students who explored the issue of the gender and racial wage gap in the United States. In this performance task, students used mathematics to examine the issue at hand, gaining valuable insight through linear modeling. They then used their mathematical findings to persuade lawmakers and politicians to make changes. To me, this is *mathematics as analysis*, where mathematics lays a foundation to better understand the problem at hand.

Chapter 11 highlighted a story of prekindergarten (PK) students designing a bridge for their indoor sensory path. The problem itself didn't need to be analyzed with mathematics at the PK level. Instead, the answer needed mathematical problem solving and reasoning as students assumed the role of bridge engineers. Mathematics played a foundational role in the *solution* to the problem.

In Chapter 4, I shared the project of second graders answering the driving question, "How can we attract pollinators to our community?" As part of the exploration of the project, students played the role of citizen scientists, gathering data as part of a statewide initiative, the Bumble Bee Brigade. Students looked at local and statewide data from previous years to bolster their knowledge of pollinators in the community, using mathematics to *analyze* the current issue. Students then moved into a solutionary state of the project, designing and building bee hotels to attract more pollinators to their community using measurement and geometry concepts. These students used mathematics to create a *solution* to the problem.

PBL PLUS TIPS

Finding the mathematics in our world means consistently posing the one big question lingering in the back of our brains: "Where's the math?"

Ask that question as you do each of the following.

☐ Scroll through your social media.

- What stories or videos stand out to you? Why? Let yourself fall into the rabbit hole as you continue to explore the depths of the World Wide Web. Perhaps set a timer so you don't become late for any important dates!

☐ Check out popular magazines for students: *National Geographic, Sports Illustrated, Popular Science, Discover, Ranger Rick,* or *Cricket Media.*

- Ask a librarian if your school or local library subscribes to these. Often, doctors' and dentists' offices still subscribe to these magazines. I'll snap pictures of interesting articles or even ask to borrow the magazine.

(*Continued*)

(*Continued*)

☐ Write down a list of problems our world is facing.

  ● Consider going to a source like Our World in Data (https://ourworldindata.org) for preliminary data. Check out the Sustainable Development Goals (SDGs) set forth by the United Nations for a global perspective on problems facing our world.

☐ Get lost in the library, especially the nonfiction section.

  ● Wander and peruse book titles. I found an entire section on Native American beading that became an incredible performance task with my students simply because I got a little turned around one day.

☐ Watch the nightly news or read the local newspaper with critical eyes and ears.

  ● What problems are facing your community? How can mathematics play a role in analyzing or solving those problems?

YOUR TURN

What project ideas come to mind when thinking about the world around you?

1.

_____

2.

_____

3.

_____

OUR STANDARDS AS INSPIRATION

"Angles."

Sitting with an insightful, dedicated fourth-grade teacher, I posed the question, "What mathematical standard do your students most need assistance in mastering?" I listened as Jasmine Valentine described her upcoming unit on angles with her students. "It's not a unit I particularly like to teach.

The curricular materials I have help students understand the mathematical concepts, but I know there is so much more I can do to engage my students."

As Jasmine described her interest in creating a project about angles, I asked her to consider how we use angles in the real world. Her first project idea centered on students creating a piece of artwork like a stained-glass window, then describing the angles formed in their art piece. Together, we decided that the project idea lacked the authenticity to fully engage her students. Although artists could create beautiful stained-glass windows, Jasmine's students would have no reason to create a stained-glass window. Additionally, Jasmine wasn't sure if she could secure the materials or experts to undertake such an in-depth art and mathematics project.

Moving on to another idea, Jasmine thought about architects who need to draw blueprints with angle measures. As we discussed this idea, she thought about asking students to create a blueprint for a home. However, we both questioned whether students would create many rooms within the home where the angle measures deviated from the traditional ninety-degree corners. Then Jasmine shared, "My classroom actually has corners that are not ninety degrees. My classroom is joined by another classroom with a common office space in between. I know this type of classroom partitioning also happened when they built the new elementary school. Do you think the students could design a school?"

This became the basis for Jasmine's fourth-grade mathematics project called *Dream School*. In her school district, financial decisions are being made about consolidating two aging high school buildings into one new school building. If this ends up happening, Jasmine's fourth-grade students will be high school students in the new building. Guided by her standards, Jasmine created a mathematically rich project. As she planned, Jasmine naturally found connections to multiplying multidigit numbers and decimals that students would need to create a budget. She also recognized many geometry standards as well as measurement and data standards could be met through this project.

When exploring academic standards, a question I ask myself is "Who uses this concept in their everyday job or career?"

In Jasmine's project, architects were a natural connection to the idea of angles being found in blueprints. However, we also talked about artists, engineers, construction workers, carpenters, and video game designers. Any one of these roles could have formed the basis of Jasmine's project. The choice of an architect solidified because of the authenticity of creating a school blueprint to present to her school district's administrators.

Not all standards are created equally, however. When looking to create a project centered on curricular standards, consider the following questions:

- To what degree do students need to understand this concept at this grade level?

- Can the standard continue to propel learning forward through inquiry?

We all know certain concepts are introduced one year, then expanded upon and mastered in subsequent school years. Right now, I'm introducing my sixth-grade students to the idea of expressions and equations, focusing on writing equivalent expressions using the distributive property. Students will continue to work on this skill throughout their middle school and high school career. Therefore, when considering project topics, I recognize that although essential to future success in mathematics, an entire project centered on writing equivalent expressions would not critically propel learning forward for sixth-grade students. I may create projects where I include writing expressions and equations, but not as the central focus.

One project-worthy topic in sixth grade is unit rates, which are foundational to many mathematical concepts in middle school and beyond. Students master unit rates in sixth grade to apply them to proportional relationships in seventh grade and eventually slopes in eighth grade. Unit rates can continue to propel learning forward as students complete investigations and activities around this authentic, rich mathematics concept. When thinking about project-worthy standards, I recognize that by incorporating critical mathematics topics into a project, students will move from memorization and understanding—the initial levels of Bloom's taxonomy—toward applying, analyzing, evaluating, and creating—the upper levels of Bloom's taxonomy (see Bloom et al., 1956). These critical movements ensure all students receive deep, mathematical learning opportunities. So take a peek at your curricular materials. Have you or your district identified power or priority standards? These would be ones to consider using as a focus of a project!

When talking about standards, another critical component to consider are the Mathematical Habits of Mind that reach to the core of embracing questioning, problem solving, exploring, reasoning, and justifying as a mathematician. While nearly every Mathematical Habit of Mind may be present in a project experience, consider focusing in on just one or two habits to intentionally develop.

YOUR TURN

What project ideas come to mind when thinking about your content standards and Mathematical Habits of Mind? Are there particular standards or Mathematical Habits of Mind that lend themselves well to creating a PBL mathematics experience for your students?

_____

_____

READILY AVAILABLE PROJECTS

Becoming a PBL mathematics designer may be a stretch for educators who in many respects are experts at using curricular materials to implement engaging lessons but have yet to dive into authentic, student-centered PBL. As you begin your quest, know that there are a lot of resources online to accompany this book, from project ideas to project management tools that you can edit and implement.

Explore these project ideas with the goal to create grade-level-appropriate connections to both content standards and the Mathematical Habits of Mind. If you choose a project from this book or another resource, ensure that the project will be engaging for your students—is it authentic to them? Will you as a learning community find joy and challenge in this project? Think about ways you can enhance the project to fit the unique needs of your students and your community while meeting rigorous standards.

 Projects and materials mentioned in this book are available for download at **https://qrs.ly/56ensfy**.

Additional Resources

An emerging number of books specific to PBL mathematics, such as the following, offer readily available projects:

- *Project-Based Learning in the Math Classroom* (K–2, 3–5, and 6–10 editions; Fancher & Norfar, 2019; Norfar & Fancher, 2022a, 2022b)

- *Rigor, Relevance, and Relationships: Making Mathematics Come Alive With Project-Based Learning* and *Project-Based Learning in Elementary Classrooms: Making Mathematics Come Alive* (Lee & Galindo, 2018, 2021)

PBL PLUS TIPS

☐ Think about the question, "Who uses this concept in their everyday job or career?"

- Reach out to area business and industry workers to ask how mathematics is used in their career. As you learn about the mathematics used in these careers, connect the mathematical skills and Mathematical Habits of Mind to your standards.

- Consider inviting an expert from that career to speak to your class (face-to-face or digitally). Have students prepare questions ahead of time.

☐ Zero in on power or priority standards. What makes them so critical to student learning? Consider ways to incorporate those standards into projects to move from surface to deep and transfer levels of learning (see Chapter 4).

☐ Explore ready-made projects that align to your standards. Make adjustments to those projects to center them on your students and your community.

CONCLUDING THOUGHTS

People often ask me why more educators, including mathematics teachers, are not designing and implementing PBL experiences in the classroom. I often cite the need for time to plan and prepare effective projects. Making those connections to experts from area businesses, universities, or service organizations takes time. Being inspired by local history, the interests of your student population, or industries in your community means that a prepackaged curriculum cannot be made.

So how will you get inspired to create projects? Consider keeping a digital or physical folder of ideas. In time, you'll be surprised just how many amazing real-world connections you can make to bring mathematics to life!

YOUR TURN

Look back at the potential project ideas you brainstormed throughout this chapter. Choose one to continue developing as you read the rest of the book. Solidify one project idea here using bullet points, sketches, and/or words.

_____

_____

PBL POINTS TO PONDER: ESP+I

Use this thinking routine to identify key areas that moved forward your understanding of designing a PBL mathematics experience as well as questions (puzzles) and struggles that remain.

☐ **Experience:** What is your current experience designing PBL mathematics experiences?

☐ **Struggles:** What struggles have you had or might you encounter as you move forward designing a project?

☐ **Puzzles:** What new questions or "puzzlings" do you have about designing a project?

☐ **+Insights:** At this point, what new or additional insights do you have about designing a project?

Launch

Apples. Blueberries. Watermelon. Avocados. Almonds. Cranberries. Honey. This assortment of food spread across the table to the wide eyes of seventeen second-grade students.

"Is this our snack today?" "Are we going on a picnic?" "Can we make a smoothie?" Questions peppered from each little mouth to the teacher, interspersed by comments like "I don't like the green one" or "I love spitting watermelon seeds."

As the students settled onto the rug, second-grade teacher Miss Allie Graumann read the book *The Thing About Bees: A Love Letter* by Shabazz Larkin (2019). The students kept asking after each page, "So what does that have to do with all the food?" As Miss Allie continued, their minds began to realize bees were responsible for pollinating all the food they saw on the table, and much more.

As the last page of the book was shared, the second graders sat quietly for a heartbeat. Then, one student raised his hand. "If there were no bees," he ventured, "we'd have to move to a different planet because there'd be no plants."

Then another student added, "There was a bee by me once. I'm afraid of bees, but I stood really still, and it didn't sting me."

Acknowledging it's okay to be scared, Miss Allie directed the students toward the food. "So, without bees, all this food wouldn't exist. Bees, and other pollinators, play a major role in our world. As we heard on the last pages of this book, there's lots we can do to help keep bees safe. So my question to all of you is this: How can we attract bees—and other pollinators—to our community?"

THE LAUNCH

Ramping up the excitement for an upcoming project is critical to student engagement. No student has ever walked into my classroom, saying, "Finally! I've been waiting twelve years to learn about surface area!" Yet, when brightly wrapped boxes sit on every desk, instantly students are intrigued to know what's going on and what it has to do with mathematics class. The goal of any launch event, whether it lasts a few minutes or a few days, is to generate interest in the project, share expectations and goals, and gather student curiosities through the form of questions.

Launching a project is an art, yet it has a simple formula for us mathematics educators to follow (see Figure 13.1).

Figure 13-1 • Launch Equation

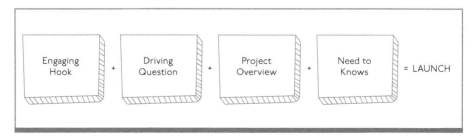

Let's examine each piece of this launch equation.

ENGAGING HOOK

Capturing the attention of your students, piquing their interest, and building momentum to the driving question are all goals of an engaging hook. At the core, a hook needs to bring student emotions to the forefront. When connected to emotion, our brains form a deeper connection, and there is a stronger transference to long-term memory. Crafting a hook takes time and a bit of creativity, but the payoff of seeing students' emotions toward the project topic—which can range from confusion to curiosity to indignation to incredulity—makes the class atmosphere palpable with excitement and momentum.

See Figure 13.2 for some general ideas for ways to hook your students along with examples from educators I've worked with across the United States.

Figure 13-2 • Engaging Hook Ideas

Engaging Hook Idea	Example
Go on a walk or field trip to explore problems in the immediate classroom, school, or community.	Ishmat gave her fifth-grade students "problem-finding" glasses, clipboards, and pencils to capture the problems they saw on a walk around their neighborhood before studying urban design principles.
Invite a guest speaker or expert to share about their work or pose the problem.	In Stephanie's prekindergarten classroom, the principal visited the preschoolers and asked the students to help her solve the problem of how to safely move from one side of the sensory path to the other, noting a gap existed in their pathway.
Use multimedia, such as TED Talks, WebQuests, Google Earth tours, 360-degree photo explorations, YouTube videos, social media postings, or songs that connect to the project.	In Alejandro's Algebra I classroom, students watched a TED-Ed talk about climate change and tipping points. Before holding an informal debate, Alejandro provided students digital resources to explore including research articles, blogs, videos, and photographs.

Engaging Hook Idea	Example
Share a letter or digital video from a community member asking your classroom for help. Ideally, this would be from a real person, but could be from a fake person or company.	Algebra II teacher Kaleo shared a letter written by the Hawaii Department of Transportation asking his students to design potential solutions to connect the Hawaiian islands, encouraging collaboration among the three divisions of maritime, aviation, and roadways.
Connect with text like books, poems, or song lyrics.	Before launching a project to create a new invention, third graders listened as their teacher Nichelle read *Whoosh!: Lonnie Johnson's Super-Soaking Stream of Inventions* by Chris Barton (2016). Nichelle worked with her school's librarian to find several more books to read throughout the project.
Engage in a simulation, game, or design challenge. Encourage collaboration and de-emphasize competition.	To begin her project on the intersection of geometry and photography, high school teacher Katy created an engaging digital breakout room where clues linked to the geometric and photographic concepts about to be explored.

PBL PLUS TIPS

☐ Create an atmosphere of wonder and excitement by redecorating the classroom, placing new objects in areas around the room, redesigning a bulletin board, hanging objects from the ceiling, or decorating the door to the classroom.

☐ Reading books is a great literacy connection and equity lever. Even middle and high school students still enjoy a good picture book if you can pull it off! Every year, I read *What Do You Do With an Idea?* by Kobi Yamada (2014) and *The Dot* by Peter H. Reynolds (2003) to my students.

☐ In addition to beginning a project, hooks can be used to introduce new units of study, like placing boxes wrapped in brightly colored wrapping paper on each student's desk to begin an exploration into surface area.

DRIVING QUESTION

"Why do we have to learn this?" "When am I ever going to need to know this?" These questions often plague mathematics educators more than any other group of teachers. The beauty of project-based learning (PBL) is that the *why* and *when* are answered! Recently, a student asked me why she needed to know the metric system when we use a different measurement system here in the United States. Before I could respond, another student piped up: "Because we need to be as precise as possible in our measurements. Millimeters are more precise than inches."

To answer the *why* and *when* questions, posing a concisely worded driving question provides the initial scaffold toward student learning in PBL. A driving question is the overarching question that guides student inquiry throughout the duration of a project. The driving question supports both the teacher and the learner in unique ways. For the teacher, the driving question focuses the inquiry of the project, conveys the goals of the project, and expresses the standards in an authentic context. For the student, the driving question generates interest and excitement for the project as well as guides student inquiry and outcomes.

Driving questions can lead to a variety of project outcomes, which I categorize as awareness, creation, or action. *Awareness* can range from educating others on a topic to exploring alternative realities; *creation* leads to a physical or digital product or a detailed plan; and *action* leaves a lasting impact on the community.

Driving questions can focus the aim of a PBL mathematics experience, thereby shaping a potential product. In Figure 13.3, I highlight how various driving question types align to project outcomes of awareness, creation, and action. Building off the work of Vincent (2014), I highlight the goal of each driving question, providing an example question and potential public product.

Figure 13-3 ◆ Driving Question Goals and Product Outcomes

	Driving Question Type	Goal	Example	Public Product
Awareness	Educate Others	Teach others through the project	How can I tell a story through data?	Visual depictions of a neighborhood with graphs or charts to tell the story of the people and locations around that area
	Form an Opinion	Explore all sides of an issue before forming and justifying a position	Should the United States adopt the metric system?	Letter to a legislator advocating for or against changing road signs to metric
	Explore a Broad Theme	Analyze big ideas about society	Do mathematicians appreciate art more than others?	Short video describing and analyzing a piece of art from a mathematical standpoint
	Be Divergent	Predict alternative timelines or scenarios	What would happen to the coastline of North America if the world's temperature increased by ten degrees Fahrenheit?	Stop-motion animation depicting the percentage of coastline impacted at each degree change
Creation	Solve a Problem	Solve a real-world problem with multiple solutions	How can we attract pollinators to our community?	2D blueprints and 3D creation of a bee hotel or butterfly house
	Embody a Role	Assume a real or fictional role to complete a task or mission	How can we, as transportation engineers, design a roadway system to connect two of the major Hawaiian islands?	Detailed scale drawings of bridge and roadway systems with mathematical functions and trigonometry

(*Continued*)

(*Continued*)

	Driving Question Type	Goal	Example	Public Product
Action	Convince or Inspire Others	Persuade an audience to take action or change their mind	How can we, as data analysts, reduce the waste from single-use items at our school?	Posters with QR (quick response) codes to videos highlighting data collection of waste that occurred due to single use items and action plan to curb single use item waste
	Make a Difference	Engage in a service project to positively impact the community	How can we help prevent childhood obesity?	Creation of an active fundraiser (run/walk, jump rope marathon) with infographic posters visually depicting issues of childhood obesity

Crafting a Driving Question

Crafting the wording of a driving question takes practice. Larmer (2018) highlights three components of a strong driving question—it should be engaging for students, open-ended, and aligned with learning goals. Let's look at some examples of driving questions and how they have been revised based on feedback and critique by others (see Figure 13.4).

Figure 13-4 • Drafts of Driving Questions

First Draft	Critique	Revised Options
Can we use trigonometry to build a bridge to connect the Hawaiian islands?	Not open-ended. Yes/no answer by starting with "Can we . . ." Vague. Which Hawaiian islands? All of them? Some of them?	How can we, as transportation engineers, design a roadway system to connect two of the major Hawaiian islands?
How can we use the golden ratio and other mathematical concepts to better understand and appreciate art?	Both narrowly defines learning goal (golden ratio) and broadly defines learning goal (other mathematical concepts). Reads like a textbook. Not engaging to students.	Do mathematicians appreciate art more than others?

First Draft	Critique	Revised Options
How can we collect data to show COVID-19 has increased the amount of single-use-item waste, and what can we, as eighth graders, do to solve this problem?	Too wordy. Unclear where data collection will occur. Global? Local? Consider adding a real-world role. Being "eighth graders" is already their role in life.	How can we, as data analysts, reduce the waste from single-use items at our school? In what ways can we, as environmental activists, reduce the waste from single-use items in our community? *Note: The two revisions slightly alter by role and location, providing different pathways to learning goals.*

When writing a driving question, center the wording on learning goals as well as the project outcome. Since the driving question is like the umbrella over the entire project, providing focus and guidance, it's critical to spend time focusing on the correct verbiage. Here are some strategies to come up with the best phrasing.

- Try a waterfall brainstorm:
  - On a piece of paper, write down as many variations of the driving question as possible, one right under the other. Underline, highlight, or circle the words and phrases that best fit your project goals. Pay particular attention to verb choice.
  - Do this individually or with a partner. Consider bringing your waterfall to other teachers or a professional learning community for refinement.

- Ask your students:
  - Chapter 6 on identity and agency highlighted working with a student project leadership team. Bring your driving question idea to the team, and ask students to provide input on drafts of the question.
  - Ask critical questions of the students such as "With this question, what sort of activities might you experience? What product or outcome does this question make you think of?"

- Reach out on social media:
  - Do you belong to a Facebook group or Twitter personal learning network? Ask your social media contacts what they think about your driving question. Consider making a poll! On Twitter, use #PBL or #PBLchat to connect with like-minded PBL educators. Connect with PBL mathematics educators using #PBLmath.

When working with mathematics educators and writing my own driving questions, a struggle that always seems to occur is ensuring the mathematics has a role in the driving question while also remaining exciting and challenging for students. Like Larmer (2018), I tend to emphasize the "engaging for students" criterion. To help with this dilemma, I ensure the mathematical goals are clearly described in my Project Overview sheet (covered in the next section), bridging any gap between the driving question and the learning goals that may not be readily apparent.

PBL PLUS TIPS

- ☐ Visibly display your driving question:
  - Post your driving question on a bulletin board or poster in your classroom, on your classroom door, on your website or learning management system, and/or in a classroom newsletter or email home.
  - Since the driving question frames the learning for the entire project, share it often.
- ☐ Revise while planning, not after sharing:
  - Writing your driving question is one of the first steps to take after mapping out your project idea and goals. Don't be afraid to revise the driving question while planning, but refrain from changing it after launching your project publicly.
- ☐ Create a driving question for a performance task:
  - A driving question can be used in a performance task to focus short-term learning, such as "How can we design a unique container to hold ten Ping-Pong balls?" Performance task driving questions may not be as open-ended as ones for a PBL mathematics experience.

PROJECT OVERVIEW

Early in my career as a PBL mathematics educator, I would hook my students through an engaging activity, pose the driving question, and gather "need to know" questions. Using this sequence, I noticed a gap between what I anticipated as "need to know" questions and what my students created. Especially lacking were "need to know" questions connecting to mathematical concepts. To bridge this gap, I now provide a Project Overview sheet to my students between revealing the driving question and gathering "need to knows." The overview highlights a few key aspects of the upcoming project:

- Project name

- Driving question

- Summary (two to four sentences about the project)

- Learning targets (content standards this project addresses)

- Mathematical Habits of Mind (mathematical practices this project enhances)

- Success skills (21st century skills this project enhances)

- Product outcomes (what students will create or do as a result of this project)

 Example Project Overview resources are available for download at **https://qrs.ly/56ensfy**.

NEED TO KNOWS

The culminating action in the launch is gathering student "need to know" questions. These are the wonderings and curiosities of students that guide learning throughout the project process. Sometimes teachers use the KWL (Know/Wonder/Learn) process to gather student questions and record student findings throughout the project. Questions students pose help the teacher assess background knowledge while generating student voice about the upcoming project process. Asking questions is a key skill in the PBL classroom, one that needs to be scaffolded for student success.

Geometry teacher Katy Weber led students in gathering "need to know" questions about a high school photography project centered on geometry concepts called *GeoPhoto*. To gather student questions, she used a digital tool called Mentimeter (see Figure 13.5). Students brainstormed questions with a partner, then added their top two or three questions to the Mentimeter. After adding questions, students chose words and phrases they felt would guide their learning, which were then compiled into a word cloud.

Figure 13-5 • Example "Need to Know" Collection Strategy

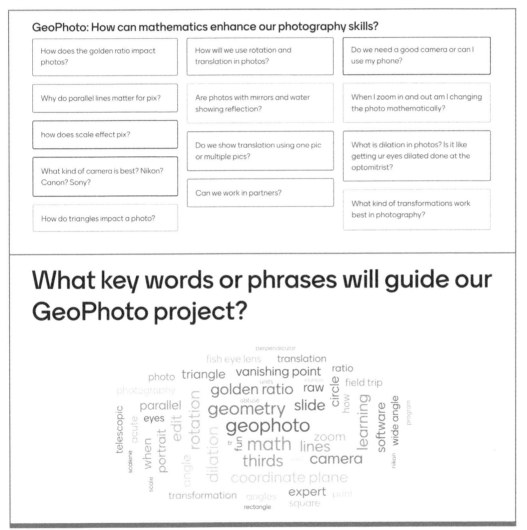

Source: Mentimeter.

Note: This figure is a reproduction of student work; spelling errors have been left in for authenticity.

Notice how the questions for this *GeoPhoto* project center on either the project logistics or the content. For example, "Do we need a good camera or can I use my phone?" is a logistical question, yet one that needs to be addressed for student learning to move forward. Content-centered questions vary in depth from "How will we use rotation and translation in photos?" to "When I zoom in and out am I changing the photo mathematically?" Both logistical and content-centered "need to know" questions are valid.

 The project featured in this vignette is available for download at **https://qrs.ly/56ensfy**.

Let's explore various ways you can gather "need to know" questions.

- Poster Paper
  - Call on students and record answers on a large piece of poster paper or chart paper.

- Think-Pair-Share or Write-Pair-Share
  - Promote conversation and dialogue about questions. Use a Think-Pair-Share strategy before calling on individuals to capture the group's thoughts.
  - Consider having students write down their questions during the "think" or "write" portion of the activity.

- Top Four
  - Ask students to write down their personal questions.
  - Partner students. Direct partners choose their top four questions.
  - Create groups of four. Each group decides on the ultimate top four "need to know" questions.
  - Ask each group to share one ultimate "need to know" question. Rotate through groups. If a question was already asked, put a check mark by it to signify that more than one group held that question.

- Sticky Notes (real or digital using Jamboard, Padlet, or Nearpod)
  - Ask individuals or groups to write down questions (one per sticky note) (see Figure 13.6).
  - Collectively sort sticky notes for general themes.

Figure 13.6 Second Grader Showing "Need to Know" Questions

"Need to Knows" Sustain Inquiry

To increase student ownership, "need to know" questions are routinely referred to throughout the project. Depending on how questions are collected, a teacher may say, "One of our 'need to know' questions was . . ." or "In order to answer Julie's question, let's explore the concept of . . ." By continuing to center the project on "need to know" questions, the inquiry process retains authenticity and student voice. The "need to know" list is an organic document, with the ability to add questions, delete questions that no longer make sense, or revise questions to better address the project topic at hand.

PBL PLUS TIPS

- ☐ Post "need to know" questions somewhere visible in the classroom, ideally close to the driving question.

- ☐ Either ask students to add their name to their questions or record names by "need to know" questions. This allows you to refer back to the individual student(s) when addressing the question during the inquiry process.

- ☐ Mark off questions as they become addressed with a check mark.

- ☐ Add new questions to the "need to know" list as they arise by marking them with an exclamation point!

YOUR TURN

Use the project topic you brainstormed at the end of Chapter 12. Create your engaging hook and driving question. Consider what information you would want to include in a Project Overview sheet. Lastly, write anticipated student "need to knows" in the form of a question.

Project Idea:	
Engaging Hook	
Driving Question	
Project Overview	
Anticipated "Need to Knows"	

CONCLUDING THOUGHTS

Although we've heard the adage, "Don't judge a book by its cover!," first impressions still play an important role in our world. This is true of the PBL mathematics world as well. As you craft the launch of a PBL mathematics experience, consider just that last word: *experience*. An experience evokes emotion. An experience leads to a lasting memory. How can you craft the launch to emotionally connect with students, to lead to a lasting memory?

PBL POINTS TO PONDER: *BE SURE TO . . .*

Use this thinking routine to envision how you will continue to grow as a mathematics educator and designer of a PBL mathematics experience.

☐ Reflecting upon this chapter, what is one idea you want to *be sure to* incorporate in a project launch?

☐ Reflecting upon this chapter, what is one idea you want to *be sure to* avoid in a project launch?

CHAPTER 14

Craft Milestones

Watching the local news one evening, high school mathematics educator Josh Wilke listened to a story about the opioid crisis and how his community was dealing with an increase in the epidemic. As Josh investigated the data cited showing the increase in opioid overdoses and deaths, he noticed linear, exponential, and logarithmic graphs. This sparked Josh's idea to create a project for his Algebra II students centered on the opioid crisis.

With an inspired project-based learning (PBL) mathematics experience in mind, Josh approached me about helping him design the nuts and bolts of the project. He wanted to launch the project with the local news story followed by a guest speaker from the Coulee Recovery Center, whose mission is to bridge the gap between addiction and recovery in Josh's local community. Wanting his students to use their mathematical knowledge to enact change, Josh thought his students could create a social media campaign to target young adults. With the launch and

Need to Knows

- How do we craft milestones to move students toward creating high-quality evidence of learning tied to the final product?

- How do we anticipate student "need to know" questions on which to center our milestones?

- How do we effectively scaffold mathematical learning in project-based learning?

213

public product in mind, Josh struggled to determine how to get from the beginning to the end of the project.

As Josh shared his idea, what I noted first was how his PBL mathematics experience connected to his students (via a social media campaign), the world (the opioid crisis), and his standards (linear, exponential, and logarithmic functions). As highlighted in Chapter 12, each of these three lenses affords us the opportunity to conceptualize a highly engaging project. I then recognized that Josh was facing the problem of how to conceptualize the "messy middle" of a project, which Larmer (2021) highlights as a common challenge for PBL practitioners.

Sitting alongside one another, Josh and I talked through two main questions: (1) What did he want his students to learn, and (2) how did he want them to learn these skills and concepts? As we focused on the *what* and *how* of his project, we began to craft what PBL practitioners call *benchmarks* (Pieratt, 2020) or *milestones* (PBLWorks, 2021). I prefer to use the term *milestones*, which also signifies an important stage in development or progress toward something—in this case the final product and culminating experience.

MILESTONES IN PBL

A **milestone** is an important event or learning experience that occurs during a project to engage students in productive inquiry in order to answer the driving question.

Milestones are important events or learning experiences that occur during a project to engage students in productive inquiry in order to answer the driving question. To embrace a student-centered project, milestones should directly connect to student "need to knows"; however, if we wait until students share their "need to knows," how can we ever plan a project? That is why we anticipate what students will ask, and craft a launch experience that moves students closer to these anticipated questions.

When I first heard this idea of anticipating questions, I thought, "*Impossible!* How do I anticipate what students might ask?" First, get to know your students. Having strong relationships with students—knowing their interests and background experiences—helps immensely in this process. Second, lead students to the questions you want them to ask through the launch experience.

For example, in the *GeoPhoto* project referenced in Chapter 13, the Project Overview sheet included specific unknown concepts such as "rule of thirds" and mathematical vocabulary like *transformations* and *angles* that led to student questions. Lastly, as students craft "need to know" questions, encourage questions you want asked by building off student conversations. I might stop by a group and point out something on the Project Overview sheet, asking questions like "What does this concept mean? Do you know how to use this idea in the context of our project?" If students say no, I say, "Sounds like a good 'need to know' question! Why don't you write it down?"

With these anticipated "need to know" questions in hand, how do we create milestones to move students toward creating high-quality evidence of learning tied to the final product? We can do this through two actions: (1) focus on the *what* (Figure 14.1) and (2) create the *how* (Figure 14.3).

FOCUS ON THE *WHAT*

Figure 14-1 • Focus on the *What*

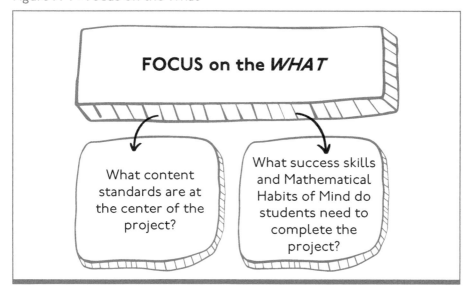

Milestones center on our content standards combined with the success skills and Mathematical Habits of Mind needed to reach high-quality evidence of learning. Not every content standard is created equally! Some of our content standards align well to project goals, including those in measurement, geometry, data and statistics, ratios and proportions, and algebraic reasoning. I often find numeracy standards (like adding, subtracting, multiplying, and dividing whole numbers, fractions, and integers) a tool used in the project but not the central focus of a project.

Additionally, as you plan a milestone, consider what success skills and Mathematical Habits of Mind will lead students to successful completion of the milestone goal. Comprehensive projects will inevitably lift up multiple success skills, such as communication, collaboration, critical thinking, and self-directed learning. To plan and implement a comprehensive PBL mathematics experience, focus on one or two Mathematical Habits of Mind to further develop a positive mathematical identity. Likewise, choose only one or two success skills, incorporating intentional practice of those skills.

As Josh and I crafted his project, we focused student learning on two key content standards, two Mathematical Habits of Mind, and one success skill (see Figure 14.2).

Figure 14-2 • The Content Standards, Mathematical Habits of Mind, and Success Skill for the *Campaign Against Opioid Addiction* Project

Project Idea: *The Campaign Against Opioid Addiction*	
Content Standards	1. Construct linear and exponential functions given a graph, a description of a relationship, or two input–output pairs.
	2. Interpret the parameters in a linear or exponential function in terms of a context.
Mathematical Habits of Mind	1. Question & Persist in Problem Solving
	2. Develop Connections
Success Skill	1. Digital Literacy

Throughout the course of a project, students will use many more content standards, Mathematical Habits of Mind, and success skills; however, this focus allows for more successful alignment to assessments and reflective opportunities.

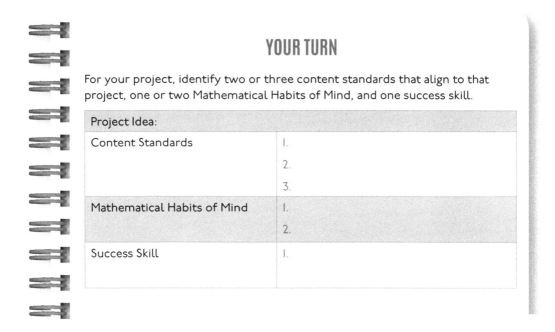

YOUR TURN

For your project, identify two or three content standards that align to that project, one or two Mathematical Habits of Mind, and one success skill.

Project Idea:	
Content Standards	1.
	2.
	3.
Mathematical Habits of Mind	1.
	2.
Success Skill	1.

CREATE THE *HOW*

Figure 14-3 • Create the *How*

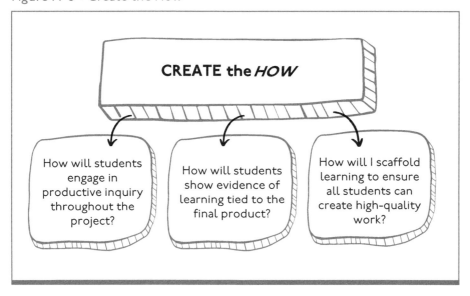

As you think about what students should know and be able to do, envision a pathway for them to engage in productive inquiry. At the start of the pathway is the *what* of the content standard, Mathematical Habit of Mind, and success skill high-lighted by a "need to know" question; at the end of the pathway is evidence of student learning, the final product or summative assessment along with a reflection. The pathway itself is the *how*, or the instructional activities—scaffolding tools, thinking routines, and timed protocols—that help students uncover and address the "need to know" question. Taken collectively, this pathway forms a milestone (see Figure 14.4). Upon completion of a milestone, students return to the "need to know" questions to continue the cycle of productive inquiry toward answering the driving question.

Figure 14-4 • Milestone Pathway

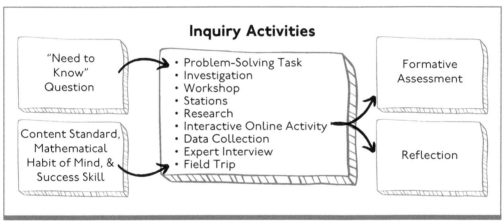

When determining the instructional activities that lead to productive inquiry, consider what activities and investigations already exist in your curricular materials. Change up instructional activities by using a variety of strategies such as rotating stations, mathematics workshops, online activities using the Desmos Graphing Calculator or GeoGebra, hands-on field trips, and expert presentations. Once you determine the instructional strategies that support student learning, determine what formative assessment can be used as evidence of learning (see Chapter 16 for ideas). Then, most importantly, consider what scaffolds are needed for all students to create high-quality work as evidence of their learning.

YOUR TURN

Using an anticipated "need to know" question you identified at the end of Chapter 13, brainstorm instructional activities to guide students toward answering that question.

Anticipated "Need to Know":	
Instructional Activities	

Scaffolding the *How*

Throughout a project, there are times when our role is to create the conditions necessary for our students to learn and grow as independent thinkers, as doers of mathematics, as productive strugglers, as triumphant perseverers. This does not mean, however, that we are "hands-off." Quite the opposite. We quietly orchestrate classroom interactions, ensuring that student learning shines. Creating those conditions requires preparation and careful planning, aided by educational tools, namely the scaffolds, routines, and protocols that boost student learning and engagement. Each of these serves a similar purpose: to help students take ownership over their learning, leading students to independently accomplish a specific task. However, there are slight differences between these three concepts, explored in Figure 14.5.

Figure 14-5 • Comparison of Scaffolding Tool, Thinking Routine, and Timed Protocol

	Scaffolding Tool	Thinking Routine	Timed Protocol
Definition	A scaffolding tool organizes student thinking, providing temporary support to move students progressively closer to a learning goal.	A thinking routine is a brief set of steps in the form of questions or short prompts, used to support and scaffold student thinking.	A timed protocol is a set of timed guidelines that follow a step-by-step format to structure learning experiences, collaborative discussions, and critique and reflection opportunities.
Example	• Frayer Model • Graphic Organizer • Chart or Table • Note-Catcher	• Notice and Wonder • "I Used to Think . . . Now I Think . . ." • Connect-Extend-Challenge (Harvard Graduate School of Education, 2015) • See-Think-Wonder	• Data Driven Dialogue (School Reform Initiative, 2002) • Good, Better, Best (see Figure 14.10) • Tuning Protocol* • Gallery Walk* • See-A-B* *See Chapter 17 for details on these critique protocols.

Scaffolding Tool

Similar to real-world construction scaffolding, an education scaffold is temporary, helping students initially access the materials, then move toward building their independence as learners. Our goal in PBL mathematics is to scaffold up, not modify down—meaning use scaffolds to build up student thinking and competency versus reducing our expectations. It's important to note, though, that some students will need a scaffold for the duration of their educational career. A scaffold is removed when no longer needed, but that is unique to each learner.

A Frayer Model is a go-to scaffold when learning new vocabulary in the mathematics classroom. This tool helps students develop a robust understanding of a term, which is especially important for our multilingual learners (Soto et al., 2023). Figure 14.6 presents an example Frayer Model from Josh's Algebra II classroom, constructed using Jamboard, as the students explored exponential functions.

Figure 14-6 • Frayer Model as a Scaffolding Tool

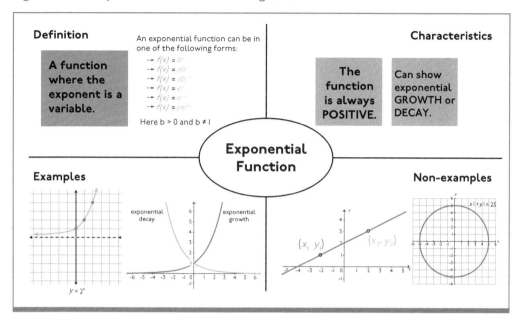

A multiplication table is a type of chart that can act as a scaffold for students. I watched fifth-grade teacher Lucas Pérez expertly use this tool with his students. Knowing that fifth graders entered the school year with varying understanding of multiplication facts, Lucas began the school year by providing a multiplication chart with every box filled in for every student. In the first few weeks of class, he had students self-assess, determining which multiplication facts they still needed support for from the multiplication chart scaffold. With a blank multiplication chart in hand, students wrote in the answers to their "top" struggle multiplication facts. Lucas expertly helped students self-identify what multiplication facts they still needed support for every two to three weeks, with the goal to help students remove the scaffold at their own pace.

Lucas developed a culture of "Challenge by Choice," where students moved away from the scaffold at their self-selected challenge level. Taking this Challenge by Choice to heart, one student created a unique strategy to self-assess her learning. She highlighted each multiplication fact as green, yellow, or pink to signify whether that fact was immediately known (green), close to being known (yellow), or still a struggle (pink). Other students adopted her idea, taking ownership of their own learning and continuing to challenge themselves. These multiplication tables were kept in a portfolio as evidence of growth in learning.

Thinking Routines

The classroom is a place of routines that help students become successful, everything from routines to take attendance to routines for how we move in the classroom or interact with one another as learners. Likewise, we can create academic routines to engage our learners, such as implementing thinking routines (see Figure 14.7). Thinking routines are a brief set of prompts or questions used to scaffold student thinking in order to make thinking visible (Harvard Graduate School of Education, 2022; Ritchhart & Church, 2020). Each chapter of this book concludes with a thinking routine. As we look at managing student learning experiences, utilizing structured thinking routines creates a sense of predictability that leads to academic safety. As students learn the routine and use it repeatedly, they internalize the habit of thinking, eventually verbalizing their thinking more freely and deeply.

A go-to strategy in the mathematics classroom is the Notice and Wonder routine. This routine asks students, "What do you notice? What do you wonder?" when examining a picture, a data set, or a mathematics problem. Here are some other thinking routines to help students engage mathematically. Each routine can be implemented based on the needs of the students and classroom by varying the type of response (written, oral) and the size of the group (individual, partner, small group, whole group).

Additional Resources

For more about these routines, explore:

- *Project Zero's Thinking Routine Toolbox* (Harvard Graduate School of Education, 2022)

- *Making Thinking Visible: How to Promote Engagement, Understanding, and Independence for All Learners* (Ritchhart et al., 2011)

- *The Power of Making Thinking Visible: Practices to Engage and Empower All Learners* (Ritchhart & Church, 2020)

Figure 14-7 • Thinking Routines

Routine	How To
"I Used to Think . . . Now I Think . . ."	Offering students these sentence stems encourages them to reflect upon misconceptions and growth, normalizing our understanding changes.
	Sixth-grade students reflected on the *Meals on Wheels* performance task using this thinking routine. One sixth grader reflected on the idea of food insecurity, sharing, "I used to think that food was a given right that all people had. Now I know that the community helps make sure everyone gets food." Another student reflected on their mathematical growth, writing, "I used to think I could always round and estimate answers. Now I think rounding down is an issue in real-world situations."
Think-Puzzle-Explore	When introducing a new topic, consider using a Think-Puzzle-Explore routine with the following question stems:
	• What do you *think* you know about this topic?
	• What *puzzles* or questions do you have about this topic?
	• How might you *explore* your puzzles?
	In his *Campaign Against Opioid Addiction* project, Algebra II teacher Josh Wilke asked his students to complete this Think-Puzzle-Explore routine after viewing tables and charts of data about opioid addiction. By asking the first question, Josh gauged student background knowledge about opioid addiction as well as student perception of data. The second prompt set up the "need to know" process of gathering student questions. The third question led students to consider additional research about opioid addiction as well as which functions may lead to mathematical models of the data.
3–2–1 Bridge (Harvard Graduate School of Education, 2019)	I've used a "mathified" 3-2-1 Bridge in the mathematics classroom as a tool for learning before and after giving a lengthy problem-solving task or performance task, especially one where mathematical modeling plays a key role. After presenting students with a task, I ask them to complete the *Before* side of a 3-2-1 Bridge. Students then fold the paper to hide the *Before* side before putting the paper away for future use. For the remainder of the class, and possibly subsequent class days, students engage in the problem-solving task or performance task.
	At the conclusion of the task, students return to the 3-2-1 Bridge and complete the *After* side without looking at their previous thoughts. Once complete, students compare their two answers, looking for growth or new understanding from the *Before* to the *After* side. See Figure 14.8 for a template of this task.

Figure 14-8 • 3–2–1 Bridge Thinking Routine

3-2-1 Bridge

Before				After
	3			
	numbers or words that are important			
	2			
	assumptions or questions I have			
	1			
	mathematical concept needed to solve this task			

Note: Fold on the dotted lines.

Timed Protocols

A timed protocol outlines agreed-upon guidelines for discussion, reading, decision making, critiquing, or presenting, providing students clear expectations for productive conversation and feedback. By using a protocol, students know the expectations and goals for the conversation and the time given to complete each goal. Timed protocols increase academic safety and lead to more engaged time on task, allowing students to work effectively and collaboratively. Protocols help students become self-directed learners, creating accountability structures for learning in small groups. Both the subsequent example milestone and Chapter 17 highlight protocols for critique. Chapter 15 highlights a decision-making protocol (Figure 15.3).

YOUR TURN

Looking at the instructional activities you brainstormed for the anticipated "need to know," identify scaffolds that would aid students in the form of a scaffolding tool, thinking routine, or timed protocol.

Anticipated "Need to Know":	
Potential Scaffolds	

EXAMPLE MILESTONE

Let's look at an example of a milestone in action. In the *GeoPhoto* project, high school teacher Katy Weber determined she would center one standard for the project on representing and describing transformations. She focused on the Mathematical Habit of Mind of Search for Patterns and the success skill of risk-taking as she knew asking students to take original photographs, find geometric transformations in their photos, and share their work required each of these skills.

In developing one of the milestones, Katy anticipated the "need to know" question, "How do mathematical transformations impact photography?" In actuality, students posed various questions that guided the photography connections to transformation, including "Are photos with mirrors and water showing math reflection?" and "How does rotation and translation get shown in a photo?" Katy expertly grouped these questions together during the "need to know" collection phase.

To investigate this "need to know" question, Katy created a series of lessons and explorations guiding students to deeper knowledge. Having preassessed students, she knew her students had limited understanding of transformational geometry, so she began by having students create a foldable—an intentional scaffold to teach the vocabulary of translation, rotation, reflection, and dilation using definitions, examples, and visual representations. Next, students applied their initial understanding of these terms to a set of curated photographs. In partners, students categorized the type of transformation represented in the photograph. Partners then chose one photograph to analyze using a digital tool, the Desmos Graphing Calculator, tracing over the image and placing it on the coordinate grid to mathematically communicate the transformation that occurred. To scaffold this process, Katy created a short step-by-step guide in both written and video format.

As students became comfortable with the process, Katy hosted students on a walking field trip around their community, where pairs of students took photographs highlighting geometric transformations. Partners then analyzed their own photographs using the same process of sketching the mathematical transformation and placing the sketch on a coordinate grid to mathematically communicate the transformation that occurred. Figure 14.9 shows an example of a photograph mathematically analyzed by two sophomore students.

Figure 14-9 • Example of Mathematical Analysis in *GeoPhoto* Project

Step 1: Original Photo

Our original photograph is of a wheel in the International Gardens. We noticed the spokes of the wheel showed a rotation.

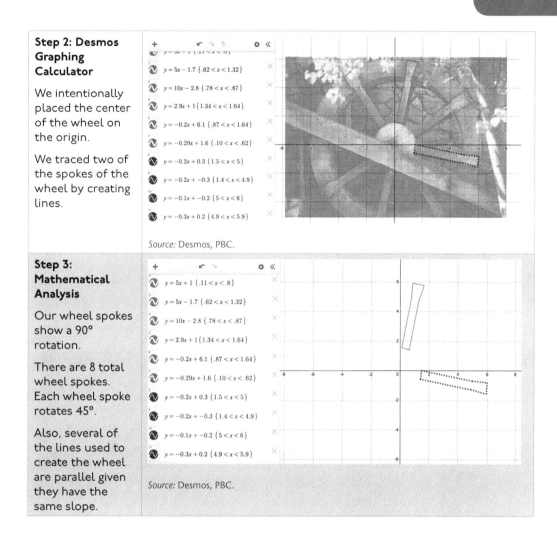

Step 2: Desmos Graphing Calculator

We intentionally placed the center of the wheel on the origin.

We traced two of the spokes of the wheel by creating lines.

$y = 5x - 1.7 \{.62 < x < 1.32\}$

$y = 10x - 2.8 \{.78 < x < .87\}$

$y = 2.9x + 1 \{1.34 < x < 1.64\}$

$y = -0.2x + 6.1 \{.87 < x < 1.64\}$

$y = -0.29x + 1.6 \{.10 < x < .62\}$

$y = -0.2x + 0.3 \{1.5 < x < 5\}$

$y = -0.2x + -0.3 \{1.4 < x < 4.9\}$

$y = -0.1x + -0.2 \{5 < x < 6\}$

$y = -0.3x + 0.2 \{4.9 < x < 5.9\}$

Source: Desmos, PBC.

Step 3: Mathematical Analysis

Our wheel spokes show a 90° rotation.

There are 8 total wheel spokes. Each wheel spoke rotates 45°.

Also, several of the lines used to create the wheel are parallel given they have the same slope.

$y = 5x + 1 \{.11 < x < .8\}$

$y = 5x - 1.7 \{.62 < x < 1.32\}$

$y = 10x - 2.8 \{.78 < x < .87\}$

$y = 2.9x + 1 \{1.34 < x < 1.64\}$

$y = -0.2x + 6.1 \{.87 < x < 1.64\}$

$y = -0.29x + 1.6 \{.10 < x < .62\}$

$y = -0.2x + 0.3 \{1.5 < x < 5\}$

$y = -0.2x + -0.3 \{1.4 < x < 4.9\}$

$y = -0.1x + -0.2 \{5 < x < 6\}$

$y = -0.3x + 0.2 \{4.9 < x < 5.9\}$

Source: Desmos, PBC.

Before turning in this formative assessment as evidence of learning, students engaged in a short critique routine called Good, Better, Best, an intentional scaffold to enhance feedback (see Figure 14.10). This critique protocol engaged students in the community agreement of critiquing the work, not the people, and allowed partners to make revisions to their own work, refining their thinking while elevating the learning of their peers.

Figure 14-10 • Good, Better, Best Critique Protocol

Activity	Description	Time
Present	Presenters share their work, explaining their mathematical transformation. Audience listens.	2 minutes
Analyze	Audience analyzes photographs and mathematical work silently.	I minute
Respond	Each audience member shares a Good, Better, Best. • What makes your work *good* is . . . • What could make your work *better* is . . . • What would make this the *best* is . . . Presenters listen and take notes.	2 minutes
Reflect	Presenters reflect on feedback and name at least one concrete action step to revise and improve work.	I minute
	Repeat process for next set of partners.	
	Total	I2 minutes

Katy used the revised student work as her formative assessment of learning. Students reflected upon their understanding using the prompt, "Rank the four types of transformations from easiest (1) to hardest (4) in terms of describing the transformation mathematically. Explain your ranking. Next, rank the four types of transformations using the same scale in terms of capturing the transformation visually in photographs. Explain this new ranking."

The reflection completed the productive inquiry for this milestone. However, as students engaged in learning about geometric transformations in photography, other geometry concepts came to the forefront, like the golden ratio and the use of parallel lines, perpendicular lines, and triangles. The activities that encompass this milestone are highlighted in Katy's planning, found in Figure 14.11.

Figure 14-11 • Example Milestone Planning

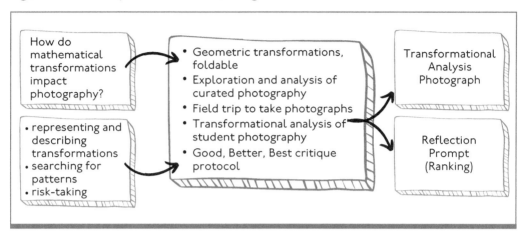

YOUR TURN

Put your design together from this chapter. Plan a milestone using the blank template that follows. What part of the planning came easily to you? Where do you need more assistance?

MILESTONE PLANNING

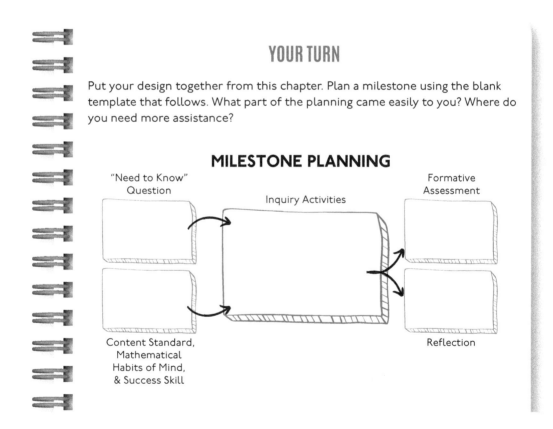

CONCLUDING THOUGHTS

As we think about our Driving Question for this book, "How can I bring project-based learning [PBL] to life in the mathematics classroom?," well-crafted milestones lead directly to sustained inquiry by our students. As we align our milestones to our content standards and skills, remember milestones show evidence of learning that answers a driving question. Milestones should connect to student "need to know" questions, necessary for the final product and culminating experience. Furthermore, milestones provide both teachers and students opportunities for assessment and feedback. In planning a milestone, create scaffolding opportunities that enhance content standards as well as the Mathematical Habits of Mind and success skills needed for the project.

PBL POINTS TO PONDER: THE FOUR Cs

In the four Cs routine, consider each of the questions as a starting point for discussion or reflection. This routine allows you to make connections, ask questions, identify key ideas, and consider application. Share your connections using #PBLmath.

- ☐ **Connections:** What connections can you draw between this chapter and your current teaching and learning practice?

- ☐ **Challenges:** What ideas, positions, or assumptions do you want to challenge or argue with in this chapter?

- ☐ **Concepts:** What key concepts or ideas do you think are important and worth holding on to from this chapter?

- ☐ **Changes:** What changes in attitudes, thinking, or action are suggested by this chapter, either for you or for others?

CHAPTER 15

Manage

"Can I have all the project managers see me up front?" My student teacher Megan Steffen gathered all the students playing the role of project manager at the front table while I worked with the budget managers on applying unit rate to the cost of accessible turf. Meanwhile, the UX (user experience) design strategists and architects busily finalized design plans for the layout of their accessible park. The energy in the room buzzed at a constant thrum as students worked on their team's preestablished daily goals, which were recorded in the team's learning log. After a few minutes, two voices rose above the rest.

"We don't have time for that. It's too late," Josephine, the architect, stated forcefully to Nora, the UX design strategist.

"It's not too late. You just do everything your way. It's not just *your* project," Nora retorted.

Before the argument became too heated, my student teacher Megan intervened. She calmly asked the entire team to move

> ## Need to Knows
>
> - How can I effectively manage the project?
> - How do I act as the manager of team dynamics?
> - How do I act as the manager of project goals?

231

to a side table where they could discuss the issue and agree to a plan moving forward. She asked the project manager to bring the team's folder, containing the team contract needed to aid in their discussion. Before discussing the conflict that led to raised voices, both Josephine and Nora read statements directly from the team contract written about how the team would make decisions and settle disagreements. They each pointed to their signatures as well, a reminder of their agreement to the team.

MANAGING THE PROJECT

One concern I hear teachers voice about project-based learning (PBL) is the lack of control they feel when students work in teams independently. As educators, we have played the role of manager as we daily manage the classroom behaviors and experiences of our students. What may be new is how to be a manager of the project process. So, how can we ensure students are successful as we move into this role?

Embracing the role of manager took time for me, yet with practice, I started distinguishing the various aspects of a project that needed overseeing, from being the manager of team dynamics to being the manager of project goals. Each of these managerial roles leads to a successful PBL mathematics experience, so let's explore strategies to embody our role of manager.

MANAGER OF TEAM DYNAMICS

Facilitating content and learning experiences, as explored in Chapter 14, is perhaps the most familiar aspect of project management. A key component of the PBL mathematics classroom is the authentic collaboration between students, making it critical to manage team dynamics. To manage teams, begin by preteaching and practicing collaboration in low-stakes environments. Consider creating roles for each member to fulfill, scaffolding team success through a team contract, and providing accountability measures by developing both team and individual products (Miller, 2011).

To increase student voice and choice, before assigning teams, I ask students to complete a short survey or set of questions that allows me to mix students together cohesively. These questions include:

- What is one strength you will bring to a team for this project?
- What is one mathematics concept you understand well that will aid your team?
- What is one mathematics concept you think will be a struggle?
- After examining the roles for this project, order your interest in each role from greatest (1) to least (4). This does not guarantee you will receive your top-choice role.

The answers to these questions help me create dynamic teams of students who can build upon one another's strengths. When I eventually share out teams, I preface the team share-out by reminding students their answers helped me craft a team based on everyone's strengths. I also remind students their interest in a specific role may or may not mean they will receive that role.

In my classroom, I distinguish the difference between teams and groups. Teams are ongoing, working together to complete the project collaboratively. I carefully consider the dynamics of a team. Groups are temporary, such as critique groups or jigsaw groups that work together for a short amount of time before returning to their team.

Practice Collaboration

Perhaps more than in any other subject, students in the mathematics classroom feel apt to give up and shut down when they encounter a challenge, perhaps because they feel they are the only one facing the struggle. By centering our instructional practices on collaboration, students begin to realize that everyone finds mathematics difficult at some point, creating a learner-centered culture where previously perceived insurmountable obstacles become collective team challenges to persevere through. Additionally, by utilizing collaborative practices, students connect ideas from instruction to the thoughts of their peers and eventually to their own thinking. This leads to higher levels of analysis and synthesis, keys to unlocking critical thinking.

Explicitly teaching success skills such as collaboration and decision making is equally as important as teaching content in the PBL mathematics classroom. To ensure successful project implementation, preteach and practice collaboration skills in the classroom in a low-stakes environment. In the first few weeks of school, I assign problem-solving tasks requiring collaboration among classmates. During these tasks, I take pictures and videos of students working together. After a few tasks, I present a small slideshow, visually representing the collaboration that occurred in the classroom. Collectively, we define what collaboration looks like, sounds like, and feels like in the mathematics classroom. We then capture our thinking in an anchor chart hung up in the classroom (see Figure 15.1).

Figure 15-1 • Collaboration Definition Anchor Chart

Collaboration in the Mathematics Classroom		
Looks Like	**Sounds Like**	**Feels Like**
• Heads together • Bodies facing each other • Eyes on the person speaking (active listening) • Messy mathematics • Only the materials you need on the table (no personal devices) • Everybody trying their best • Working together • Trying lots of strategies • Pictures and numbers • Taking turns	• "Building off what you said . . ." • "I don't understand. Can you explain it again?" • "I respectfully disagree because . . ." • "It's okay to make mistakes." • "I have an idea I'd like to share." • "What's your idea, _____?" • "Let's try _____'s strategy."	• Being part of a team • Accomplished • Successful • Respectful • Active • Supportive • Dynamic • Challenging

A collaboration strategy I use takes a twist on the traditional Think-Pair-Share. Developed specifically to support multilingual learners, Soto (2021) created a Think-Pair-Share 2.0 strategy to support inquiry-based approaches in the classroom (see Figure 15.2). In this strategy, students more intentionally highlight what each partner is thinking, then work together to reach consensus on what to share out to their classmates. Soto highlights four options for this consensus: (1) whatever partner 1 said, (2) whatever partner 2 said, (3) a combination of both ideas if they were similar, or (4) a completely new idea. Regardless, whatever students decide to share must be discussed and agreed upon by both partners.

Using this structure, I have found student conversations to be more focused and productive. I regularly highlight that during a Think-Pair-Share 2.0, students are working on the community agreement to "Listen to everyone's ideas. Work to understand their thinking" (Chapter 10). As students engage in a PBL mathematics experience, this Think-Pair-Share 2.0 strategy can be used as evidence of learning not only of mathematical content but also of the success skill of collaboration.

Figure 15-2 • Think-Pair-Share 2.0

Question or Prompt	What I Thought (*Speaking*)	What My Partner Thought (*Listening*)	What We Will Share (*Consensus*)

Source: Adapted from Soto (2021).

Use Roles

Using roles that exist as jobs or careers heightens the authenticity of a project while providing a structure leading to stronger classroom management and student self-management. When students know the expectations of their role, they can work more confidently and diligently.

Developing roles for a team project does not have to be fake. Using the authentic context of a situation, consider what careers or roles already exist in that environment. Here are some general roles I use in projects:

- Project manager
- Budget manager or financial planner

- Marketing executive

- Social media director

- Reporter or journalist

- Analyst

- Designer or artist

- Measurement specialist

- Organizational agent

- Featured speaker or lead presenter

- Content strategist

- Problem solver

- Innovator or creator

YOUR TURN

Considering your ongoing project, which roles make sense for students to embody during the project? How would those roles enhance accountability and authenticity?

_____

_____

_____

Each project takes on a different need in terms of team size or organization. I find the ideal size of a team to be three or four students. In the *Accessible Park* project, I created teams with four roles (see Figure 15.3). After placing students in their *Accessible Park* teams, I created a decision-making protocol for students to determine roles in an effective manner, respecting each student's voice. Before this protocol, I referenced our community agreements including "Collaborate effectively" and "Listen to understand."

Figure 15-3 • *Accessible Park* Decision-Making Protocol

Activity	Details	Time
Individual Reflection	Using the project roles overview sheet, review each role. Rank your choices from 1 to 4 (1 being the top choice).	1 minute
Share-Out	Each group member has 30 seconds to share out what role they would like as their top choice, giving reasons why they would be a strong candidate. Then, each member shares their second choice. The rest of the team listens silently while each member speaks.	2 minutes
Team Discussion	As a team, determine who will embody each role. Sign your name to the role on the team contract. If time permits, begin brainstorming a team name.	4 minutes
Tiebreaker	If a team consensus cannot be made, individuals will engage in Rock, Paper, Scissors for unclaimed roles, with the "best out of three" winner choosing their top role.	1 minute
	Total:	8 minutes

This process laid down the foundation for successful teams. Using this protocol for the *Accessible Park* project, all but one team came to a consensus before the tiebreaker round.

Team Contracts

After students determined roles, teams worked through a team contract. Team contracts can be short, such as reading a set of predetermined team agreements with each member signing their name to the document, perhaps allotting some time for teams to add an idea or two to the team agreement.

Given the extended time students would engage in teams for the *Accessible Park* project, I asked teams to give more thought to their team structure. I developed a short, one-page contract for teams, facilitated by the project manager, budget manager, UX design strategist, and architect. The roles of UX design strategist and architect were specific to this project as a major goal was for students to engage in thinking about children and people with disabilities as they designed a blueprint for a playground or park.

As part of a team contract for the *Accessible Park* project, students discussed the team agreements as well as our classroom's community agreements. Led by the student role of project manager, teams had the opportunity to add any agreements specific to their team. Then, team members discussed how to make decisions collaboratively, predicting potential conflicts and ways to resolve those conflicts. Finally, students shared an action plan for potential team struggles. An example team contract is available for download at https://qrs.ly/56ensfy. By establishing team agreements signed by students, the foundation for a successful project is established.

> online resources   The project featured in this vignette is available for download at **https://qrs.ly/56ensfy**.

Accountability Through Products

A common hesitation around PBL mathematics, and honestly group projects in general, is the fear that one student will do all the work. To alleviate this fear, I intentionally scaffold projects to provide clear individual and team accountability (Piper, 2012). In the *Accessible Park* project, each role had a designated item to submit as evidence of learning (see Figure 15.4). By designating individual projects, students participating in team collaborative learning can rest assured that their learning and assessment will not be negatively impacted by a fellow classmate.

Additionally, this designation of individual products provides the teacher opportunities to engage students in smaller "expert" or "jigsaw" groups. In the *Accessible Park* project, all students explored the concept of unit rate; however, I created additional mini workshop materials for the budget managers to apply that content knowledge to determine the cost of accessible turf.

Figure I5-4 • *Accessible Park* Roles

Role	Description
Project Manager *Student:*	Responsible for team organization, team communication, cohesiveness of design from user experience to layout to budget, and final presentation. Conducts interviews with each member of the team to determine accuracy of mathematics application. Evidence of Learning: Submits learning logs, interview notes, and final presentation. Expert Skills: General mathematical knowledge, organization, communication.

Role	Description
Budget Manager *Student:*	Responsible for creating a budget proposal, including the cost of each play equipment item, approximate cost of turf, and approximate cost of pavement for parking or pathways. Evidence of Learning: Submits budget proposal and all documents showing mathematical research and processes. Expert Skills: Unit rate, decimal addition and multiplication, detail orientation.
UX Design Strategist (*UX = User Experience*) *Student:*	Leads research of play equipment items. Determines dimensions of play area, rounds play equipment to a useful unit, and determines fall zone and usage area that satisfy safety and Americans with Disabilities Act (ADA) regulations. Works with architect to determine scale for blueprint. Evidence of Learning: Submits UX design cover sheet and all UX draft designs. Submits safety regulations inspection sheet focused on measurement and area. Expert Skills: Area, measurement, research savvy.
Architect *Student:*	Translates UX design strategist draft designs into final blueprint. Works with UX design strategist to determine scale for blueprint. Oversees the creation of the *Accessible Park* project blueprints and coordinate grid graphing. Evidence of Learning: Submits blueprint drafts, scale calculations, and coordinate points plot map. Expert Skills: Coordinate grid graphing, scale, artistic design.

online resources   The resource is available for download at **https://qrs.ly/56ensfy**.

MANAGER OF PROJECT GOALS

As a project extends over multiple days or weeks, creating structures to manage project goals helps students track their progress. Managing the project goals also ensures the project does not extend over more curricular time than allotted. Teachers can implement various tools to ensure clear, structured project goals, including using a visual benchmarking system, a scrum board, checklists, or daily learning logs. Lastly, support students by asking them to reflect on what they need to move forward via a help desk ticket.

Benchmarking System

Even though we aim for students to move through a project at a similar pace, inevitably, some teams will move faster than others. To help teams chart their progress, consider making a visual benchmarking system. Pieratt (2020) highlighted a visual clip chart that breaks milestones down into manageable subgoals. Begin by using a long strip of butcher paper and dividing it into sections marked with each subgoal. Label a clothespin or binder clip with each team name or number. Move the clip along each milestone as teams progress through each subgoal.

Scrum Board

Sometimes in a project, individual teams create specific goals that slightly differ from those of other teams. In this instance, use a scrum board to manage a team's progress. A scrum board has been used in the business world as a tool to focus project groups. There really is no right or wrong way to "scrum," but generally, a scrum board features a large table with column headers such as To Do, In Progress, Review & Revise, and Done. Underneath those headers are rows dedicated to each team, where teams can post sticky notes with individual goals written on them, moving the sticky notes through the columns as they progress through tasks. Figure 15.5 shows an example of a scrum board during the *Accessible Park* project.

Checklist

Checklists give students a way to organize actionable items for a project, driving accountability for students. By organizing items into a checklist, teachers can assign and communicate what needs to be accomplished in an easy-to-use format at a team or individual level. Consider creating a checklist with escalating action items, meaning items that need to get completed first happen before the next items on the list, ensuring students and teams complete the most critical items first.

Figure 15-5 • *Accessible Park* Scrum Board Example

Scrum Board

Team	To Do	In Progress	Review & Revise	Done
1	determine scale & complete calculations		get feedback on initial design idea	
2	complete budget proposal	find area to determine cost of accessible turf		
3		determine dimensions of fall zone		scale calculations
4		create coodinate grid for blueprints	get feedback on budget proposal	

Learning Logs

One responsibility of a project manager is organizing the beginning and end of work time, which can be accomplished through the aid of a learning log. Students in Jasmine Valentine's fourth-grade *Dream School* project used daily learning logs to record what learning in the project occurred each day and a goal for the following class period (see Figure 15.6). The project manager led these conversations and recorded team thoughts. Learning logs allowed Jasmine a quick, succinct way to review team progress each day.

Figure 15-6 ◆ *Dream School* Learning Log Example

Dream School Learning Log

DATE	WHAT DID YOU ACCOMPLISH TODAY	WHAT IS A GOAL FOR NEXT SESSION
5-18-22	Must and May's, and we accomplished the 1st floor.	Starting the 2d floor
5-19-22	Idea's for 2d floor	Not get distracted
5-20-22	Most of second floor	To finish 3d floor and not get distracted AGAIN!
5-23-22	We finished drawing the second floor.	To finish the math for the first floor.
5-24-22	Angles for first and second floor.	Angles for 3d floor.
5-25-22	Angles for 3d floor.	Finish presentation.

Help Desk Ticket

Scene: Classroom during work time. A hand is raised. The teacher swiftly moves over to a table of students, dodging backpacks and workbooks strewn on the floor.

Student: "I need help."

Teacher: "Help with what?"

Student (*unsure*): "Ummm . . . Everything."

Teacher (*hopeful*): "Can you be a bit more specific?"

Student (*getting frustrated*): "I don't know. I just need help!"

I think we can all relate to this scene. In reality, the words "I need help" are not very helpful, especially in a PBL mathematics experience. In order to support students to become more specific in their request for assistance, I have created a help desk ticket (see Figure 15.7). Similar to filling out a help desk ticket when stuck with an online issue or calling a customer service person to assist in troubleshooting, the help desk ticket provides students more concrete ideas of how I can support their learning. These can be used individually or in teams not only during PBL mathematics experiences but also during problem-solving tasks or performance tasks.

When teaching students how to use these, I point out the ticket will be "returned" and remain "unfilled" if the "I/We have tried . . ." section is left blank. As a class, we brainstorm strategies to try before using a help desk ticket, creating an anchor chart highlighting ideas such as asking another team, reviewing the Project Overview sheet, or drawing a picture of our thinking. These help desk tickets provide strong evidence of growth in the Mathematical Habit of Mind of Question & Persist in Problem Solving. Consider sending the help desk ticket home (physically or via a photo) with a positive note highlighting how students persevered in learning.

Figure 15-7 • Help Desk Ticket

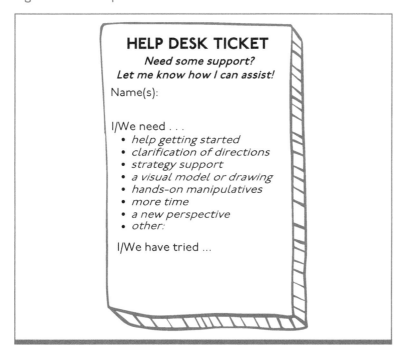

HELP DESK TICKET
Need some support?
Let me know how I can assist!
Name(s):

I/We need . . .
- *help getting started*
- *clarification of directions*
- *strategy support*
- *a visual model or drawing*
- *hands-on manipulatives*
- *more time*
- *a new perspective*
- *other:*

I/We have tried ...

YOUR TURN

Consider the project you continue to develop. What tool(s) would best keep students and teams accountable throughout the project? What role on the project team would take charge of this accountability measure?

_____

_____

_____

CONCLUDING THOUGHTS

Managing a project can seem daunting at first, but in time, structuring the project with these management tools increases student agency. I have found the more students clearly understand the project expectations, the more time I dedicate to teams via conferencing, and the less I engage in behavior management with individual students. Planning management techniques is equally as important as planning the content of a lesson.

PBL POINTS TO PONDER: GLOWS & GROWS

We often critique ourselves negatively without pausing to reflect on all our amazing qualities. Use this protocol to highlight the way you *glow* as an educator and areas to *grow* your practice.

☐   Glow: In what ways do I *glow* in my ability to manage students as self-directed learners?

☐   Grow: In what ways can I *grow* in my ability to manage students as self-directed learners?

CHAPTER 16

Assess

"The rubric says we need to show evidence of each type of angle on our blueprints. I know we labeled the right angles, but have we labeled all the acute and obtuse angles?" asked one fourth grader of his team members, who were collaboratively designing their dream school.

A team member replied, "Do we need to just label the angles, or do we have to measure them with the protractor?"

Need to Knows

- What do formative and summative assessments look like in the project-based learning mathematics classroom?

- How do we create a culminating experience?

"I'm pretty sure we have to do both. I'll start labeling the angles if you go find a protractor," a third team member clarified before asking, "What angle does a circle have?"

Students in this fourth-grade classroom used a rubric, co-created between the students and their teacher Jasmine Valentine, to self-assess their progress on creating blueprints for their dream school (see Figure 16.1). Using the rubric to guide their conversations, teams of students assessed their summative products of a blueprint and accompanying oral presentation, which was scheduled for two days from that class period, in front of a panel of experts. The pressure was on, and self-assessment using the rubric provided students the opportunity to achieve goals based on project requirements.

Figure 16-1 • *Dream School* Self-Assessment

Dream School

Grows	Meets Expectations	Glows
remembering re write them Down	**Angles** • Labels **20 right angles** using right angle symbol • Accurately uses protractor • Measures and labels **5 acute angles** • Measures and labels **12 obtuse angles**	Good at finding the angles
Have not started the area yet	**Area** • Accurately calculates area of every room, hallway, or learning space • Labels areas correctly (squared measurements) • Area total does not exceed 350,000	good measurment
need working on loud Speaking voices	**Speaking & Presentation Skills** • Speaks loudly and clearly with expression in voice • Holds attention of audience with direct eye contact • Shows confidence and practice through strong body language (gestures, stance)	good presentation

ASSESSMENT IN PBL MATHEMATICS

As explored in Chapter 8, meaningful assessment contributes to a classroom dynamic centered on providing students a *why* behind their learning. Being clear about the *why* helps both the students and the teacher make progress toward a final product highlighted at the culminating experience. To clarify expectations for assessments, having a robust rubric is essential.

Let's look more closely at how to co-create a rubric with students, adding a sense of student agency to the project.

Rubric (Co-)Creation

As a project-based learning (PBL) mathematics practitioner, I have grown over time from developing a rubric *for* students to sharing the art of rubric creation *with* my students. I have co-created a rubric with students as young as second grade. With time and practice, students can engage in the art of rubric co-creation. So, what does this process look like?

1. ***Determine Categories:*** Review the project outcomes and learning goals for content, Mathematical Habits of Mind, and success skills. Create a category name for each goal. This can be done independent of the students; however, consider revisiting the Project Overview sheet with students to review project goals. In total, I like to use four to six categories. More than that feels overwhelming. Fewer than that may indicate lack of depth in a PBL mathematics experience, potentially indicating a performance task instead of a project. Content categories might be Application of Unit Rate or Analysis of Statistical Findings. To ensure rigorous content, I focus on my verb choices, using active verbs at the application level. I rarely use the phrase "Understanding of" as the goal in a PBL mathematics experience is *application* of content knowledge. Choose two or three content categories. Although you may have touched on several content skills, consider which knowledge led to new learning for students or was most needed for project completion. Mathematical Habits of Mind are critical to address in a rubric as well; choose one or two categories to assess. These categories might include Use Tools Strategically or Question & Persist in Problem Solving. Essential to PBL mathematics is lifting up success skills. Students probably engaged in many success skills, including collaboration, communication, perseverance, creativity, and adaptability. Choose one or two skills essential to the success of the project to include in the rubric.

2. ***Brainstorm Descriptors:*** Share a model descriptor with the students, perhaps one for a category in the current rubric or a category from a previous rubric. Showing a model allows students to see what a high-quality

descriptor looks like. Either as a whole class or in small groups, ask students to complete a Y-chart activity, describing what their given descriptor looks like, sounds like, and feels like. Use these ideas to write a descriptor for each category (see Figure 16.2).

Figure 16-2 • Student Example of Rubric Descriptor: Precise Measurement

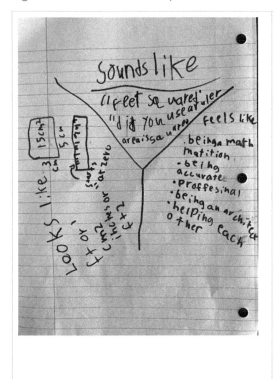

[*Descriptions of student work pictured*]

Sounds like:

- "feet squared"
- "did you use a ruler"
- area is squared

Looks like:

- ft or ´
- cm2
- inches or "
- ft2
- 15cm^2 [*written within a rectangle labeled* 3cm *by* 5cm]
- starts at zero [*with an arrow pointing to zero on a drawing of a ruler*]

Feels like:

- being a mathmatition
- being accurate
- proffesinal
- being an architect
- helping each other

Note: This figure is a reproduction of student work; spelling errors have been left in for authenticity.

3. **Create Draft:** Use student descriptors and brainstorms to create the first draft of a rubric. Do this outside of class as rubric creation takes too much time as a whole class. Also, if you repeat this process with more than one class period, this allows all student thoughts to come together in one document. I like to label my rubric as a draft, highlighting to students they still have final say in the rubric.

4. **Present Draft (and Revise as Necessary):** The following class period, present the draft rubric to students. Provide students time to ask any clarifying

questions or make suggestions for revision. In my experience, revisions are often minor, but this process provides students ownership over the final rubric.

Personally, I like to use single-point rubrics, where I create only one descriptor for each category. I then leave space for feedback and assessment.

 An example of co-created rubrics is available for download at **https://qrs.ly/56ensfy**.

Assessments Tied to "Need to Know" Questions

The assessments of a project should connect to student "need to know" questions, which are aligned to the project milestones. Let's explore what this looks like at both an elementary and a high school level.

Elementary: Fourth-Grade *Dream School* Project

"Need to Know" Question	Activity and Assessment
How many students fit in a high school classroom?	Students took a field trip to a local high school. In small groups, students measured the dimensions of the classrooms (all rectangular except the planetarium) and calculated the area. Students interviewed the high school principal to learn about classroom size and capacity.
	To highlight formative evidence of learning, students submitted drawings of their measurements, mathematical calculations of area, and an estimate of how many classrooms their dream school needed based on their projected school size.
How do we measure angles that aren't ninety degrees?	Students learned the vocabulary of *acute*, *obtuse*, and *right* using a graphic organizer. Students used a protractor on paper to learn how to use the tool.
	Using the teacher's classroom, which was trapezoidal in shape, students measured the angles of the room using special construction protractors. Students created mini blueprints of the classroom, diagramming the obtuse corners of the room, acute angles made by doorways and room dividers, and right angles formed by bookshelves.
	As formative evidence of learning, students submitted diagrams of the room with degree measurements and angle type labeled (*acute*, *obtuse*, *right*).

(Continued)

(*Continued*)

"Need to Know" Question	Activity and Assessment
How do we find the area of a room that is not a rectangle?	Students measured and designed rooms that were a combination of rectangles, trapezoids, and other polygons. The fourth-grade standards only asked students to understand the area of a rectangle. To foster student agency, fourth-grade teacher Jasmine Valentine created a "Challenge by Choice" workshop. Students who wanted to explore area of composite shapes, like two rectangles composed together or rectangles and triangles composed together, attended the workshop, while other students engaged in a "Math With Technology" lesson, continuing to explore the concept of the area of a singular rectangle. Each group of students was given a short quiz as a formative assessment. Note that quizzes still have their place in the PBL mathematics classroom. However, a quiz or test should not be a summative assessment or the only means of assessment.

High School: *Wage Gap* Performance Task

"Need to Know" Question	Activity and Assessment
How do we know if the data are accurate?	Students analyzed sources and websites to find the data to complete their research. Students discussed research bias and how data can be manipulated to fit an organization's needs or goals. To show formative evidence of learning, students submitted two sources that provided information on the wage gap, highlighting similarities and differences. Students wrote a short paragraph explaining why they thought differences in the data existed, based on classroom discussions and personal research.
How can we accurately estimate when women and men are equal in pay?	Students learned how to graphically model data over time. Given the data over time for the wage gap were fairly linear, students learned how to use the slope-intercept form of a line in context of a situation. As formative evidence of learning, students modeled the data of earnings by white women compared to white men using the Desmos Graphing Calculator, annotating their findings using Desmos Studio tools (see Figure 16.4).
Is there a difference in pay for BIPOC men and women? What about LGBTQ+ people? How do their data compare to data on white men? When will equality be reached by all?	Students split into small groups to explore data on a focused population of people and the wage gap that exists within that population (e.g., LGBTQ+ compared to heterosexual people). Students grappled with incomplete data sets, making judgments about whether enough information existed to form a complete picture of the situation. As part of their summative evidence of learning, students created advocacy letters written to lawmakers highlighting the inequities in wages, using linear modeling to show when their focus population would achieve equal pay. Students submitted advocacy letters online to several local, state, and national politicians.

FORMATIVE ASSESSMENTS AS EVIDENCE OF LEARNING

As explored in Chapter 8, formative assessments provide both students and teachers a quick check of progress in ongoing learning. Formative assessments can take less than one minute, like a quick Fist to Five (Keeley & Tobey, 2011), or a few minutes, like a Muddiest Point (Chapter 5). In a PBL mathematics experience, all student work that leads up to the final product is considered formative. For that reason, let's explore more in-depth formative assessment options that show evidence of student learning at major benchmarks.

- ABC Book Page
  - Depending on the topic of study, there might be enough vocabulary words that connect to a letter of the alphabet. In this formative assessment, ask students to pick a letter of the alphabet and sketch out a page of a book that would connect to that letter. With the class, establish minimum requirements for each page, such as the word, a definition, an example, and a picture. There is no "right" or "wrong" way to create pages. Use the same letter two or three times as needed.
  - Example: In an eighth-grade project, students studied bivariate statistics to determine what quantitative attributes contributed to the "ideal athlete." Figure 16.3 highlights some of the words students used to create their page of the ABC Book. Not every letter led to a word in the book; some letters had multiple words.

- Learning Logs and Analysis
  - Learning logs can be filled out as an individual or a team. By spending each day writing down a short summary of what was learned, students can analyze their mathematical learning and growth over the course of a project. I like to ask students at two points during the project to write a short analysis of their learning using their learning logs. Students write about struggles they have faced, how their learning has deepened, or aha moments in the project. This reflective analysis focuses students on content learning.

Figure 16-3 ◆ ABC Book Page Words

A analysis	B bivariate	C correlation, Cartesian plane, cluster	D dependent	E
F fit	G	H	I independent	J
K	L linear	M	N negative, numerical data	O outlier
P population, positive	Q quantitative	R random, regression	S scatter plot, sample, strong correlation	T trend, table
U univariate	V variable	W weak correlation	X x-axis	Y y-axis

- Poster
  - A go-to formative assessment tool, posters can be hung around the room and reflected upon using a Gallery Walk (see Chapter 17). I like when students show their mathematical work with written annotations or helpful tips, such as "Here's how I found the unit rate" or "Always label area in units squared." "Convince Me" posters ask students to show at least two ways students know their mathematical work is correct, such as through a visual model and algorithm.

- Annotated Graphs or Charts
  - Graphs or charts show a deep understanding of a concept. However, as I've grown in my PBL mathematics practice, I have found students may accurately make a graph or chart but not understand how it connects to the project topic. This led me to ask students to annotate their work, making thinking visible.
  - One way to annotate a graph digitally is to use the Graphing Calculator by Desmos Studio. In the *Wage Gap* project performance task, students added notes to their graph to highlight mathematical thinking (see Figure 16.4).

Figure 16-4 • Annotated Desmos Graphing Calculator *Wage Gap* Graph Example

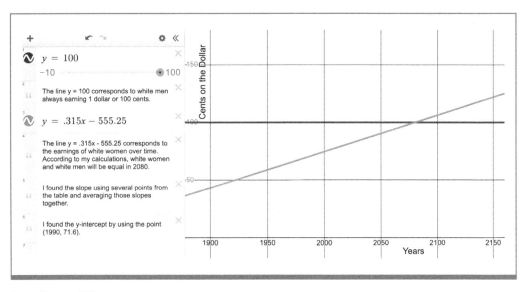

Source: Desmos, PBC.

- Sketches or Diagrams
  - As they prepare to make final products, ask students to brainstorm what the product looks like through a sketch or diagram. These sketches highlight important components of a final product such as potential materials, approximate size, design or layout choices, or technology needed.

- Prototypes
  - Whether physical or digital, prototypes of final products provide teachers the opportunity to check for understanding of concepts. Prototypes should not be fancy. Cardboard, construction paper, paper towel rolls, popsicle sticks, straws, pipe cleaners, and lots of glue and tape make for some creative yet efficient prototypes.
  - Using a prototype, students share their understanding of mathematical concepts including measurement, shapes (both two- and three-dimensional), angles, area, perimeter, and scale. If possible, I ask students to post sticky notes on or around their prototype to explain their application of these concepts.

SUMMATIVE ASSESSMENT: PUBLIC PRODUCTS AS EVIDENCE OF LEARNING

As explored in Chapter 8, summative assessments in the PBL mathematics classroom often take the shape of a public product displayed or implemented during a culminating experience. The public product should highlight each of the Six Essential Attributes of the PBL mathematics classroom in action. Upon deciding what public product best fits a project, consider Rigorous Content, Productive Inquiry, Identity & Agency, Authentic Connections, Meaningful Assessment, and Growth Through Reflection. How will the public product provide opportunities to reflect upon each of these attributes? How will the public product lift up rubric categories of content knowledge, Mathematical Habits of Mind, and success skills? Lastly, how will the culminating experience highlight the public product? Check out Figure 16.5, including the following expanded list of ideas, for potential public products, and see Figure 16.6 for a student example.

- Debates
  - Debates about critical topics provide students an outlet to combine research into a topic with mathematical research and knowledge.
  - A high school statistics class partnered with an English class to host mathematical debates. Students debated gun control laws, lowering the voting age, raising the driving age, and marijuana legalization, among other topics. In partners, students researched available information, paying particular attention to the organization and potential statistical bias. Students developed and implemented their own surveys, analyzing data and preparing graphs to support their position. On the day of the debate, students presented information using the debate structure and techniques learned in their English class.
- Game Creation
  - Students of all ages love playing games. Why not give them ownership by creating the rules and game boards? Creating a game explores mathematical concepts of fractions, percentages, probability, geometric concepts, and measurement. Students in upper grades can share

their games with younger children to play and evaluate the effectiveness of their game.

- Cautionary note: Remember that in PBL mathematics, students learn through the process and creation, not simply by the end product, so a game that reviews mathematics concepts probably is not a true PBL mathematics experience.

- Infographic
  - Whether physical or digital, students of all ages can create an infographic, highlighting information learned and visually representing data. My students use Canva to create infographics. Canva is free and provides hundreds of templates to get creative juices flowing. Infographics can be printed and hung around the school or the community.

- Interviews
  - We don't know what we don't know. That's something I tell my students often. An interesting assessment idea is to ask students to interview someone in the community about how they use mathematics in their life. Whether the mathematics is used in a home situation or at work, all mathematics should be uplifted in these interviews. This builds a positive sense of identity and agency in students, who can appreciate the value mathematics plays in a person's everyday life.

- Mathematical Art
  - Mathematics and art pair naturally. Art-based items include jewelry, sculptures, weavings, clothing, fashion accessories, stationery or greeting cards, murals, photographs, and comics.
  - I love showing my students the innovative fashion company Diarrablu, a brand that merges the rich colors and patterns of Africa with mathematical algorithms and concepts. The founder, Diarra Bousso, considers herself a "Creative Mathematician," an incredible embodiment and enactment of mathematical identity.

- Public Service Announcement (PSA)
  - Students love making videos, and creating a PSA allows students to share their learning with the school community, families, or the larger community.

     ○ Students in sixth-grade mathematics studied food labels and created PSAs using their mathematical knowledge of fractions, decimals, percentages, and unit rates to inform the public about healthy eating choices.

- 3D Creation

     ○ Physical or technology-based, three-dimensional items provide hands-on, tangible ways to apply mathematical concepts. The sky truly is the limit on these ideas, but may include scale model energy-efficient homes, new business products, three-dimensional printed objects, vehicle designs, robots or coded items, obstacle courses, or toy designs.

- Website

     ○ Websites act as a digital tool for teams to capture their work. Collaborative website platforms such as Google Sites make it easy for students to work simultaneously. Websites can promote student small businesses, advocate for change based on data and research, or share new learning.

     ○ Websites can easily be promoted to an authentic audience through a school's social media, family communication newsletters, or QR (quick response) codes posted around the school or community.

Figure 16-5 • Public Product Ideas List

Public Product Ideas List

- 3D Creation
- Blog
- Blueprints
- Brochure or Pamphlet
- Book (children's, fiction, nonfiction, comic, graphic novel)
- Budget or Financial Plans
- Coded Video Game or Robotics
- Debates
- Dioramas to Scale
- Event or Fundraiser Plans
- Game Creation
- Infographic
- Interviews
- Letter to Government Official or Policymaker
- Maps
- Mathematical Art
- Models of Natural Phenomenon
- Mural
- Musical Composition
- Podcast
- Poetry
- Public Service Announcement
- Social Media Campaign
- Software Development
- Statistical Analysis
- Survey
- Website

Figure 16-6 • Example Public Product: Fourth-Grade *Dream School* Blueprint

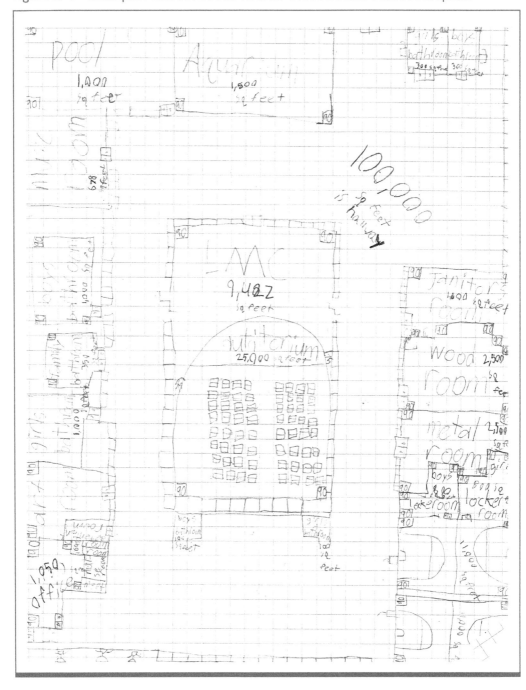

YOUR TURN

Describe the final product you envision students creating. Consider drawing pictures or diagrams of the final product.

_____

_____

_____

CULMINATING EXPERIENCE IDEAS

Creating an authentic product is a major goal in the PBL mathematics classroom; however, if that product does not leave the classroom, then authenticity is not elevated. As PBL mathematics educators, thinking beyond the four walls of a classroom is part of the project process. In today's multimedia age, finding ways to authentically share products digitally becomes increasingly easier when using social media, emails, QR codes on posters, or links on school websites. Remember to check family permissions for videos or photos of students before posting digitally.

As you plan for an audience for your culminating experience, consider inviting in experts who shared during the project process. Family members, administration, and other educators in the school are always a good audience. Business owners, nonprofits, and career professionals may be interested in student projects, especially if the project ties into that organization's mission or vision. I have an ongoing connection to local university professors who are always eager to engage preservice teachers in authentic experiences.

Here's a list of culminating experience ideas to inspire highlighting the public products with an authentic audience in mind, adapted and extended from Pieratt (2020).

- Informative or persuasive presentation to audience members or panelists

- *Shark Tank*–style pitches

- Schoolwide or community exhibition

- Visual display at an art gallery or local library

- Book-signing party at school or a local bookstore

- Red carpet–style screening of films or documentaries

- Local media: nightly news, newspaper article, or magazine article

- "Reveal" or ribbon-cutting ceremony

- Small business sale: consider partnering with a local farmers' market, craft show, or artisan sale

- Trade show–style event, highlighting new products

- Fundraiser or community event

YOUR TURN

What might an authentic culminating event look like for your project? Who would be invited? What role would students have in designing the event?

_____

_____

_____

CONCLUDING THOUGHTS

Having an authentic product, audience, and culminating experience raises the bar for students. When we set high expectations and provide the necessary scaffolds and structures, students rise to the occasion. Time and time again, I have witnessed students persevere and put their best foot forward to meet and often exceed the expectations of a project. Truly, PBL mathematics is an equity lever in our classrooms. Now, more than ever, the time is right to rethink our assessment practices to meet the needs of our unique learners.

PBL POINTS TO PONDER: "I USED TO THINK . . . NOW I THINK . . ."

Given your background knowledge and ongoing understanding of assessing a PBL mathematics experience, complete the following sentence stems regarding the notion of meaningful assessment in the classroom.

☐   I used to think . . . Now I think . . .

Now, reference the statement you wrote at the end of Chapter 8. How have you grown in your understanding of meaningful assessment since reading that chapter? Share your growth using the hashtag #PBLmath.

CHAPTER 17

Reflect

"I learned how big to make the bridge and count really high," shared DeSean excitedly. In his hardhat and vest, four-year-old DeSean described his learning as he measured the length of the hallway using cubes, blocks, and LEGO bricks. DeSean and his classmates determined the length of the bridge for their indoor sensory pathway. They completed their prototypes of the bridge a parent would later construct for the school. To gather student reflections as they neared the end of their project, I spent my morning talking to students individually or in pairs about their bridge design and learning.

261

Talking to two little bridge constructors, I asked questions about their bridge design, the mathematics they learned, and a success they had in the project. Both Clara and Sierra, pictured in Figure 17.1, were eager to share their thoughts.

"Tell me about your bridge. How did you come up with the design?"

"We drewed it out on paper. Clara and me worked together, and Mrs. Umberger helped us put it together," replied Sierra.

"What kinds of shapes did you use in your bridge?"

"It has a rectangle and arches and squares. This rectangle is bigger than the squares 'cause it goes on top," Sierra said, pointing to the rectangle pathway.

"And these are rectangles and we taped them down to make arches," shared Clara, pointing to the three arches on their bridge prototype.

I probed a little deeper: "Fill in the blank. We chose these shapes because . . ."

Sierra jumped in. "It would make it long, and it matched the pictures," she shared, referencing the bridge pictures students saw in the books they read and at the activity stations they participated in daily.

I looked at Clara, who at this point always responded after Sierra, and started the sentence again, prompting her to respond, "Because they would make the bridge strong."

"Wow. Those were good ideas. One last question. What is one thing you did well during this project? I want to hear from each of you, starting with you," I said, pointing to Clara first this time.

"I was good at counting all the animals that went on the bridge," replied Clara, highlighting an activity where students tested the safety of their bridge.

"I was good at everything!" giggled Sierra. Asking her to be more specific, Sierra shared, "I was good at being a friend to Clara and making the shapes."

 The project featured in this vignette is available for download at **https://qrs.ly/56ensfy**.

Figure 17-1 • Prekindergarten Students Share Their Public Product

REFLECTION EXPLORATION

As we know, reflection looks and feels different at each stage of a student's learning process. As educators, we should carefully consider student reflection and provide varied reflection techniques, regardless of the age of the students we teach.

What Are Students Reflecting On?

Spencer (2022) highlighted several aspects of a project where students should engage in self-reflection. Using several of Spencer's ideas and adding in specific goals for the project-based learning (PBL) mathematics classroom, I created a set of questions or sentence stems to engage students of various ages (see Figure 17.2). Returning to ideas explored in Chapter 9, reflective moments should occur both formally and informally throughout the project process, not just at the end of the project.

Figure 17.2 • Reflection Questions and Sentence Stems

Reflection Area and Description (adapted from Spencer, 2022)	Questions or Sentence Stems to Prompt Reflection
Reflection on Content Learning *Students reflect on their growth in learning key content applicable to the project.*	• What were the main mathematical concepts or ideas you learned? • How did you apply those concepts in your project? • What is a mistake or misconception you or a classmate had that helped you learn? • A new vocabulary word or concept I needed to know for this project was _____. This word/concept was essential because _____. • Today I went to Station _____. At this station, I learned _____. My favorite part was _____ because _____.
Reflection on Goals *Students reflect on the initial goals they set individually or as a team, the change in goals, and steps taken to achieve goals.*	• Initially, we had a goal of _____. We now realize the goal should be _____. • One goal that has stayed the same is _____. • One goal that needs to be rewritten is _____. Here is the new goal: _____. • In order to meet our goal, here is a list of three concrete steps that need to happen: _____. • When I met my goal to _____, I felt _____. • I knew I would successfully meet my goal because _____.
Reflection on Project Progress *Students reflect on how they are progressing toward meeting key deadlines or completing products.*	• Circle the best descriptor of your progress: on track, ahead of schedule, somewhat behind, far behind. • Fill out your progress bar showing what percent of the project you have completed. • Are you learning while doing, instead of learning then doing? How is this impacting your progress?

Reflection Area and Description (adapted from Spencer, 2022)	Questions or Sentence Stems to Prompt Reflection
Reflection on the Creative Process *Students reflect on the journey of the project process, not the quality of work.*	• What has been the most challenging part of the project process? • What part of the project process did you feel was easiest? Why? • If you compared your role throughout the project to a car, what part of the car were you? Explain.
Reflection on the Product *Students reflect on the quality of their product, including the focus on research, the diversity of ideas during brainstorming, and the quality of their prototype.*	• How are you making choices about your products? • How are you ensuring a diversity of ideas and perspectives is included in your final product? • How have your ideas changed from initial brainstorm to prototyping to finished product? Why did these ideas change? Were the changes better or due to constraints? • By creating a prototype, I learned _____.

Reflection on Team Dynamics
 	
Students reflect on the collaborative process and decision-making process.
	• Write a thank-you note to a team member who helped you grow as a learner, describing in detail what that team member did or said to help you.
	• Describe a time when your team struggled to make a decision. How did you work through that moment?
	• Check all that apply. When we make decisions as a team:
	   ○ We each present our ideas before making a decision.
	   ○ We take a vote.
	   ○ We argue a lot.
	   ○ We debate the pros and cons of each idea.
	   ○ We draw out our thinking.
	   ○ We jump in quickly and excitedly.
	   ○ Other: _____
	• Draw a picture to represent how your team is functioning.
	• Are you asking your team members questions? How does this feedback loop help your project develop?

(Continued)

(Continued)

Reflection Area and Description (adapted from Spencer, 2022)	Questions or Sentence Stems to Prompt Reflection
Reflection on Identity as a Mathematician or Change Agent *Students reflect on how they embodied the role of a mathematician as well as how they can use mathematics to be a change agent in society.*	• I felt most like a mathematician when I _____. • I used to think mathematicians _____, but now I think _____. • I do/do not consider myself a mathematician because _____. • I can use math to _____. • Without mathematics, I would not be able to _____. • One way I can use math to help my community is to _____.

Reflection on Mathematical Habits of Mind
 	
Students reflect on the habits of mind that mathematicians exhibit.
	• You've shown a lot of perseverance in problem solving. Fill in the blanks to capture your work.
	
	  ○ One strategy that didn't work out was _____ because _____. Even though it didn't work out, I learned _____.
	
	  ○ I've tried _____ and _____, but I haven't tried _____.
	
	• Is communicating mathematically a strength or an area of growth for you? Why?
	
	• Describe the mathematics tools you used to complete the project. Which mathematics tool was most important? Why?

Reflection on Success Skills *Students reflect on skills such as collaboration, communication, organization, empathy, and adaptability.*	• I grew in my ability to communicate effectively by _____. • A strategy we used to stay organized was _____. I can use this strategy in my own life when I need to _____. • There is a famous saying, "The only constant in life is change." How did you or your team have to change or adapt your project? How did you respond to that change? • How did completing this project help you better understand another human being? • How are you taking responsibility for your learning? • How are you celebrating your learning with others (peers, friends, family, teachers, pets)?

Obviously, giving students an extensive list of questions for reflection is not ideal. Consider three things when reflecting: *short*, *varied*, and *often*. Short reflections help students focus on the most pertinent aspect of the project. If you notice a lot of tension among team members, pause to help all students reflect on team dynamics. If students recently engaged in mini workshops or a series of stations presenting a new concept, ask students to reflect on content learning. Depending on the length of the project, refer students back to their initial goals; help them clarify how goals have changed, perhaps rewriting or revising goals.

How Are Students Reflecting?

As explored in Chapter 9, providing students with a variety of ways to reflect engages them throughout the learning process. Even our youngest learners should engage in reflection, using more verbal or visual options. Consider including shorter, more frequent opportunities to reflect throughout a project. Here is a list of ideas for ways to capture reflection in the PBL mathematics classroom.

- Mathematics Journal or Notebook
  - Prompting ongoing reflection and the ability to reference prior thoughts, ask students to use a mathematics notebook or journal. This could be physical or digital. Digital platforms allow students to quickly and easily share their reflections with teachers or peers, such as Seesaw for younger students or Google Docs, Sites, or Slides for older students.

- Exit Ticket
  - Consider using only one question or sentence stem to keep the reflection narrowly focused. I often use a notecard or a half sheet of paper to physically remind myself and my students to keep the reflection short.

- Survey
  - A survey helps students reflect quickly by choosing an answer from a list. Sometimes open-ended questions overwhelm students, so providing numerical options, categories, or rating scales aids students in a quick pulse

check. A survey also provides the teacher with a quick snapshot of the entire class. Using Google Forms or SurveyMonkey makes it quick and easy to gather and display data.

- One Word
  - Ask students to share one word (or phrase) that captures their learning for the day. This can be shared in a popcorn style (students randomly shout it out) or as a wrap-around (start with one student and sequentially move around the room). Digitally capture these words using Answer Garden, which creates a cloudlike wordle highlighting the most common words shared.

- "I Used to Think . . . but Now I Think . . ."
  - This thinking routine from Project Zero (Harvard Graduate School of Education, 2022) provides students a scaffolded sentence to consider how their thinking has changed. This normalizes the fact that new learning brings new thinking, emphasizing growth.

- Progress Bars
  - Want a way to bring fractions or percentages into reflection? Provide students with an empty progress bar (think of this like the battery bar on your device). Ask students to shade in the progress bar showing the fraction or percent of the project or specific task they have completed.

- Analogies
  - I have a set of nearly twenty cards showing different hats—like a wizard hat, hardhat, artist beret, top hat, racecar helmet, and pilot's hat. I lay these pictures out and ask my students, "What hat matches your project work style right now?" In my sixth-grade classroom, one student chose the artist beret, saying, "I'm tapping into my creativity as I design my accessible zoo," while another student picked up the pilot's hat, replying, "It was a bumpy takeoff, but I'm finding smooth air

now that I've gotten farther into the project." Using analogies like the hats provides students a starting point (like a sentence stem), but freely allows them to make unique connections to share their thinking.

- Think-Ink-Pair-Share
  - After posing a question or providing a sentence stem, students pause for reflection, write their thoughts, then share with a neighbor. Writing and verbalizing a reflection solidifies learning and growth.

- Rubric Calibration
  - Ask students to compare their current work to the criteria on the rubric. Students can use the rubric to set goals. For example, a student might reflect, "I am currently *emerging* in my application of unit rate and would like to be *proficient*. To meet this goal, I need to . . ." The reflection on quality may lead to self-assessment, so ensure students set goals for action.

- Drawings or Sketches
  - Students convey a lot through drawing. Spencer (2022) shares a favorite way to capture reflective drawings from students, providing students a "handout of a mind and the prompt, 'Sketch what's going on in your mind right now as you think about this project.'"

When planning for a project, encourage students to reflect at critical learning moments throughout the project. Having a set of reflection options provides you flexibility to embed reflective moments when they naturally occur. Reflective activities like One Word are perfect to embed quickly at the end of a class period. Implement activities like Analogies during work time, while walking around the classroom or hosting students for mini conferences. What's important is that students reflect frequently, recognizing reflection as a tool for growth and continued learning.

YOUR TURN

Consider two questions: (I) *What are students reflecting on?* and (2) *How are students reflecting?* Think about a specific opportunity for reflection in the project you brainstormed. Plan for intentional reflection answering those two questions.

What are students reflecting on?	How are students reflecting?

GROWTH THROUGH CRITIQUE AND REVISION

Critique and revision opportunities become apparent with ongoing reflection. While reflection occurs throughout the entire process, critique and revision focus on the products of learning. Sometimes revision happens naturally, such as when a student recognizes and corrects a mathematical mistake. More often than not, though, as educators, we need to provide the conditions and structures for our students to revise their work.

Critique

Before engaging in critique, ensure community agreements for critique have been established and practiced in low-stakes environments. One of my favorite videos to show students how to critique is *Austin's Butterfly*, developed by Ron Berger, the chief academic officer of EL Education (2016). In this video, Berger highlights his three rules for critiquing work: be kind, be specific, and be helpful. These three rules apply no matter the age of students in the classroom. I also use a community agreement: "Critique the work, not the person."

This centers the feedback on the actual products created, not the person or people who created them. These community agreements can and should be practiced early and often in the mathematics classroom.

As students feel ready to engage in critique, here are some scaffolds, routines, and protocols that can be incorporated into the PBL mathematics classroom.

- Compare Examples
  - Whether you have saved student work from prior years or you create an example yourself, have students compare these examples to their product as well as the products of other students or teams. Ask questions such as "What makes each product unique? How does the example show high-quality work? What steps do you [or another student/team] need to take to show that same degree of quality? Based on the example, what parts of the product still need finalizing?"

- Glows & Grows
  - Ask students to engage in this critique routine by sharing verbally or in writing *glows* (strengths) and *grows* (areas for improvement) for another student's project. Depending on the students' age, I may require a number of each type of feedback statement—for example, at least two glows and one grow per project. Sentence stems lead to even stronger critique sentences by students. For example, "My favorite part of this project is . . ." leads to a *glow*. "One thing you might consider is . . ." leads to a *grow*.

- Good, Better, Best
  - Pieratt (2019) created a critique routine called Good, Better, Best based on the mantra "Good, better, best—never let it rest." This routine, similar to Glows & Grows, allows students to provide both positive and constructive feedback.
    - ❖ Good: "One *good* aspect of this project is . . ."
    - ❖ Better: "Something that would make this project *better* is . . ."
    - ❖ Best: "To make this project the *best* it can be, consider . . ."

- Gallery Walk
  - During a Gallery Walk, display products throughout the room like at an art gallery. On sticky notes, notecards, or slips of paper, students provide feedback to peers. Feedback is collected on or near the product, ideally facedown so no other student peeks at the feedback. Ask students to write on the back of a sticky note before posting to keep feedback hidden.

- See-A-B
  - This protocol focuses on the skill of observation. Both partners "see" (look at, examine, explore, observe) Partner B's product for a designated amount of time. Then, Partner A provides feedback to Partner B. This feedback could be scaffolded as Glows & Grows or Good, Better, Best. Finally, Partner B responds to the feedback, developing at least one goal based off the feedback from Partner A. Roles then switch.

- Tuning
  - Originally developed by the School Reform Initiative (2021) and adapted heavily by several PBL schools and organizations, the Tuning protocol helps students fine-tune their projects. I have used this protocol with kindergarten through high school students, slightly changing the timing or altering steps to be developmentally appropriate. As the teacher, I call time for each "step" of the Tuning protocol so students focus on the critique experience, not the timing.
  - Tuning protocols with three participants per group is ideal. One student plays the role of presenter while two students play the role of the audience. Roles are switched, with the protocol happening three times so each participant can play the role of presenter. See Figure 17.3 for a sample Tuning protocol geared for upper elementary through high school students as well as Figure 17.4 for an abbreviated Tuning protocol used with early elementary students.

Figure 17-3 • Tuning Protocol for Upper Elementary Through High School Students

Step	Description	Timing
Presentation	Presenter shares overview of the project, highlighting both key concepts and skills learned. Presenter shares a struggle, whether current or past. Audience listens silently.	5 minutes
Clarification	Audience asks clarifying questions. Presenter responds. • Can you tell me more about . . . ? • I was confused by . . . • What did you mean when you said . . . ?	2 minutes
Gather Thoughts	Audience writes down thoughts they want to share. Audience uses rubric to determine what parts of the project are "in tune" with the project goals. Presenter sits quietly. If culturally appropriate, presenter turns their chair to the side or faces backwards to visually and physically practice the art of listening, not responding, during the next two steps.	1 minute
"I like . . ."	Audience shares what they liked. • I like . . . • When [presenter name] said _____, I felt . . . • [Presenter name] was good at . . . • One of the most powerful ideas was . . . Presenter listens.	2 minutes
"I wonder . . ."	Audience shares concerns or possible ideas. • I wonder . . . • One thing I might consider changing is . . . • I'm not sure _____ was the most effective choice. • When [name] said _____, I was wondering if . . . • [Name] could use more/less of . . . Presenter listens.	2 minutes
Reflection	Presenter reflects on useful feedback. • Thank you for _____. • When you said _____, I felt . . . • I definitely want to include the idea to . . . Audience listens.	1 minute
Final Thoughts	Presenter and audience engage in final thoughts, including potential ideas to continue or enhance the project.	2 minutes
	Total:	15 minutes

Figure 17-4 • Abbreviated Tuning Protocol for Early Elementary School Students

Step	Description	Timing
Presentation	Presenter shares overview of project, highlighting both academic learning and product creation. Audience listens silently.	3 minutes
Questions	Audience asks questions. Presenter responds. • Why did you . . . ? • How did you . . . ? *Note:* Consider question stems along the five *W*s (*who, what, where, when, why*) and one *H* (*how*).	2 minutes
"I like . . ."	Audience shares what they liked. • I like . . . • The best part was . . . Presenter thanks audience members after sharing comments.	I minute, 30 seconds
"I wonder . . ."	Audience shares concerns or possible ideas. • I wonder if . . . Presenter thanks audience members after sharing comments.	I minute, 30 seconds
	Total:	8 minutes

Revision

It's equally important to highlight the revision process. I remember my English class in middle school when we learned revision symbols such as capitalizing a letter, inserting a comma, or indenting a paragraph. When turning in a final paper, I needed to include all the drafts, including the peer-reviewed drafts. In the PBL mathematics classroom, students show how growth has been achieved through revision. Here are some strategies to highlight the revision process.

- Before & After Photos
  - This revision strategy asks students to take a photo before and after revising a product. Then, students annotate the photo or add a caption describing the revisions that occurred and why the changes led to a stronger, more mathematically accurate product.

- Calculation Annotation
  - Ask students to recheck all mathematical calculations. Have students explain verbally or in writing why they believe their solutions are reasonable. Ask students to annotate solution points along the way. This directly connects to the Mathematical Habit of Mind of Reason & Justify.

- Portfolios
  - Whether digital or physical, asking students to save work during a project to put into a portfolio of learning is an authentic way to capture the revision process. Seeing iterations of work, from sketches to prototypes to final products, highlights the natural revision process that occurs.

- Revision Reflections
  - Ask students to share a short written or verbal reflection about the revisions they made to their product. Provide sentence stems such as "Based on the feedback by a peer to _____, I decided to _____" or "After reviewing the rubric, I realized I needed to revise _____ in order to _____."

YOUR TURN

Critique and revision should occur at least once before the final product and culminating event. How do you want students to engage in critique? What about revision?

_____

_____

_____

CONCLUDING THOUGHTS

As we think about our Driving Question for this book, "How can I bring project-based learning [PBL] to life in the mathematics classroom?," consider the role of reflection and critique. In time, reflection in the PBL mathematics classroom should become second nature to students. Growth in content understanding, Mathematical Habits of Mind, and success skills comes after intentional reflection with an implementable plan of action. A defining characteristic of a PBL mathematics experience is the use of critique as a means for students to reflect upon next steps and revise work. What can you try in your classroom to engage more frequently in reflection for growth?

PBL POINTS TO PONDER: WHAT? SO WHAT? NOW WHAT?

Consider your current experience with using critique and reflection in the mathematics classroom as well as your ongoing learning of how to use critique and reflection in the PBL mathematics classroom. Share your *Now What?* using the hashtag #PBLmath.

☐ **What?** Describe what you have done in terms of critique and reflection in your current classroom.

☐ **So What?** Make meaning of those experiences. What impact did critique and reflection have on your students? On your teaching practice?

☐ **Now What?** With your growing understanding of critique and reflection, plan forward by identifying actions and implications for you and your students.

CHAPTER 18

Design the Experience

Eight bus stops and fifteen local businesses later, my crew of seventh-grade students were exhausted yet elated. They had just delivered personally designed mugs to local business owners and employees as prototypes of promotional items for their stores. For six weeks, these seventh graders communicated with their clients at these local businesses, crafting a mug to meet the needs of their client. Presenting each client with the mug and celebrating their hard work through a daylong schedule of stops throughout our city, these students deservedly felt a sense of accomplishment. As their teacher, I joyfully watched each presentation, seeing the pride on their faces as they shared their final product. Yet, how did this day come to be? How did these students engage in this authentic *Mugs O' Math* project?

Planning a project from start to finish may seem overwhelming, yet with the support of all the ideas presented in this book, and this concluding chapter, you can successfully develop a high-quality project-based learning (PBL) mathematics

> ## Need to Knows
>
> - How do I plan a project-based learning mathematics experience for my students from start to finish?

experience for your students. To aid your design of a project, let me share my planning process for the seventh-grade *Mugs O' Math* project.

This chapter will explore step-by-step how to plan a project, referencing all the ideas from the previous chapters. You can find templates of this planning process on the companion website at https://qrs.ly/56ensfy.

 Templates are available for download at **https://qrs.ly/56ensfy**.

BRAINSTORM

Remember as a student all those times your teachers asked you to brainstorm before writing a paragraph or an essay? Well, creating a project starts with that same process. Let's brainstorm! Brainstorming takes on many forms, from mind maps to doodles to bulleted lists. As you brainstorm your PBL mathematics experience, consider how each of the Six Essential Attributes impacts the overall project. Figure 18.1 highlights my project brainstorm for the *Mugs O' Math* project.

MAP THE PROJECT

After a project brainstorm, consider mapping out the entire project. This is like creating a large outline or road map that highlights the essential experiences that move students from Point A (the project launch) to Point B (the project conclusion).

 The project map template is available for download at **https://qrs.ly/56ensfy**.

Figure 18-1 • *Mugs O' Math* Project Brainstorm Example

PROJECT BRAINSTORM

Brainstorm project ideas by considering the top three Essential Attributes first. Ensure the Rigorous Content, Authentic Connections, and Meaningful Assessment are aligned, forming a cohesive project.

Rigorous Content

What content standards will this project meet? What Mathematical Habits of Mind and success skills will students engage in?

content standards:
- surface area & volume of 3D objects
- circumference & area of a circle
- formal writing

Mathematical Habit of Mind:
- Communicate Mathematically

success skill:
- design thinking (emphasize iteration)

Authentic Connections

What will be my authentic situation or problem? What audience might care about this topic?

authentic situation:
- small businesses need support marketing their business
- small businesses owners may not have time or finances to create marketing materials

authentic audience:
* small business owner Downtown Mainstreet Inc.
* marketing majors from local universities
* businesses that develop promotional items & materials

Meaningful Assessment

What product will my students create? What culminating experience will highlight student work?

product ideas:
- formal introductory letter
- client intake form
- ongoing correspondence
- orthographic sketches
- Tinkercad designs & video
- mathematical specifications sheet (aka spec sheet)
- 3D-printed mug

culminating experience ideas:
- visiting each small business
- short presentation by students to business owner or employee
- #socialmediablitz
- local news coverage

Using your brainstorm of the first three Essential Attributes, brainstorm ways you will engage students in Productive Inquiry, enhance student Identity & Agency, and promote Growth Through Reflection.

Productive Inquiry

What activities will engage students in learning about content? How will students develop the Mathematical Habits of Mind and success skills needed for the project?

activities:
- investigation of promo items
- nets of 3D shapes
- surface area & volume of a cylinder exploration
- converting cubic cm to fluid oz
- professional writing & communication
- how to use 3D printing software (Tinkercad)

potential experts:
- Designz (local promotional item business)
- university marketing majors
- In*Tech Integrated Marketing Services

Identity & Agency

How will students develop a mathematical identity or increase their sense of agency through this project?

identity:
- students embody role of a marketing professional
- student identity as a mathematician elevated through communicating mathematics with client (small business owner or employee)

agency:
- students use mathematics to positively impact a small business
- students choose businesses run by diverse family or community members, helping these local businesses thrive & compete against larger businesses

Growth Through Reflection

How will students engage in critique? How will students use reflection to grow in content understanding and skills?

critique opportunities:
- ongoing feedback from client (small business owner or employee)
- Gallery Walk of initial sketches (Glows & Grows)
- See-A-B protocol with draft of Tinkercad designs
- Tuning protocol before submitting finalmug design

reflection opportunities:
- after receiving feedback from client
- after each critique protocol (above)
- after presentation of mugs to local business owners: audio reflection

YOUR TURN

How is the project you brainstormed in Chapter 12 aligned to the Six Essential Attributes of the PBL mathematics classroom?

PROJECT BRAINSTORM

Brainstorm project ideas by considering the top three Essential Attributes first. Ensure the Rigorous Content, Authentic Connections, and Meaningful Assessment are aligned, forming a cohesive project.

Rigorous Content	Authentic Connections	Meaningful Assessment
What content standards will this project meet? What Mathematical Habits of Mind and success skills will students engage in?	What will be my authentic situation or problem? What audience might care about this topic?	What product will my students create? What culminating experience will highlight student work?

Using your brainstorm of the first three Essential Attributes, brainstorm ways you will engage students in Productive Inquiry, enhance student Identity & Agency, and promote Growth Through Reflection.

Productive Inquiry	Identity & Agency	Growth Through Reflection
What activities will engage students in learning about content? How will students develop the Mathematical Habits of Mind and success skills needed for the project?	How will students develop a mathematical identity or increase their sense of agency through this project?	How will students engage in critique? How will students use reflection to grow in content understanding and skills?

PLAN THE LAUNCH

Start your engines! Time to plan that engaging project launch. Remember, a project launch has four key pieces: the engaging hook, driving question, project overview, and "need to know" questions.

Driving Question

I like to begin by writing, revising, and refining my driving question first. Remember, a strong driving question is engaging to students, open-ended, and aligned to learning goals. Here are a few iterations of the driving question of my *Mugs O' Math* project. To make my thinking visible, I've included annotations of why I made each change. After reading my example in Figure 18.2, try creating several iterations of your driving question!

Figure 18-2 • *Mugs O'Math* Project Driving Question Iteration

Iteration Number	Possible Driving Question (DQ)	Reason to Change
1.	How do businesses create promotional items that attract and retain customers?	This DQ doesn't really align to my project goals. Based on my wording, the emphasis is on how and why businesses create promotional items, not on how students could do this.
2.	How can we use mathematics to create a mug for a local business?	This DQ is moving in the right direction. It brings the student (we) into the action. It specifies a product and is aligned to learning goals. This DQ doesn't sound engaging to students. The students know they will be using mathematics, so I don't need to say that.
3.	How can we, as seventh graders, create promotional items to help local business owners attract and retain customers?	This is really close to what I want! I can think of a better role because my students are already seventh graders. The end of the question gets a little wordy.
4.	How can we, as marketing professionals, partner with local business owners to create a promotional item?	Final choice! I like the role as I imagine students in teams of two or three, where they pretend they are a marketing agency and have even more specific roles within their agency. I like the change in word choice to *partner* with local businesses to emphasize the collaboration about to happen.

Engaging Hook + Project Overview + "Need to Knows"

Now that I have a driving question, I determine the rest of the launch experience (refer back to Chapter 13). To kick off the *Mugs O' Math* project, I decided to rearrange and redecorate my room to jolt students into an immediate sense that something was different. I arranged my room so that my desk acted like a "reception desk" near the entrance to the classroom. I then put student desks into pods of three (previously they were pods of four). I printed table tents that looked like office name plates to signify where each student would sit initially before moving into their official team. All around the room, I placed promotional items I had accumulated such as mugs, pens, drawstring bags, stress balls, sticky notes, stickers, and water bottles. This dramatic change of scenery shocked students as they entered class, leading to a discussion of promotional items and a successful kickoff of the launch experience.

I know for every launch that I need to provide students with a project overview. In planning, I consider what is the best means to share this information. For *Mugs O' Math*, I considered the following options:

- A one-page project overview sheet—students could peruse in pairs or as a whole class

- A slideshow of project goals and expectations—facilitated by me with the whole class

- Information loaded onto a website—could be pairs or whole class

- A document loaded onto the school's learning management system—should be done no matter what

I decided to create a one-page project overview sheet, which I also loaded onto our school's learning management system. Additionally, this project overview sheet was easily shared via email with the families of my students, providing clear communication between home and school.

Lastly, I needed to decide how I would collect "need to knows." I decided to use a Write-Pair-Square-Share method. Individually, students recorded their "need to know" questions on a sticky note. Students partnered with a classmate to compare and consolidate questions. Partners then "paired up" again, forming groups of four. These small groups presented their top four "need to know" questions to the entire group to capture a classroom list.

How will you engage your students from the onset of the project? How will you share vital project information? How will you orchestrate the "need to know" process?

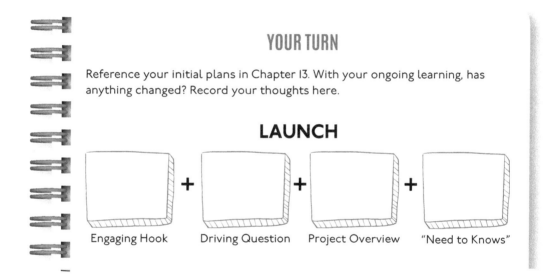

YOUR TURN

Reference your initial plans in Chapter 13. With your ongoing learning, has anything changed? Record your thoughts here.

LAUNCH

Engaging Hook　+　Driving Question　+　Project Overview　+　"Need to Knows"

PLAN THE PROJECT CONCLUSION

I love musical theater! As a child, I grew up acting, singing, and dancing under the hot lights of the stage. To embrace the role I received in a show, I always began by envisioning myself on stage as this character. What was I wearing? How was my hair fashioned? How did I walk? How did I talk? How did I interact with other characters on stage? How did the audience view me: As a hero? A villain? A supporting character? How did I feel after a successful performance?

Visioning the end of an experience is not unique to my time in theater. Sports teams mentally walk through a successful game. Content developers engage in a cognitive walkthrough of new apps, games, and websites. Wedding planners vision the happy couple's experience from the start to the end of their wedding day. Business professionals walk through major presentations.

Planning with the end in mind for a PBL mathematics project is one way to strengthen the conclusion of a project. A project conclusion includes the final opportunity for critique and revision, a final product, a culminating experience, and a reflection opportunity.

In your mind, zoom in on the final product and culminating experience. Let's see how this can be enhanced by completing a cognitive walkthrough. Try it now!

YOUR TURN

Vision what you want the culminating experience to look like, sound like, and feel like for your students. What does the final product look like? Who is part of this experience? How do students know they have been successful? What does success look like? How are students communicating mathematically?

_____

_____

_____

When I envisioned my culminating experience for the *Mugs O' Math* project, I initially visioned all students choosing a local business represented by one of our Rotary Clubs. I thought students would be excited to attend a Rotary Club meeting or luncheon, sharing their experience by revealing their mugs. As I continued to create the project, I changed this vision as I realized student choice of a business was key to engaging students and developing agency. Therefore, I chose not to limit students to businesses that were part of the Rotary Club. However, the idea of presenting each business owner with a mug face-to-face remained a central goal of the culminating experience, as highlighted by the introductory story to this chapter.

MAP THE MILESTONES FROM LAUNCH TO CONCLUSION

Now that the launch and project conclusion have been mapped, it's time to plan the milestones (see Chapter 14). Each milestone should be connected to student "need to know" questions, or what we anticipate students will ask. These "need to knows" should align to the project's content and skills goals, highlighting evidence of what students know and are able to do as a result of their learning through the project.

One technique to start developing milestones is to put yourself in the mind of your students. *I know: Kinda scary, right?* Try picking two or three students who represent different pockets of your classroom. What kinds of questions would each of these students ask? Make a list of these questions, then determine which questions might serve as anticipated "need to knows" and which questions will help develop the scaffolds needed to support students throughout the project.

Figure 18.3 shows my attempt to explore questions from three different perspectives. I've listed salient characteristics of each student to create a picture of their needs.

Figure 18-3 • Student Perspective to Brainstorm *Mugs O' Math* Project "Need to Knows"

Student A: Seventh-grade boy, lots of energy, hands-on learner, loves Minecraft, works hard in class, understands mathematics conceptually but struggles with numeracy	Student B: Seventh-grade girl, personable, kind, empathetic, struggles with writing, strong mathematics skills and positive mathematics identity	Student C: Seventh-grade girl, very social with friends, artistic, verbally says she hates mathematics but will give effort when working one-on-one, strong family ties
• Will we be making mugs out of clay? • Will everyone get to design a mug? • Do mugs have to be cylindrical, or can we make them any shape we want, like a cube? • Do we get to work on laptops or iPads? • Do we get to use a calculator?	• How will we talk to businesspeople, on the phone or through email? • How will we know what the businesspeople want? • How will we know how many ounces go into the mug without printing it? • How big can the mug be?	• Can I choose my aunt's hair salon? • Do I have to email my aunt if I already know her? • Do we get to choose our team? • Will we be making 2D or 3D mugs? • Can I be the drawer? • Do we get to dress up to visit the businesspeople?

Writing these questions from my students' perspectives helped me determine which questions and ideas would lead to strong milestones. I used questions from my brainstorm in the mind of my students to develop four project milestones centered on an anticipated "need to know" question:

- How do we communicate effectively with business professionals?

- How can we design a mug using geometric shapes that promotes the business?

- How do we ensure the mug meets the specifications of the business?

- How do we balance artistic license and creativity with feedback from the business professionals?

Now that I had questions to guide each milestone, I considered what activities would guide students toward answering each of these milestone "need to knows" (see Chapters 15, 16, and 17). I perused my curriculum for lessons, mini workshops, and station activities connected to my content goals. I included problem-solving tasks aligned to content standards as part of a milestone. I thought about what scaffolding sheets, thinking routines, and timed protocols would lead all students to create high-quality evidence of learning for each milestone. Using a rubric detailing what high-quality evidence of learning would look like for each standard, I determined what formative assessment would encapsulate each milestone, including how students would reflect upon their growth.

This process takes time and practice. Not a project goes by that I don't bounce ideas off my colleagues for, seeking their wisdom and insight into the project activities.

Explore my completed planning map in Figure 18.4 to see how the *Mugs O'Math* project unfolds from launch to project conclusion. Try mapping out your own project milestones using the templates available for download at https://qrs.ly/56ensfy.

Figure 18-4 • *Mugs O'Math* Example Planning Map

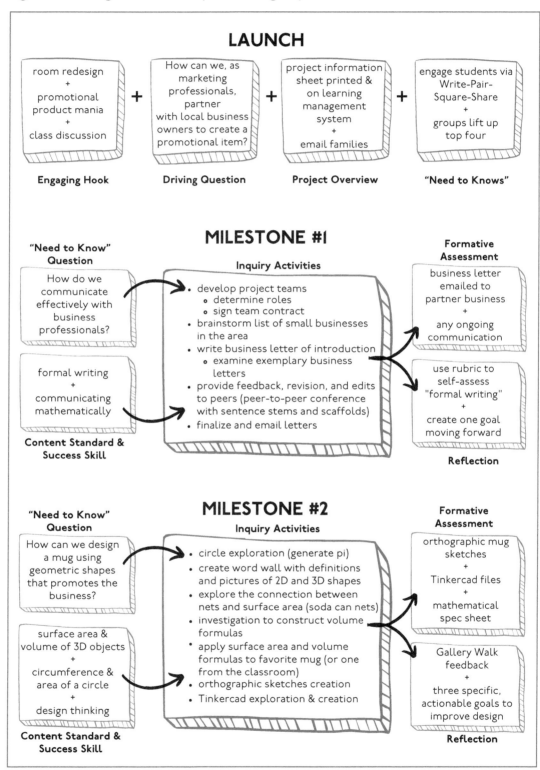

(*Continued*)

(*Continued*)

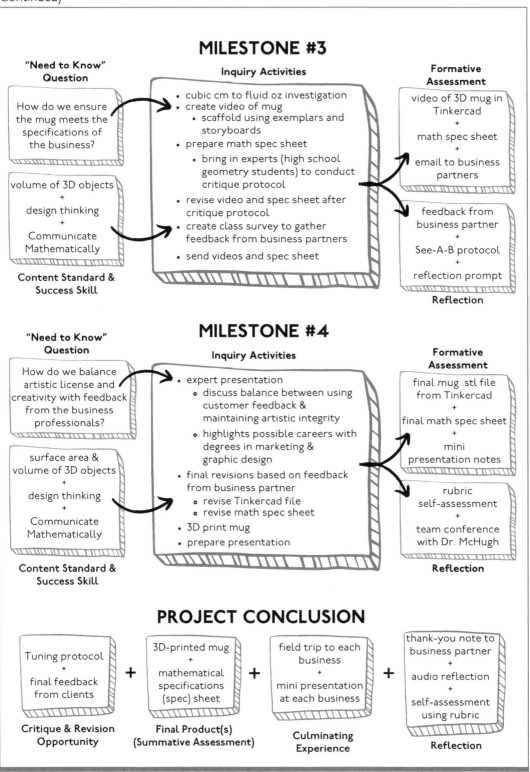

MILESTONE #3

"Need to Know" Question

How do we ensure the mug meets the specifications of the business?

volume of 3D objects
+
design thinking
+
Communicate Mathematically

Content Standard & Success Skill

Inquiry Activities

- cubic cm to fluid oz investigation
- create video of mug
  - scaffold using exemplars and storyboards
- prepare math spec sheet
  - bring in experts (high school geometry students) to conduct critique protocol
- revise video and spec sheet after critique protocol
- create class survey to gather feedback from business partners
- send videos and spec sheet

Formative Assessment

video of 3D mug in Tinkercad
+
math spec sheet
+
email to business partners

feedback from business partner
+
See-A-B protocol
+
reflection prompt

Reflection

MILESTONE #4

"Need to Know" Question

How do we balance artistic license and creativity with feedback from the business professionals?

surface area & volume of 3D objects
+
design thinking
+
Communicate Mathematically

Content Standard & Success Skill

Inquiry Activities

- expert presentation
  - discuss balance between using customer feedback & maintaining artistic integrity
  - highlights possible careers with degrees in marketing & graphic design
- final revisions based on feedback from business partner
  - revise Tinkercad file
  - revise math spec sheet
- 3D print mug
- prepare presentation

Formative Assessment

final mug .stl file from Tinkercad
+
final math spec sheet
+
mini presentation notes

rubric self-assessment
+
team conference with Dr. McHugh

Reflection

PROJECT CONCLUSION

Tuning protocol
+
final feedback from clients

Critique & Revision Opportunity

+

3D-printed mug
+
mathematical specifications (spec) sheet

Final Product(s) (Summative Assessment)

+

field trip to each business
+
mini presentation at each business

Culminating Experience

+

thank-you note to business partner
+
audio reflection
+
self-assessment using rubric

Reflection

PLAN FOR DAILY LESSONS FROM LAUNCH TO CONCLUSION

The last step in planning a project is to take your project map and create daily lessons for each phase of the project, from launch to milestones to project conclusion. The map provides an excellent overview of the entire project. Now, it's time to move from big-picture to detailed planning.

Most teachers feel comfortable planning daily lessons. Use your expertise of your students, your teaching experience, your curriculum guides, and your colleagues to guide daily planning. Refer back to the ideas from Chapters 13–17 to enhance daily planning specific to PBL mathematics.

Here are a few additional considerations to take into account as you plan your project. Think about the following questions centered on *time* and *resources*:

- How many class periods total can the entire project take? How many class periods should each phase of the project take: launch, each milestone, and project conclusion?

- What work time will be given in class? What work (if any) is expected to be completed outside of class?

- What experts can help my students grow in content knowledge? What experts can provide feedback to my students? How will these experts interact with my students (face-to-face, Zoom, at their place of work)?

- What opportunities do I have to connect the project to field trips? When can those be scheduled? What is the cost?

- What access do I have to materials needed for this project? What financial cost, if any, will this pose to my students? How can I ensure equitable access to high-quality materials or technology for all students?

- How can families play a role in supporting this project?

CONCLUDING THOUGHTS

I remember implementing my first PBL mathematics experience. There were some great successes, but as I wrapped up the project, I realized what I hoped to accomplish differed from what actually transpired. Was it a failure? No. Was it a raging success? Not at all. That first project was just okay. Had I not been committed to PBL in my mathematics classroom, I maybe would have stopped after that first project. The amount of time, energy, and planning to develop the project at first did not seem worth the outcome. However, in time, with reflection and continued practice, my projects became more and more successful, as evidenced by student engagement and academic growth.

One strategy I use to embrace the journey of designing and implementing a PBL mathematics experience is to be transparent and honest with my students. From the beginning, I share with my students this is a new experience, asking for their input on ways to improve the project. I usually pause for a midpoint calibration with the students, pausing to examine the learning goals and project objectives. Do they align? What adjustments do we need to make? Then, at the conclusion, I ask for feedback on the entire project. This often takes the form of a survey, with a Likert scale prompting student responses to questions such as the following:

- The launch captured my attention. [*I usually remind students of the launch experience.*]

- By the end of the project, I could answer the driving question.

- The project topic interested me.

- I enjoyed creating the product.

- The mathematics applied in the project helped me grow as a learner.

Designing and implementing your first project is exciting. Hold on to that excitement. Accept struggles as opportunities for growth. Daily, we ask our students to try something outside of their comfort zone, to embody that role of learner and mathematician. Now it's your turn! Embrace the experience.

PBL POINTS TO PONDER: CIRCLE OF VIEWPOINTS

Consider two different viewpoints: (1) a student with a positive mathematical identity and (2) a student who struggles with mathematics. Use the following script (numbers 1–3) to consider what it would be like to engage in your project. Then proceed to the wrap-up.

1. I am thinking of engaging in this project from the point of view of ...

2. I think ... [*Describe your project experience from your viewpoint. Take on the character of your viewpoint.*]

3. A question I have from this viewpoint is ... [*Ask a question from this viewpoint.*]

Wrap-up: What new ideas or insights do you have about your project you didn't have before? What new questions do you have? What implications are there for your project moving forward?

Conclusion

Congratulations! Throughout the book, our Driving Question was "How can I bring project-based learning [PBL] to life in the mathematics classroom?" How fully can you answer this question? As you engaged in the interactive sections of the book, you should now possess a robust PBL mathematics experience planned for your students. Now what? Time to put that project into action. Try it with your students. Reflect upon the experience. Celebrate successes. Embrace opportunities for growth. Remember no project will ever be perfect. Just like our students, we must give ourselves the space to make mistakes and learn from them. This is what makes teaching both an art and a science.

In the end, though, when you see your students the following school year, at high school graduation, in the grocery store as adults, or on whatever social media platform is still going ten, twenty, thirty years from now, know the ultimate goal of any project is to be an experience—an experience to share with your students; to develop a stronger, more authentic relationship with your students; to help your students realize their full potential; to light a fire for learning in your students; to bring change to the community and possibly the world. Experiences, like those created in the PBL mathematics classroom, live on in the hearts and minds of our students years after the daily lessons have faded. Embrace the experience.

References

Adams, H. (1918). *The education of Henry Adams*. Houghton Mifflin. https://www.gutenberg.org/files/2044/2044-h/2044-h.htm

Aguirre, J., Mayfield-Ingram, K., & Martin, D. (2013). *The impact of identity in K–8 mathematics learning and teaching: Rethinking equity-based practices*. National Council of Teachers of Mathematics.

Ani, K. (2021). *Dear Citizen Math: How math class can inspire a more rational and respectful society*. Damascus Rodeo.

Appleton, J. J., Christenson, S. L., Kim, D., & Reschly, A. L. (2006). Measuring cognitive and psychological engagement: Validation of the student engagement instrument. *Journal of School Psychology, 44*, 427–445.

Bartell, T., Yeh, C., Felton-Koestler, M. D., & Berry, R. Q. (2022). *Upper elementary mathematics lessons to explore, understand, and respond to social injustice*. Corwin.

Barton, C. (2016). *Whoosh!: Lonnie Johnson's super-soaking stream of inventions*. Charlesbridge.

Becker, H. (2018). *Counting on Katherine: How Katherine Johnson saved Apollo 13*. Henry Holt.

Bergeron, H. (2022, March 3). *Using PBL to build a strong learning community*. Edutopia. https://www.edutopia.org/article/using-pbl-build-strong-learning-community

Berry, R. Q., III, Conway, B. M., IV, Lawler, B. R., & Staley, J. R. (2020). *High school mathematics lessons to explore, understand, and respond to social injustice*. Corwin.

Bloom, B. S., Engelhart, M. D., Hill, W. H., Furst, E. J., & Krathwohl, D. R. (1956). *Taxonomy of educational objectives: The classification of educational goals*. Handbook I: Cognitive domain. David McKay.

Boaler, J. (2015). *Mathematical mindsets: Unleashing students' potential through creative mathematics, inspiring messages and innovative teaching*. Jossey-Bass.

Boaler, J., Dance, K., & Woodbury, E. (2018). *From performance to learning: Assessing to encourage growth mindsets*. YouCubed. Stanford University. https://www.youcubed.org/wp-content/uploads/2018/04/Assessent-paper-final-4.23.18.pdf

Boss, S., & Larmer, J. (2018). *Project based teaching: How to create rigorous and engaging learning experiences*. ASCD.

Brown, M. J. (2017). *The concept of "situation" in John Dewey's logic and philosophy of science*. https://www.matthewjbrown.net/professional/papers/situation-science.pdf

Carpenter, S. (1998). *The three billy goats gruff* (Illustrated ed.). HarperFestival.

Common Core State Standards Initiative. (2020). *Key shifts in mathematics*. http://www.corestandards.org/other-resources/key-shifts-in-mathematics/

Conway, B. M., Id-Deen, L., Raygoza, M. C., Ruiz, A., Staley, J. W., & Thanheiser, E. (2022). *Middle school mathematics lessons to explore, understand, and respond to social injustice*. Corwin.

Defined Learning. (2015, April 10). What is a performance task? (Part I). *Performance Task PD With Jay McTighe*. https://blog.performancetask.com/what-is-a-performance-task-part-1-9fa0d99ead3b

Dewey, J. (1933). *How we think: A restatement of the relation of reflective thinking to the educative process*. Henry Regnery.

Dewey, J. (1938). *Logic: The theory of inquiry*. Henry Holt. https://ia601604.us.archive.org/20/items/JohnDeweyLogicTheTheoryOfInquiry/%5BJohn_Dewey%5D_Logic_-_The_Theory_of_Inquiry.pdf

DiNoia, D. (2021). Math: When am I ever going to use this stuff? *Mr. D Math.* https://mrdmath.com/math-when-am-i-ever-going-to-use-this-stuff/

Discovery Education. (n.d.). *Directed inquiry versus guided inquiry.* https://static.discoveryeducation.com/techbook/pdf/DirectedInquiryvsGuidedInquiry.pdf

Eisberg, A. (2018, March 28). *PBL versus product-based learning.* PBLWorks. https://www.pblworks.org/blog/pbl-vs-product-based-learning

EL Education. (2016, October 4). *Austin's butterfly: Models, critique, and descriptive feedback* [Video]. YouTube. https://www.youtube.com/watch?v=E_6PskE3zfQ&ab_channel=ELEducation

Fancher, C., & Norfar, T. (2019). *Project-based learning in the math classroom: Grades 6–10.* Prufrock Press.

Fennell, F., Kobett, B., & Wray, J. (2017). *The formative 5: Everyday assessment techniques for every math classroom.* Corwin.

Ferlazzo, L. (2021, April 19). Don't "make the math classroom a project-based-learning-free zone." *EducationWeek.* https://www.edweek.org/teaching-learning/opinion-dont-make-the-math-classroom-a-pbl-free-zone/2021/04

Field, S. (2021, March 11). 4 equity levers in project based learning. *Gold Standard PBL: Teaching Practices.* PBLWorks. Buck Institute for Education. https://www.pblworks.org/blog/4-equity-levers-project-based-learning

Fletcher, G. (n.d.). *3 act task file cabinet.* https://gfletchy.com/3-act-lessons/

Fredricks, J. A., Blumenfeld, P. C., & Paris, A. H. (2004). School engagement: Potential of the concept, state of the evidence. *Review of Educational Research, 74,* 59–109.

Gojak, L. M. (2013, February 5). What's all this talk about rigor? NCTM *Summing Up.* https://www.nctm.org/News-and-Calendar/Messages-from-the-President/Archive/Linda-M_-Gojak/What_s-All-This-Talk-about-Rigor_/

Gruber, M. J., & Ranganath, C. (2019, November 6). *How curiosity enhances hippocampus-dependent memory: The prediction, appraisal, curiosity, and exploration (PACE) framework.* Trends in Cognitive Sciences. https://doi.org/10.1016/j.tics.2019.10.003

Guinness World Records. (2022). *Fastest tortoise.* https://www.guinnessworldrecords.com/world-records/77951-fastest-tortoise

Gutstein, E., & Peterson, B. (Eds.). (2013). *Rethinking mathematics: Teaching social justice by the numbers.* Rethinking Schools.

Harvard Graduate School of Education. (2015). *Thinking routine: Connect, extend, challenge.* Project Zero. http://www.pz.harvard.edu/resources/connect-extend-challenge

Harvard Graduate School of Education. (2019). *Thinking routine: 3–2–1 bridge.* Project Zero. https://pz.harvard.edu/sites/default/files/3–2–1%20Bridge_0.pdf

Harvard Graduate School of Education. (2022). *Project Zero's thinking routine toolbox.* Project Zero. http://www.pz.harvard.edu/thinking-routines

Hattie, J., Fisher, D., Frey, N., Gojak, L. M., Moore, S. D., & Mellman, W. (2017). *Visible learning for mathematics: What works best to optimize student learning, grades K–12.* Corwin.

Heiligman, D. (2013). *The boy who loved math: The improbable life of Paul Erdos.* Roaring Brook Press.

HQPBL. (2018). *High quality project based learning.* https://hqpbl.org/

Hua, H. (2020, July 26). *"I am a math person" frame.* https://howiehua.wordpress.com/2020/07/26/i-am-a-math-person-frame/

Illustrative Mathematics. (2016, May 4). *Jamir's penny jar.* https://tasks.illustrativemathematics.org/content-standards/2/NBT/B/5/tasks/1071

Institute for Habits of Mind. (2022). *What are Habits of Mind?* https://www.habitsofmindinstitute.org/learning-the-habits/

Kaplinsky, R. (2019). *Open middle math: Problems that unlock student thinking, 6–12*. Stenhouse.

Keeley, P., & Tobey, C. R. (2011). *Mathematics formative assessment, Volume 1: 75 practical strategies for linking assessment, instruction, and learning*. Corwin.

Kersaint, G. (2015). *Orchestrating mathematical discourse to enhance student learning*. Ready Curriculum Associates. https://ttaconline.org/Document/zxbIhX_YCJNP0qvIYsAjT0x-qdzE3VlX/WP-Curriculum_Associates%20Orchestrating_Mathematical_Discourse.pdf0.pdf

Koestler, C. (2022). *Early elementary mathematics lessons to explore, understand, and respond to social injustice*. Corwin.

Krall, G. (2018). *Necessary conditions: Teaching secondary math with academic safety, quality tasks, and effective facilitation*. Stenhouse.

Krall, G. (2021, June 28). *A rubric masterclass*. Emergent Math. https://emergentmath.com/2021/06/28/a-rubric-masterclass/

Larkin, S. (2019). *The thing about bees: A love letter*. Readers to Eaters.

Larmer, J. (2012, June 5). *PBL: What does it take for a project to be "authentic"?* Edutopia. https://www.edutopia.org/blog/authentic-project-based-learning-john-larmer

Larmer, J. (2018, July 13). *A tricky part of PBL: Writing a driving question*. PBLWorks. https://www.pblworks.org/blog/tricky-part-pbl-writing-driving-question

Larmer, J. (2021). *27 tips for managing the "messy middle" of a project*. PBLWorks. https://www.pblworks.org/blog/27-tips-managing-messy-middle-project

Lee, J. S., & Galindo, E. (2018). *Rigor, relevance, and relationships: Making mathematics come alive with project-based learning*. National Council of Teachers of Mathematics.

Lee, J. S., & Galindo, E. (2021). *Project-based learning in elementary classrooms: Making mathematics come alive*. National Council of Teachers of Mathematics.

Levasseur, K., & Cuoco, A. (2003). Mathematical habits of mind. In H. L. Schoen (Ed.), *Teaching mathematics through problem solving: Grades 6–12* (pp. 23–37). National Council of Teachers of Mathematics.

Liljedahl, P. (2021). *Building thinking classrooms in mathematics*. Corwin.

Lomax, K. (n.d.). *3 act tasks*. Learning From Children. https://learningfromchildren.org/3-act-tasks/

Lucas Education Research. (2021). *Rigorous project-based learning is a powerful lever for improving equity*. https://www.lucasedresearch.org/wp-content/uploads/2021/08/Equity-Research-Brief.pdf

Magnify Learning. (2022). *What are benchmarks in PBL?* https://www.magnifylearningin.org/benchmarks

Matthews, L. E., Jones, S. M., & Parker, Y. A. (2022a). *Engaging in culturally relevant math tasks: Fostering hope in the elementary classroom*. Corwin.

Matthews, L. E., Jones, S. M., & Parker, Y. A. (2022b). *Engaging in culturally relevant math tasks: Fostering hope in the middle and high school classroom*. Corwin.

McDowell, M. (2017). *Rigorous PBL by design: Three shifts for developing confident and competent learners*. Corwin.

Meyer, D. (n.d.). *Category: 3 acts*. https://blog.mrmeyer.com/category/3acts/

Miller, A. (2011, September 14). *20 tips for managing project-based learning*. Edutopia. https://www.edutopia.org/blog/20-tips-pbl-project-based-learning-educators-andrew-miller

Morgan, A., & Barden, M. (2015). *A beautiful constraint: How to transform your limitations into advantages, and why it's everyone's business*. Wiley.

Mosca, J. F. (2018). *The girl with a mind for math: The story of Raye Montague*. Innovation Press.

National Council of Teachers of Mathematics. (2010). *Why is teaching with problem solving important to student learning?* [Research brief]. https://www.nctm.org/Research-and-Advocacy/Research-Brief-and-Clips/Problem-Solving/

National Council of Teachers of Mathematics. (2014). *Principles to actions: Ensuring mathematical success for all.* https://www.nctm.org/PtA/

National Council of Teachers of Mathematics. (2018). *Catalyzing change in high school mathematics: Initiating critical conversations.* National Council of Teachers of Mathematics.

National Council of Teachers of Mathematics. (2020a). *Catalyzing change in early childhood and elementary mathematics: Initiating critical conversations.* https://www.nctm.org/Standards-and-Positions/Catalyzing-Change/Catalyzing-Change-in-Early-Childhood-and-Elementary-Mathematics/

National Council of Teachers of Mathematics. (2020b). *Catalyzing change in middle school mathematics: Initiating critical conversations.* https://www.nctm.org/Store/Products/Catalyzing-Change-in-Middle-School-Mathematics/

National Gang Center. (2011). *National youth gang survey analysis.* https://nationalgangcenter.ojp.gov/survey-analysis

National Governors Association Center for Best Practices & Council of Chief State School Officers. (2010). *Common Core State Standards for mathematics.* https://learning.ccsso.org/wp-content/uploads/2022/11/ADA-Compliant-Math-Standards.pdf

Nguyen, F. (2020). *Visual patterns.* https://www.visualpatterns.org/

Norfar, T., & Fancher, C. (2022a). *Project-based learning in the math classroom: Grades K–2.* Routledge.

Norfar, T., & Fancher, C. (2022b). *Project-based learning in the math classroom: Grades 3–5.* Routledge.

Orr, J., & Pearce, K. (2019, December 7). *Spark curiosity, fuel sense-making, and ignite teacher moves!* Make Math Moments. https://makemathmoments.com/framework/

PBLWorks. (2018, July 28). *Resource list: Assessment in PBL.* https://www.pblworks.org/blog/resource-list-assessment-pbl

PBLWorks. (2019, June 5). *Tiny house project* [Video]. YouTube. https://www.youtube.com/watch?v=B2gBFlPEZ2Q&ab_channel=PBLWorks

PBLWorks. (2021). *Project-based learning handbook for elementary school: Creating projects to ignite learning for every student.* PBLWorks.

PBLWorks. (n.d.). *Gold Standard PBL: Essential project design elements.* https://www.pblworks.org/what-is-pbl/gold-standard-project-design

Pearce, K., & Orr, J. (n.d.). *3 act math tasks.* Tap Into Teen Minds. https://tapintoteenminds.com/3act-math/

Pieratt, J. (2019, February 10). *How to teach students to critique in project-based learning.* CraftEd Curriculum. https://craftedcurriculum.com/how-to-teach-students-to-critique-in-project-based-learning/

Pieratt, J. (2020). *Keep it real with PBL, elementary: A practical guide for planning project-based learning.* Corwin.

Piper, K. (2012, September 18). *Practical PBL: The ongoing challenges of assessment.* Edutopia. https://www.edutopia.org/blog/practical-pbl-challenges-of-assessment-katherine-piper

Ray-Riek, M. (2013). *Powerful problem solving: Activities for sense making with the mathematical practices.* Heinemann.

Reid, K. (2017, April 11). *Water within reach: Compare two 5-year-olds' walk for water.* World Vision. https://www.worldvision.org/clean-water-news-stories/compare-walk-for-water-cheru-kamama

Reynolds, P. H. (2003). *The dot.* Candlewick.

Right Question Institute. (2022). *What is the QFT?* https://rightquestion.org/what-is-the-qft/

Ritchhart, R. (2015). *Creating cultures of thinking: The eight forces we must truly master to transform our schools.* Jossey-Bass.

Ritchhart, R., & Church, M. (2020). *The power of making thinking visible: Practices to engage and empower all learners.* Jossey-Bass.

Ritchhart, R., Church, M., & Morrison, K. (2011). *Making thinking visible: How to promote engagement, understanding, and independence for all learners.* Jossey-Bass.

Ritchie, H., & Roser, M. (2021). *Clean water and sanitation.* Our World in Data. https://ourworldindata.org/clean-water-sanitation

SanGiovanni, J. J., Katt, S., & Dykema, K. J. (2020). *Productive math struggle: A 6-point action plan for fostering perseverance.* Corwin.

School Reform Initiative. (n.d.). *Data driven dialogue.* Developed by the Teacher Development Group, 2002. https://www.schoolreforminitiative.org/download/data-driven-dialogue/

School Reform Initiative. (2021). *Tuning protocol.* https://www.schoolreforminitiative.org/download/tuning-protocol/

Singh, S. (2018, November 29). *Mathematics waits for everyone, but few wait for mathematics.* Q.E.D. https://medium.com/q-e-d/mathematics-waits-for-everyone-but-few-wait-for-mathematics-7095c86cda70

Soto, I. (2021). *Shadowing multilingual learners.* Corwin.

Soto, I., Sagun, T. R., & Beiersdorf, M. (2023). *Equity moves to support multilingual learners in mathematics and science, grades K–8.* Corwin.

Spencer, J. (2022, April 11). *How to guide students in self-reflection during a project.* John Spencer. https://spencerauthor.com/reflection-pbl-process/

Stanford Graduate School of Education. (2019, April 2). *And I'm a mathematician (K-12+).* YouCubed. https://www.youcubed.org/resources/and-im-a-mathematician-k-12/

Sztabnik, B. (2015, May 7). *A new definition of rigor.* Edutopia. https://www.edutopia.org/blog/a-new-definition-of-rigor-brian-sztabnik

Teaching Channel. (2015). *My favorite no: Learning from mistakes.* https://learn.teachingchannel.com/video/class-warm-up-routine

University of Cambridge. (2022). *NRICH.* https://nrich.maths.org/

U.S. Census Bureau. (2011). *Race and Hispanic origin and the 2010 census.* https://www.census.gov/newsroom/blogs/random-samplings/2011/03/race-and-hispanic-origin-and-the-2010-census.html

Vincent, T. (2014, October 10). *Crafting questions that drive projects.* Learning in Hand. https://learninginhand.com/blog/drivingquestions

Webb, N. (1997). *Criteria for alignment of expectations and assessments on mathematics and science education* [Research monograph no. 6]. Council of Chief State School Officers.

Wedekind, K. O. (2011). *Math exchanges: Guiding young mathematicians in small group meetings.* Stenhouse.

Wiernicki, M. (n.d.). 3 act tasks. *Under the Dome: Thoughts About Teaching.* https://mikewiernicki.com/3-act-tasks/

Yamada, K. (2014). *What do you do with an idea?* Compendium.

Yousafzai, M. (with Lamb, C.). (2013). *I am Malala: The girl who stood up for education and was shot by the Taliban.* Little, Brown.

Zager, T. J. (2017). *Becoming the math teacher you wish you'd had: Ideas and strategies from vibrant classrooms.* Stenhouse.

Index

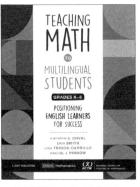
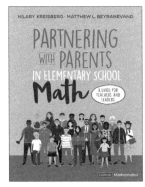

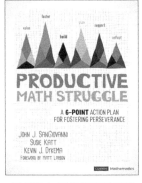

**JENNIFER M. BAY-WILLIAMS,
JOHN J. SANGIOVANNI, ROSALBA SERRANO,
SHERRI MARTINIE, JENNIFER SUH**

Because fluency is so much more
than basic facts and algorithms

Grades K–8

**KAREN S. KARP,
BARBARA J. DOUGHERTY,
SARAH B. BUSH**

A schoolwide solution for students'
mathematics success

Elementary, Middle School, High School

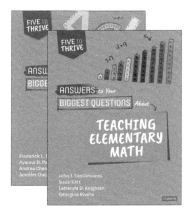

**JOHN J. SANGIOVANNI, SUSIE KATT,
LATRENDA D. KNIGHTEN, GEORGINA RIVERA,
FREDERICK L. DILLON, AYANNA D. PERRY,
ANDREA CHENG, JENNIFER OUTZS**

Actionable answers to your most
pressing questions about teaching
elementary and secondary math

Elementary, Secondary

**SARA DELANO MOORE,
KIMBERLY RIMBEY**

A journey toward making
manipulatives meaningful

Grades K–3, 4–8

A SAGE Publishing Company

Helping educators make the greatest impact

CORWIN HAS ONE MISSION: to enhance education through intentional professional learning.

We build long-term relationships with our authors, educators, clients, and associations who partner with us to develop and continuously improve the best evidence-based practices that establish and support lifelong learning.